America's Working Poor

Monotype by Douglas Kinsey

America's Working Poor

THOMAS R. SWARTZ
KATHLEEN MAAS WEIGERT

University of Notre Dame Press
Notre Dame and London

Manufactured in the United States of America

Library of Congress Cataloging-in-Publication Data

Swartz, Thomas R.
America's Working Poor / edited by Thomas R. Swartz and Kathleen Maas Weigert.
p. cm.
ISBN 0–268–00648–2 (hc. : alk. paper) 0–268–00649–0 (pa. : alk. paper)
1. Working class—United States. 2. Poor—United States.
3. United States—Social conditions—1980– I. Weigert, Kathleen Maas, 1943– . II. Title.
HD8072.5.S82 1995
305.5'69'08623—dc20 95–9128
CIP

The paper used in this publication meets the minimum requirements of the American National Standard for Information Sciences—Permanence of Paper for Printed Materials, ANSI Z39.48–1984.

Book design by Will Powers
Set in Minion and Cushing types
by Stanton Publication Services, Inc.

For our spouses, Jeanne and Andy

For our daughters:

Mary Elizabeth
Karen Ann
Jennifer Lynne
Anne Marie
Rebecca Jourdan
Karen Rose
Sheila Marie

Contents

Preface

The essays found in this book offer both a review of the current status and research on the working poor and the policy options that are available to address the problems of those who suffer under these conditions. After reading these essays, we are confident that you will share our high regard for the contributions made by our participants. We are equally confident that you will share in their conclusion: if we are to solve the problem of the working poor, we must all participate. The poor must upgrade their skills and training, more research must come from the academic community, more good paying jobs must be generated by the business sector, more innovative public policy must be implemented by our elected officials, and each of us must recognize that some of us live the American nightmare rather than experiencing the American dream.

We are particularly grateful for the enthusiastic participation of our principal contributors: Eli Anderson, Becky Blank, Sheldon Danziger, Peter Gottschalk, Sandy Hofferth, Jack Kasarda, Becky London, and Jim Sterba. In addition to their formal papers, that form the substance of this book, nearly all of these very, very overly committed individuals were able to visit our campus to share their vast experiences with our students and colleagues.

We must hasten to add that we are also indebted to many of our friends and colleagues here at the University of Notre Dame, most significantly, the members of the "Urban Poverty Study Group." This interdisciplinary group of scholars was convened by Don McNeill, C.S.C., in the fall of 1992. During the following eighteen months we greatly benefited from the support and good counsel of John Borkowski, Jay Brandenberger, Ben Giamo, Dick Lamanna, Clark Power, John Roos, Roland Smith, and Fred Wright. We are also indebted to many others here at Notre Dame. Chuck Craypo read and commented on many early drafts of our contributors and was always ready to provide answers to our technical questions in the field of labor economics. David Hay made all the arrangements for our visitors, hosted them while they were on campus and coordinated a one credit-hour course which incorporated their lectures. Douglas Kinsey, whose wonderful monotype graces this book, expresses in art what we cannot express in words. With remarkable insightfulness, our University Press editor Carole Roos identified our remaining problems and negotiated this manuscript over and around what sometimes appeared to be insurmountable publication obstacles. And finally, a special thanks goes to Sherry Reichold. She converted our computer discs, typed and retyped many of the papers and tables, formatted all the papers, and endured without complaint Swartz's terrible handwriting.

Financial support for this project came from the Institute for Scholarship in the Liberal Arts; the academic departments of Economics, American Studies, African and African American Studies, and Sociology; the Office of Multicultural Affairs; the Center for Social Concerns; and from a generous grant from the Paul M. and Barbara Henkels Visiting Scholars Series.

T. R. SWARTZ
K. M. WEIGERT
1995

1

A Rich Nation and Its Poor Workers: Introduction and Overview

KATHLEEN MAAS WEIGERT

"If you work hard and honestly at your job, you will be able to meet your essential needs and those of your family." Most Americans believe in that basic bargain. It does not promise riches over night or the resources to live in the best neighborhood tomorrow, but it *is* supposed to be that a job provides a decent wage.

The problem is that for some Americans the formula doesn't hold: they work yet find themselves in poverty. Who are these poor workers? How can this happen in the United States? What can be done about it? It is these questions this book attempts to answer. Too little attention has been paid to the plight of the "working poor" and the research that is available is often anecdotal in nature or disciplinary-based. Yet the social reality is considerably more complex. To provide a much-needed interdisciplinary perspective, we invited scholars from urban ethnography, economics, social policy, sociology, and philosophy to describe and analyze the current situation of the working poor and to evaluate the frameworks and policy alternatives for addressing their situation.

Two basic themes provide a background to their essays. First is the issue of jobs in the ever-changing national and global arenas; second is the topic of the growing inequality in the United States. After examining each of these, I profile the seven essays that follow. The textured picture that emerges from their analyses deepens our understanding of the social and economic challenges that face not just the working poor but all of us in the United States as we fast approach the twenty-first century.

Changing Jobs at Century's End

With an increasingly interconnected global system, political borders are more permeable than ever and talk of a "national" economy seems obsolete.[1] From financial markets to communications, far-reaching changes are rapidly affecting the organizations, structures, and processes of daily living. Part of this global transformation is spurred by technological innovations. While such changes are often seen as good in the long run, in the short run, some people lose their jobs. Will they find work? And will their new jobs be good ones?

New jobs *are* being created in the United States but increasingly these jobs provide only low-wage work. One of our authors, Elijah Anderson, recounts the story of his father who, with very little education, earned the 1994 equivalent of $28,000 a year for a job in the 1950s at the Studebaker auto plant in South Bend, Indiana. That story is not likely to be replicated in the 1990s when the opportunity for high-wage unskilled and semi-skilled work is rapidly disappearing from the workplace. The more well-paying jobs of the manufacturing world are giving way to the less well-paying service sector jobs like child care, food service, and home health.[2] Unlike Professor Anderson's father, even high school graduates find it increasingly difficult to break into a labor market that has seen wages for their educational level plunge over the last two decades.

A related phenomenon complicates the picture: an increase in what is called the "contingent" work force, that is, those who are involuntarily part-time workers, temporary workers, leased employees, homeworkers, and "independent" contractors. As many as 25 to 30 percent of the American civilian labor force may be contingent workers. Few would classify such jobs as "good" when these workers do not share in the once taken-for-granted protections like occupational safety and health regulations, unemployment insurance, and safe pension funds.

For many Americans there is no choice but to work at more than one job. Multiple job holding is growing in the United States. Today some 7 million Americans (6.8 percent of the work force) hold fifteen million jobs. Most of these workers are married and they number nearly as many men as women, according to government data. One indicator of the importance of the growth in this area is that the Labor Department is now, for the first time, compiling surveys of multiple job holders every month.

While some will benefit from these dramatic changes in labor markets, too many will not. Those who can least afford it suffer the negative consequences of our new economic system. Their plight is manifested in the reality that economic inequality continues to grow.

Growing Inequality

Disparities in wealth and income have always characterized our country but during the last decades of this century, we are becoming a more rigidly two-

Table 1.1

Share of Aggregate Income in 1967 to 1992 Received by Each Fifth and Top 5 Percent of Households

Year	Number (thous.)	Percent distribution of aggregate income					
		Lowest fifth	Second fifth	Third fifth	Fourth fifth	Highest fifth	Top 5 percent
TOTAL							
1993	97,107	3.6	9.1	15.3	23.8	48.2	21.0
1992	96,391	3.8	9.4	15.8	24.2	46.9	18.6
1991	95,699	3.8	9.6	15.9	24.2	46.5	18.1
1990	94,312	3.9	9.6	15.9	24.0	46.6	18.6
1989	93,347	3.8	9.5	15.8	24.0	46.8	18.9
1988	92,830	3.8	9.6	16.0	24.3	46.3	18.3
1987	91,124	3.8	9.6	16.1	24.3	46.2	18.2
1986	89,479	3.8	9.7	16.2	24.3	46.1	18.0
1985	88,458	3.9	9.8	16.2	24.4	45.6	17.6
1984	86,789	4.0	9.9	16.3	24.6	45.2	17.1
1983	85,290	4.0	9.9	16.4	24.6	45.1	17.1
1982	83,918	4.0	10.0	16.5	24.5	45.0	17.0
1981	83,527	4.1	10.1	16.7	24.8	44.4	16.5
1980	82,368	4.2	10.2	16.8	24.8	44.1	16.5
1979	80,776	4.1	10.2	16.8	24.7	44.2	16.9
1978	77,330	4.2	10.2	16.9	24.7	44.1	16.8
1977	76,030	4.2	10.2	16.9	24.7	44.0	16.8
1976	74,142	4.3	10.3	17.0	24.7	43.7	16.6
1975	72,867	4.3	10.4	17.0	24.7	43.6	16.6
1974	71,163	4.3	10.6	17.0	24.6	43.5	16.5
1973	69,859	4.2	10.5	17.1	24.6	43.6	16.6
1972	68,251	4.1	10.5	17.1	24.5	43.9	17.0
1971	66,676	4.1	10.6	17.3	24.5	43.5	16.7
1970	64,374	4.1	10.8	17.4	24.5	43.3	16.6
1969	63,401	4.1	10.9	17.5	24.5	43.0	16.6
1968	61,805	4.2	11.1	17.5	24.4	42.8	16.6
1967	60,446	4.0	10.8	17.3	24.2	43.8	17.5

Source: U.S. Bureau of the Census CD-ROM, *Income and Poverty:* 1993, Table H-1.

tiered society.[3] Not since the 1930s have we seen such an economically stratified society as America is today. Compared with other industrial nations, the United States has the greatest economic inequality and it is growing more unequal at a faster pace. Current poverty and income data illustrate the seemingly relentless march toward a less egalitarian society.

In 1993 there were 39.3 million people (15.1 percent of the population) living below the official government poverty level (which was $14,763 for a family of four). This was the largest number of individuals suffering poverty since 1962 when 39.6 million (22 percent) were poor. But while much of the poverty at mid-century entrapped the elderly, today it is the children. In 1992, 21 percent of all children were poor, with 46 percent of African-American children and 39 percent of Hispanic youngsters living in poverty. One startling comparative note: our child poverty rate is four times the average of Western European countries.

The story of income concentration is clearly seen in the data presented in Table 1.1. As the table indicates, a change occurred in household income shares around 1979. Prior to that time, we saw a shift in income away from the relatively affluent to the relatively poor. After that, a reversal occurs and we find resources moving away from the relatively poor and toward the relatively well-off. The most recent data from the Census Bureau provide no relief. In 1993 the bottom fifth of households received only 3.6 percent of U.S. income while the top fifth amassed 48.2 percent, the widest gap since the Census Bureau started keeping track in 1947.

While there is a broad consensus about the changing labor markets and the growing inequality, there is not much agreement on how to account for these phenomena. Some claim that international competition is the culprit. The United States has lost its competitive edge in the global arena and unless it is recaptured, the argument goes, the situation will not improve for anyone, least of all for poorer people. Others argue that the real villains are in the domestic arena. Here some cite the decline in the numbers and power of unions and the adverse effects of automation. Others point to the tax reforms and the decrease in social spending in the 1980s. With the new Republican majority in Congress, they fear the likelihood that such policies will be expanded, further exacerbating the situation.

If there is little agreement on what produces the changes, there is even less on what to do about them—if anything. But that increasing pressures are placed on the working poor as a result is beyond dispute.

Seven Views of the Future for America's Working Poor

Who are the working poor and what can be done about their situation? In answering these two central questions, the contributors to this book help broaden the picture of America's working poor and carefully examine policy alternatives that might alleviate their situation. In the initial essay, Elijah Anderson helps ground this reality through a vivid portrait of a social type in his "The Black Inner-City Grandmother: Transition of a Heroic Type?" Employing an ethnographic approach, Anderson offers a brief history and analysis of the central role of the grandmother in the black community. He observes that in the contemporary context there are really two types of grandmothers: the "decent" and the "street-oriented." We then hear the story of one of the grandmothers, a woman Anderson calls "Betty." As Betty's story unfolds, it becomes apparent that the grandmother status and role are in a precarious position. Various social forces combine to constrict the resources of these women who have freely accepted, or have had thrust upon them, this traditionally respected position. Betty's struggles to care for the children, her own and her daughters', become a prism for the reader to view the pressures the grandmother experiences in an impoverished inner-city community where work opportunities are severely limited.

We move from a social type to a "descriptive framework" of the working poor over the last decade in John D. Kasarda's essay, "America's Working Poor: 1980–1990." Employing a unique data source, the 5 Percent Public Use Microdata Sample (PUMS) from the 1980 and 1990 Censuses of Population, Kasarda traces the changes in the magnitude of this group. He argues that it is more in keeping with ordinary citizens' views to define the "working" poor in terms of those who are in fact employed at some job for at least some reasonable period over a given year yet are in families below the poverty line. He suggests two standards (one based on 20 hours of work per week for 27 weeks; the other based on 35 hours per week for 50 weeks) and documents the growth in the number of working-poor people under each measure. He then describes the size, composition, and distribution of the working poor and examines the leading industries and occupations where poverty-wage jobs are concentrated, noting especially the higher proportions of women in poverty-wage work.

Sheldon Danziger and Peter Gottschalk focus on prime-age male workers in the nation's largest metropolitan areas during the 1980s in their essay, "Hardly Making It: The Increase in Low Earnings and What to Do about It." They find that the incidence of low earnings and earnings inequality increased in most metropolitan areas. After examining the trends in the level and distribution of earnings, they turn to policy alternatives that would aid low earners. While they agree that economic growth is important, given its uneven and slow development, it is insufficient in itself to help low earners.

More immediate promising approaches include the Earned Income Tax Credit and the expansion of child-care subsidies.

Rebecca M. Blank and Rebecca A. London look at the working-poor population with special attention to policy changes over the past fifteen years. In their essay, "Trends in the Working Poor: The Impact of Economy, Family, and Public Policy," they examine the extent of employment among the poor in light of changes in the U.S. economy. In exploring the impact of policies on work behavior among this segment of our population, they offer a detailed examination of three different policy options beginning with programs that directly attempt to increase employment among low-income adults through job placement and training. Then they discuss anti-poverty programs and the incentives and disincentives embedded in them. Finally, they examine tax policy to supplement earnings, focusing especially on the Earned Income Tax Credit, a policy they argue is "potentially the most important policy change for the working poor of the last decade."

In the next essay, entitled "Out-of-School Time: Risk and Opportunity," Sandra L. Hofferth focuses on the important issue of child care. She uses two different definitions of working poor, one tied to the poverty level and work status of the head of household, spouse or both; the other based on those whose family incomes lie between the poverty line and $25, 000. Any decision by poor parents to seek employment, Hofferth contends, has to be made in the context of the needs of their children. Hofferth examines child care for one group not frequently examined, namely, adolescents. Using data from two recent national studies, she argues that much more attention needs to be given to such issues as parental work schedules and the availability, affordability, sponsorship, and type of child-care programs if we are going to encourage poor parents to consider entering the work force or strengthening their commitment to it.

As the nation addresses the empirical realities of the working poor and tries to fashion appropriate policies, one way of helping advance that conversation is to frame it in a larger way. Whether explicit or not, policies are often rooted in and shaped by more abstract ideas about justice. What is fair? What do people have a right to? In his essay, "The Right to Welfare of the Working Poor," James P. Sterba examines five alternative conceptions of justice to determine whether they support a right to welfare in general and a right to welfare for the working poor in particular. In critically evaluating each of the perspectives—libertarian, socialist, welfare liberal, communitarian, and feminist—Sterba finds that even though they differ in many and substantial ways, there is within each an understanding that can lead to the support of a right to welfare especially for the working poor. In these conflicting times, such a fundamental idea may help in building the common ground so critically needed for fashioning creative policies that assist the working poor.

The final chapter, "The Working Poor and the Prospect of Welfare Reform 1995 Style," is by Thomas R. Swartz, who speculates about the future of the working poor as it would be shaped by various welfare reform proposals. Although it is not yet clear which proposals will finally be enacted by Congress, it is clear that compared to the Clinton proposals, the policy agenda of the Republican congressional leadership is far more threatening to the economic well-being of America's working poor. Swartz concludes that only time will tell how those who cling to the bottom rung of the economic ladder will respond to these changes and how we as a society will be judged for our actions.

These essays move us beyond the current state of knowledge about the economic and social realities of the working poor. In the richness of the interdisciplinary work, they provide insights about that world and evaluate current research and policy alternatives that might make a difference. In the rapidly changing global and national scenes, the opportunities for this segment of our population seem limited at best. That some among us can work and still be poor challenges all of us to reflect on what can be done and what should be done to alleviate their predicament. There is a role to play for everyone and each of us must do what we can to lessen the burdens on our neighbors: poor workers in this rich nation.

Notes

1. See Kennedy (1993), Krugman (1994), and Reich (1992) for insightful analyses of these developments.

2. Mishel and Bernstein (1993) and Yates (1994) provide detailed information on these changes.

3. Barlett and Steele (1992), Bernstein (1994), and Phillips (1991) supply empirical support for the growing bifurcation of our society.

References

Barlett, Donald L. and James B. Steele. 1992. *America: What Went Wrong?* Kansas City: Andrews and McMeel.

Bernstein, Aaron. 1994. "Inequality: How the Gap between Rich and Poor Hurts the Economy." *Business Week*, August 15: 78–83.

Kennedy, Paul. 1993. *Preparing for the Twenty-First Century.* New York: Random House.

Krugman, Paul. 1994. *Peddling Prosperity: Economic Sense and Nonsense in the Age of Diminished Expectations.* New York: W. W. Norton.

Mishel, Lawrence, and Jared Bernstein. 1993. *The State of Working America, 1992-93.* Economic Policy Institute Series. Armonk, New York: M. E. Sharpe.

Phillips, Kevin. 1991. *The Politics and Rich and Poor: Wealth and the American Electorate in the Reagan Aftermath (1990)*. New York: Harper Perennial.

Reich, Robert B. 1992. *The Work of Nations: Preparing Ourselves for 21st Century Capitalism (1991)*. New York: Vintage Books.

Yates, Michael D. 1994. *Longer Hours, Fewer Jobs: Employment and Unemployment in the United States*. New York: Monthly Review Press.

2

The Black Inner-City Grandmother: Transition of a Heroic Type?

ELIJAH ANDERSON

From slavery onward, in the most trying of circumstances, the mother—and by extension, the grandmother—has been an extremely important source of support for the black family (Jones 1973; Gutman 1976). Correspondingly, the black grandmother holds a special place among her people, both in folklore and in real life. Through the generations, many have characterized her as the anchor holding the family and indeed the whole kinship structure together. Frazier (1939) sums her role up nicely:

> In her explanation of why the responsibility of "her chillen" falls upon her, this old woman [a 77-year-old ex-slave] expresses the characteristic attitude of the grandmother in her role as "oldest head" in the family. Where the maternal family organization assumes such importance as among a large section of the Negro population, the oldest woman is regarded as the head of the family. Some of these grandmothers will tell you of their courting, which sounds very much like that of their granddaughters' today [1939]. Often, instead of having been a prelude to marriage, it culminated in motherhood and the responsibilities which it imposed. Even when they married, sometimes marriage was of short duration, and the responsibility of rearing and supporting their children fell upon them. Thus it has been the grandmother who has held the generations together when fathers and even mothers abandoned their offspring. (p. 150)

This essay seeks both to paint an ethnographic picture of this traditional pillar of strength in the black community and to indicate the reasons, structural and personal, for the grandmother's resilience through changing forms of adversity from slavery through the onslaught of the impoverished conditions of today's inner city. The lack of jobs brought about by the economic shift from a manufacturing to a service base and by the growth of the global economy—particularly widespread joblessness and the appearance of crack cocaine as a central feature of the ghetto underground economy—has greatly exacerbated the problems with which the grandmother has been called upon to do battle. How she has been able to manage and why her position is now threatened to a greater extent than perhaps it has ever been I believe sheds light on the very nature of the black community and what is necessary to sustain and nourish it. For, although the network of grandmothers continues to form a communal safety net, that net is imperiled and has been weakened. Young women are still maturing into the traditional grandmother role, but their numbers are increasingly fewer, making their obstacles proportionately greater.

An Ethnographic Approach

A note on the method of ethnography is perhaps in order. Ethnography seeks to paint a conceptual picture of the setting under consideration through the use of observation and in-depth interviews. The researcher's goal is to illuminate the social and cultural dynamics that characterize the setting: the local way of life, but especially how the people in the setting perceive their situation, the assumptions they bring to their decision making, the behavior patterns that result, and the cultural consequences of those behaviors. An important aspect of the ethnographer's work is that it be as objective as possible. This is not easy since it requires the researcher to set aside his or her own values and assumptions about what is and is not morally acceptable and what prism should be used to view a given situation. By definition, one's own assumptions are so basic to one's perceptions that it may be difficult to see their influence. The ethnographic researcher, however, has been trained to recognize underlying assumptions, his own and those of his subjects, and to override the former and uncover the latter (see Becker 1958, 1970; Geertz 1983).

For the present study, I interviewed numerous inner-city grandmothers, their children, and their grandchildren. I also spoke with other inner-city residents, attempting to obtain their perspectives on the role of the black grandmother and how that role has changed over time. In what follows, I depict that role as I have come to understand it.

The Role of the Grandmother: Then and Now

In the days of slavery and then of sharecropping when black men generally were unable to achieve economic independence, the black grandmother was often a heroic figure whose role required great sacrifice. The black man was often, but not always, emasculated, weakened, or simply neutralized by the social control efforts of the wider white society, thereby reducing him as a competitive force in a male-dominated society (see Gutman 1976; Stampp 1989; Blassingame 1972; Furstenberg et al. 1981; Lemann 1991). But the black woman was not usually perceived to be as much a threat as the black man to the hegemony of the white man. And, according to folklore, such women were then allowed to develop into strong, independent, willful, wise, and omniscient matriarchs who were not afraid to compete with men when necessary.

With the advent of the industrial economy, black men became better able to support themselves and their women and children and began to function less ambiguously as head of the family (see Frazier 1939; Wilson 1987; Jaynes 1986). Accordingly, over time the grandmother's traditional role was gradually diminished but never completely dismantled. Even in the "good old" days of available jobs at decent wages, the grandmother was there in a crisis to pick up the slack when difficulties arose (Jones 1973; Jackson 1971b), and at times she even competed with the man for dominance within the family (see Alice Walker's *The Color Purple* for a fictional treatment of this theme). Traditionally, her meager savings and her home were at the disposal of family members who used them as extras or necessities during temporary hard times.

Today, with the loss of well-paying manufacturing jobs and the introduction of drugs (particularly crack) and the violent drug culture into the ghetto, the black grandmother is once again being called upon to assume her traditional role (see Wilson 1987, 1995; Hershberg 1973; Anderson 1990). As in the past, the heroic grandmother comes to the aid of the family, taking responsibility for children abandoned by their own parents, asserting her still considerable moral authority for the good of the family, and often rearing the children herself in conditions of great hardship.

The grandmother's central role has become institutionalized in the black community and carries with it a great deal of prestige but also a great deal of stress (Jackson 1971a; Register and Mitchell 1982). However, because this role is imbued with such prestige and moral authority and is so firmly entrenched in the culture, many of those who assume it see it as highly rewarding and necessary, if not critical for the survival of the black inner-city family.

A review of the literature on grandparenthood reveals that the existence of this institutionalized grandmother role is a major feature of black family life, particularly among the poor. Among inner-city blacks, because of this strong tradition, it appears to be a mandatory role with established rights, obligations, and duties (Burton and Bengston 1985; Bengston 1985; Jackson 1971b), and those who refuse it may be judged by many in the local black community as having abdicated an extremely important responsibility. Hence, when called upon, black grandmothers appear constrained to play out their role.

Traditionally, grandmothers have served as "kin keepers" for the extended family. This function seems much greater among poor blacks (Bengston 1985; Cherlin and Furstenberg 1986; Troll 1971) and is de-emphasized among the middle and upper classes (see Kornhaber and Woodward 1981). Extensive kinship networks in general are more in evidence among poor black families (see Drake and Cayton 1962; Hays and Mindel 1973; Stack 1974; Heiss 1975), and tend to diffuse with upward mobility. Even so, women in general appear to be resilient, protective of home life and culture, and much more important to the workings of the family than many men are wont to acknowledge. The stereotype of the meddling mother-in-law, which has become well established in general popular culture—for blacks, it finds comedic expression in the Sapphire figure and her mother in *Amos and Andy* or, more recently, *The Jeffersons*—is an expression of this important, yet sometimes resented, position. However, the popular stereotypical portrayals represent a very small part of the black female's actual familial role.

Because the role of grandmother has such communal support—even public acknowledgment and expectation—unmarried teenage mothers of fifteen or sixteen easily turn to their own mothers for help, which is generally forthcoming (Dunston et al. 1987; Presser 1980). In this social context, depending on the age and maturity of the new mother, the experienced grandmother may take over the care of the newborn, partly because she may lack full confidence in her daughter's ability to be a mother and to be an adult, and partly to help keep her daughter from being as deviant as she would be otherwise, at times even helping her to resume her social life (Anderson 1989). In addition, the grandmother may take pleasure and pain in revisiting the role of a mother in a more than simply vicarious way. For many of these reasons, the tendency is for such girls to achieve a new, if provisional, status in their mother's eyes once they become an unwed mother (Williams 1991). At the same time, through the trials and tribulations of motherhood, such girls often gain a new appreciation of their mother (Rickel 1989), as well as of themselves.

In addition, the community is prepared to make a conceptual distinction between a biological and a "real" mother. A common neighborhood saying goes that any woman can have a baby; it takes caring, love, and "mother wit" to be a "real" mother. Regardless of the circumstance, the birth of a baby is genuinely considered to be a truly blessed event. And accordingly, a profound female bonding takes place as the mother begins to pass down her wisdom and experience to the daughter. At social gatherings, neighbors, relatives, and friends often augment this knowledge with their own fond remembrances and tales of maternity, attempting to effectively socialize the new mother into the socially preferred role of "real" mother. At the same time, they try to prepare her to survive on her own terms, with or without a man. Given the high rate of family dissolution among poor inner-city blacks, the fact that women often retain custody of the children, and the fact that many of these women then prevail upon their extended family members and friends—often other females—for moral, emotional, practical, and financial support, the familial experience among the poorest may be described as matriarchal. Hence, kinship ties, fictive or real, cemented through the grandmother become the backbone of the inner-city extended family, and by implication the local community (see Stack 1974). Mothering—nurturing the family, particularly young children—becomes an extremely important, perhaps the preeminent, domestic female role in the community.

The community consistently looks to the mother or grandmother to play or strongly support this mothering role, a duty which has been handed down to her through traditions and by her own socialization. Typically, as a young girl with a limited outlook and sense of options for the future, she often is easily enlisted into playing this role. In conditions of persistent poverty, she may look forward to the rewarding role of mother, and by extension, to that of grandmother. Young men sometimes come to expect such young women to bear their children and to make few claims on them in the process; at the very least, birth control is viewed as the woman's responsibility, as a matter of "taking care of herself." A common view in the inner-city poor community is that bearing and raising children is the business of women and that men should be only marginally involved except in matters of discipline and finances, which are almost always in short supply.

Today, the grandmother increasingly plays the role of a hero who has been waiting in the wings and has now been activated by the social and economic crises besetting the poor black family. When more options and choices become available to poor blacks, and the miseries of poverty, drugs, and violence recede, the "heroic" grandmother may once again retire to the wings precisely because there is perceived to be a decreasing need for her role, socially and economically. This, then, is a role that has developed, that has been nurtured, supported, and legitimated over time, in part because of the impoverished ghetto family's persistent lack of resources, its subsequent vulnerability, and particularly the inability—or unwillingness in many cases—of young men to fulfill their parental obligations and responsibilities.

Inside the Impoverished Ghetto Community and Outside the Mainstream

A severe lack of resources is probably the defining characteristic of an impoverished ghetto community. Members of the lower or working class have always lived in or within the reach of poverty, but today there is widespread destitution of a different order due to changes outside the local community. The country is currently undergoing a profound economic transformation, particularly as the employment base changes from manufacturing to service (see Wilson 1987) and jobs requiring sophisticated technical skills. For many who would be breadwinners, there is simply no gainful work. The jobs that are available are usually low paying or highly insecure. All this has worked to create great numbers of persistently poor people who are utterly unable to adjust effectively to these economic changes. Often the cultural adaptations such people make in effort to survive and live well further complicate their lives and make it even more difficult to get beyond their distress. These adaptations include drug dealing and participation in the alternative underground economy. Children growing up in these circumstances are typically characterized by extreme social isolation and marked by an inability to distinguish "right" from "wrong." Many of the social problems that beset the poor urban black community originate with this situation, which is further complicated by lingering racism and active discrimination.

Much of the social distress in the black ghetto stems from this economic reality. The need for every individual to garner a sufficient share of the inadequate available resources often results in a battle mentality which pervades inner-city neighborhoods. Life for many residents is truly a fight for survival, a contest that often pits person against person and at times family against family. The primary basis for solidarity is kinship (although, as indicated above, kin can be loosely defined to include close friends who may be viewed as "fictive" kin).

The Importance of Family

The family becomes the primary bastion of support against the consequences of the fight for survival, which is played out on the streets of the community. The community lore is that every resident must be constantly vigilant; all are potential prey for drug dealers looking for customers, pimps looking for prostitutes, street criminals and various scam artists looking for victims. It is difficult to convey to those unfamiliar with the setting the overwhelming nature of the situation in which impoverished inner-city blacks live—the hopelessness many feel about any chance of improvement and the expression of this in antisocial behavior. Many residents here are living on the edge and are aware that one false move—a date with the wrong man, an inadvertent display of disrespect—is enough to drag one irrevocably into the dog-eat-dog culture of the streets. As the resources of the community shrink and it becomes ever more difficult for young people to live meaningful lives in ways consistent with the norms of the wider community, people adapt to those limited avenues left open to them.

In spite of these realities, numerous young men are solidly imbued with the work ethic, strong family values, and an abiding faith in God. Many of these young men strive to marry and form enduring families. Such families try to uphold humane, communal, and "decent" values. Typically, the young man works hard at his often menial job, perhaps as a parking-lot attendant, busboy, porter, fast-food restaurant worker, or even an auto mechanic, factory worker, security guard, or construction worker. Some work multiple jobs. When they become involved with female partners, many of these young men strive to be the "good man," trying to "do right"—including paying child support and participating in the rearing of their children.

But this is no easy task. Often, such a young man is likely to have divided loyalties and responsibilities—one to his present family, another to his young son or daughter from a previous affair or marriage. This duality places tremendous strain on the young man, yet he often meets his obligations for as long as he is able. Especially worrisome to him is the fact that he must give up money for support but is unable to obtain anything tangible in return, such as sexual favors, affection, or wifely duties. At times, the woman, in full cognizance of this issue, will try to satisfy some of the man's needs, which then works to complicate the situation still further.

Equally important, the young man's situation is sometimes highly unstable. Due to his limited degree of what may be called "human capital" (Coleman 1988), he may easily fall victim to the forces impacting upon the ghetto. For instance, a case of mistaken identity by the local police landing him "in trouble with the law," an argument with a co-worker, a negative work report for being tardy so many times—any of these developments may cost him his job, fundamentally changing his family status. Often, it is just such sets of problems that make it very difficult for even the "decent," able, and willing young men to meet their domestic responsibilities. In addition, there is also a very limited amount of support for married life among inner-city male peer groups; to get married and have a family is viewed as deviant by so many young men.

The case of Martin is germane:

> Martin is a young man of about 25 who has a steady job as a furniture mover for a secondhand store downtown. He has been going with a young woman named Joyce for a number of years. When Martin met Joyce, she already had a son, Rashan, by a man who took his parenting obligations lightly. After they had been seeing each other for a year, Martin and Joyce had Tommy. Unlike Rashan's father, Martin visited Joyce regularly, helping to support financially and physically take care of both boys. He particularly enjoyed playing with the children, roughhousing with them in the house and taking them on outings. For all intents and purposes he was Joyce's husband and Rashan and Tommy's father, but at first he saw no reason to get married. This decision received no sanctions from anyone, neither his friends nor his family.
>
> Martin comes from a strong, decent family. Several of his aunts are fully in the traditional grandmother role; one is even pastor of a church attended predominantly by people who are in some way related to each other. In Martin's family, kinship ties are strong and encompass men as well as women. As a result, as he was growing up, Martin had his share of male role models, including his father and a number of uncles, who played ball with him and counseled him in the ways of the world.
>
> It appears that after several years of his informal arrangement with Joyce, Martin's sense of family asserted itself. He began to feel that since he loved Joyce and was prepared to be responsible for her and her children, he ought to marry her. The notions of decency and of responsibility with which he had been raised became entwined with his love for Joyce, and he felt that the proper expression of this feeling was marriage. When he announced his intention to his friends, however, it was met with scorn rather than support. The young men with whom he socialized see marriage as a loss of freedom and derided Martin for wanting to "put his head in the noose." They tend to believe that he is unable to meet the responsibilities of being a husband but also that he is putting himself in a position of being exploited by a woman. But Martin's family was supportive. His aunt, the pastor, received the couple at her church, counseled them briefly on marriage, and gave them her blessings. In the end, Martin chose his family's support over his friends' objections and married Joyce.

Martin's story is important for the light it sheds on his background and the men and women in his life. Martin had the benefit of both traditional men and women serving effectively as caretakers and role models. But in impoverished inner-city areas, such relatively advantaged young men are unusual. Yet, as I've seen in my research, the attempt by many young men at some point in life to become a family man is common. They want desperately to play this domestic role but simply fail at establishing and maintaining intact families, largely for economic reasons. Still, they keep trying with other women.

Some young men commonly adapt by giving up on a domestic role, largely because they are unable to financially support families or, in their words "play house," to provide for women and children in a way that allows them to command an adequate amount of deference and respect from all concerned (Anderson 1990). Many assume that a man requires an effective financial position to be able to be a decent husband and father. From a woman's point of view, a suitable male partner or "good man" is often primarily a man who has a decent job. Accordingly, if he has a good job, he may have a say in what goes on in the domestic scene and be respected in the home. Without a job, he feels he loses that prerogative. When men do get married and are unable to establish domestic control, physical abuse sometimes follows. There can even be a cascade effect in which the abused wife then abuses the children. Hence, the economic nexus operates as the keystone of so many domestic relationships, pointing to the importance of the successful breadwinner role.

The current welfare system, particularly AFDC, fits with these considerations. Among the very poor, both women and men make use of the welfare system as a way to support themselves; many learn to work the system. This is not to say that they necessarily take their lead from the welfare system, but rather people do what they can to survive. Consistently, public "aid," as residents call it, contributes to family breakup by paying money to women who have more babies without a male breadwinner. It is also true that some women do look forward to welfare and have babies because of it. The welfare system is one of the few sources of money for the community, and the most desperate people exploit in various ways.

Predatory Males

The predatory inner-city male is a response to this situation. One especially sinister social type that has emerged recently is the drug-dealing loan shark, who advances drug-addicted young girls money on their "aid" checks, taking their welfare cards as collateral and ultimately a significant portion of their welfare money as his profit. On the day the welfare checks arrive, he goes with his girls to the cash exchange and gets what is owed him before letting them take the remainder (if there is any). He is constantly on the lookout for young girls to hook up with the drug trade. He will move through the neighborhood looking for a likely prospect at local taverns, at school playgrounds, and on the streets. When he finds one, he will follow her and try to entice her into love affairs and drugs. His object is to manipulate her into a position of vulnerability and then to use her for his own financial gain.

Some financially desperate inner-city men develop a string of women who receive their welfare checks on "Mother's Day." Typically, they play up to the women just before the checks arrive but ignore them the rest of the time. They visit the women a few days before the end of the month, "play daddy" with their children, acting like an upstanding man around the house, and provide the women with sexual satisfaction. Then after receiving the money, sexual favors, and whatever else they want, they leave. This scenario is well known in the community and happens monthly like clockwork. As part of this scheme, some actually try to get girls pregnant in order to claim some of their ensuing welfare benefits. As they confront an unyielding social environment, many young men make little emotional investment in these essentially predatory activities. They exploit the vulnerable and leave behind a trail of casualties, young women and their children, whose lives may be irreversibly altered if not ruined by drug addiction and early pregnancy. One informant elaborated the male perspective:

> He taking her money. I done seen some of that now and then. The guy playing up to her, and the others say, "Man, how you gone take that lady's aid, Jack. That money's for the kids!" But I done done it so I can't a, a . . . I know what they doing. They got it planned ahead of time. They know just about when the check coming, and they just sit there and before the check come. And they willing and everything, and they say, "Now, baby, I got have this so and so, and when you get the money [check], I'm gone take it, I gon' flip it [invest it to double it], I'm gon' double it. Most times, they just tell 'em how they gon' flip it [often through a drug deal]. They get that leverage on 'em, 'cause they got to have 'em some kinda frame of mind, telling 'em it's [money] gon' make more money. Then they [women] can give it up. So that's the game. It's how most of 'em is gettin' the money. They gon' buy some cheap watches, some dope, or something. She then gives up the money, thinkin' something gon' happen. The women, being so poor, have to be under the impression that they will get something in return. They so poor that they reluctant to just give they money away. The man gets the woman to believe he gon' give 'em something back. 'Cause they [the welfare women] ain't got nothin' else coming in. So they got be, they have to put 'em in that frame o' mind that they gon' give it back to 'em. The man runs a game, saying we gon' make this or we gon' buy that after we make money. They be all kinds of games they play on these women. It's always a loan. The women think they given it to 'em for a while, and they gon' need it back. Then he goes out, and she may never see the money again.

> But this "loan" ties her to him, and that's what she wants. He becomes obligated to her. He be coming and staying at her house, you know. And she gettin' what she wants. Probably sex is what she wants out of it. But probably what she really wants is a man. She wants somebody to come in there and be daddy. 'Cause she already got a kid or two, you know. And the other daddy's gone. And then she wanta daddy so bad, she let him move right on in. To keep him, she'll give 'im whatever he want. For that, he'll play the role of daddy. Takes care of the kid, spank him, tell him what to do. He becomes a play-daddy. He *got* to play daddy. He *got* to be daddy while he there, that's right.

The Pull of the Streets

These behaviors must be viewed as adaptations to persistent poverty and are all aspects of the street culture. The cultural life of the streets exerts a strong draw on the various institutions of the black community, especially the family, on which it has a destabilizing effect. The family's weakest members are vulnerable and often succumb to the draw of the street culture, which is at odds with upward mobility (Anderson 1991) and often survival itself. For many such youths, it is important to be tough, daring, and hip, the lessons for which are taught on the inner-city streets. Such lessons are mixed with the need and strong desire to survive. In these circumstances, the street culture becomes a magnet that draws people who are not anchored in the strong emotional unit of the family and other "decent" institutions such as the church. But one of the primary reasons the street is so powerful is that the wider society has not been receptive to many of these people who lack the sense of personal responsibility, skills, education, outlook and wherewithal to survive through legitimate means.

The exodus of middle-class blacks out of the inner city has left many without solid and successful examples (see Wilson 1987; Anderson 1990). And many of the remaining "decent" blacks will have little to do with those who exhibit any indication that they possess a "street" orientation. Moreover, from the perspective of the street, the white society is increasingly culturally bankrupt and square. So the denizens of the street are effectively locked out of mainstream society and form an impoverished group that basically festers and feeds on itself.

Grandmothers as "Godfathers"

In many cases, vulnerable family members turn to close friends and their families when they are threatened by predators. The grandmother is often the most reliable support. Given her traditional role, it is generally believed that she cares, that she will marshal family resources, she will call the authorities, she will even mobilize the community in some instances to mount an organized protest against those plying the drug trade in the community. In any case, she will know what to do. These beliefs help to form the conception that family members as well as community residents tend to have of her role, stereotypically defining her and giving support for the positive community roles she would play. Today, in playing such roles, some of these women actually lead marches down the street and picket crack houses. In a literal sense, they fight to preserve their neighborhoods and especially the lives of the neighborhood's children.

This social context is important in understanding the role of the grandmother. As noted, the role has been a part of a long tradition but has at times been diminished. If there is a resurgence of it now, it is largely because the social context—the dearth of able male breadwinners, the rise of crack-addicted daughters and male predators, and the general encroachment of the street culture into the fabric of the community—demands it. In her *traditional* role, the grandmother really may be viewed, romantically at least, as a selfless savior of the community. Her role may be compared to a lifeboat. If she is pressed into service, it is because the ship is sinking. And, to so many residents, the inner-city ghetto community does seem to be sinking into ever more entrenched poverty, increasingly undermined by the realities of the street culture as the mainstream culture slips further away.

The Grandmother as a Social Type: The "Real" One vs. the "Nothing"

In the minds of many local residents, a strong dichotomy between the streets and the decent world works to organize the community (see Anderson 1994). Community social organization is based on interactions that determine local status (Anderson 1978). The outcome of many interactions is that people become associated with decency or with the street. Those associated with the street are generally thought of as "lowlife" or of very limited respectability, and those associated with decency are viewed as respectable. Of course, even people who think they are decent can be judged by others as falling short of the standards of decency, which may include regular church attendance, involvement in close and extended families, low-income financial stability, espousal of the work ethic, and a desire to get ahead and "have something" in life. The ideal traditional grandmother is generally viewed as "decent," or a "real" grandmother, and thus represents mainstream society. The one who shirks the role that is expected of her is considered a "nothing," but particularly if she is associated with the street. The extent to which grandmothers deviate from the traditional role may be an indication of the extent to which the social type is itself falling victim to persistent poverty and to present realities. It may also indicate the diminished ability of the community to produce citizens who can function adequately in the wider society.

The Traditional Grandmother

Conceptually, two types of grandmothers may be discerned: the decent and the street-oriented. The decent ones tend to be much better off financially. Accordingly, they are able to marshal various props of decency and to make claim on wider values like the work ethic, propriety, and church and to gain affirmation of a sort through these connections, which further serve to enhance their authority. This type of grandmother is very far from the street and she generally likes it that way. She tends to be somewhat suspicious of and careful with most anonymous black people she encounters for the first time; her doubts begin to dissipate only when she gets to know them better and determines they are more decent than street.

Along with church and religion, she espouses abstinence or at least moderation; often she does not drink or smoke. She takes religion very seriously, and pictures of Jesus, Martin Luther King, Jr., and sometimes John F. Kennedy grace her walls. An aura of decency is all about her, and these emblems attest to her decency, as anyone who visits her quickly learns. The word "decency" is an important part of her vocabulary and conversation. In her presence, everyone defers. Usually she has an effective financial position. Whatever its source, whether it be a pension, social security, or welfare, she has an income and tends to manage her money well enough that she is known to have a "stash." With this reputation she is able to exert some leverage over family members. Depending on how they behave, she metes out favors, giving them things, tangible and intangible. Her grown children may make more money than she does, but they tend to run through it more quickly. Carefully managing her money, she is often thrifty and wise and has the ability to live within her means so the little she has may seem like a lot and go a long way.

In addition, in times of family distress or real trouble, this grandmother is often able to assume the role of an activator. Not only does she have resources of her own to commit to family needs, she has the moral authority to prod other members of the family into committing their own resources of time, money, and care to aid the family member in trouble or need. In one family I interviewed, when one of the daughters became addicted to crack, her siblings initially responded simply with expressions of "shame, shame" and little more. But their mother was able to prevail on them to help out materially and even to take in one of the daughter's children. And she "went to work" on the girl, counseling her strongly and offering "tough love."

In addition, due to their normally better educational background, the "decent" people usually have more resources than the street-oriented people and this goes for grandmothers as well. Such grandmothers are generally more able to obtain help from the system. They are the ones who can deal with the welfare agency and have their addicted daughter's benefit checks diverted to them so that the money actually goes to the children and not for drugs. They not only provide help themselves but know to whom to turn in order to get even more.

Racism, the changing economy, unemployment, and changing social values all affect the people in this community. But the grandmother, particularly if she is middle-aged or elderly, often takes an ideologically conservative view and tends to have little tolerance for structural explanations. Given her prior experience in the local community in the days of the manufacturing economy, in matters of idleness and unemployment she is ready to blame the victim because she feels that there is work to be had for those who are willing to do it and that people can abstain from doing wrong if they want to. It is her belief that the various social problems plaguing the community stem more from personal irresponsibility than from any flaw in the wider system. At times, she may feel she is paying the price for failure of family members. As one 78-year-old grandmother rather vehemently expressed herself:

> Well, I don't have too much sympathy about these drugs. Everything is drugs, drugs, if it wasn't for the drugs. As long as someone is not holding you down, prying your mouth open, and pourin' it down your throat, you don't have to take it. So you take it because you want to take it. And nobody else has beat the habit so what makes you think you're stronger than the other fellow? You see what it has done to his life. Now if you're forced into it, then you're a victim of circumstance.

The Emerging Role Model: Adapting to Crisis

But there are also certain women who wake up one day and find themselves in this role and may at best be ambivalent about it. Yet they are constrained to try to enact it because of the forces of tradition and of present-day circumstances. What else can they do? Not to do something would be to seriously abdicate their responsibility to their kin. With very limited resources, they may experience bitterness and stress, at times resenting their daughters and grandchildren, yet they work to help their kin because that is their place, one that they largely accept.

Still other women completely abdicate or are indifferent to their traditional responsibility with respect to their grandchildren and this role. Often, though not always, they are associated with the street. These "street" grandmothers are much more at the mercy of circumstances that are often beyond their control. These tend to be people who are deeply invested in the "rough" street culture. They tend to drink, smoke, take drugs, cavort with men, and generally engage in behavior that discredits them in the eyes of others, who then say things like, "She's weak," or "She's not ready," readily measuring her with respect to the ideal *traditional* grandmother role—which is loving and decent. The label "weak" or "not ready" may be simply describing the inability to define one's self according to the role. Even those who shirk the grandmother role know that they have deviated from a norm. Some feel enormous guilt, which often prods them to attempt to play this positive role as best they can in spite of their personal circumstances. Hence, the traditional grandmother role has become something of a standard, a conceptual capstone of the value system into which many young girls are initiated and actively grow.

All of this has resulted in a core cadre of black women in poor inner-city neighborhoods who are fountains of strength, reservoirs of resilience. In the communities, especially the poorest communities, they assume this script and play out this strong decent role, becoming a kind of rock that others have learned to depend on and even to mythologize. When the family is intact, this woman is often the person other family members praise and look to for authority and direction; she gives advice and others take it. If the family is broken, she keeps the pieces as least loosely together. She may have little in the way of resources, but she has enormous moral authority and spiritual strength.

On the average, a woman becomes a grandmother at about the age of 37, with some doing so at 33 or 34, though some are, of course, elderly. Typically single, she may have a steady boyfriend or sporadic male company. Thus some semblance of nuclear family life is apparent but there may be no formal domestic ties. Her home is a social center, a kind of nest for the family, with her grown children regularly coming and going. Generally her daughters are still living with her when they begin to have babies, further complicating the home's social activity. The woman herself may be employed but often in a low-level service or clerical occupation, such as nurse's aid, while the daughters may be working at a fast-food restaurant. By pooling their resources, they cope, but barely. Concerned about helping out the family, together they buy clothes and toys for the kids, take responsibility for child care, and when necessary give moral support to the mothers. In addition, the grandmother draws social sustenance from her female friends, her church, and her neighborhood. At local coffee and liquor gatherings, they sometimes exchange the latest gossip about others in the neighborhood and share accounts of their own family problems. They speak of who is going with whom, who is working, and whose child is "on the pipe" (attested to by a clear loss of weight). As they engage in such talk, important social and moral lessons are drawn, and children are carefully instructed in the rules of right and wrong. Children who grow up in this kind of household learn the rules and values of communal family support and they are strongly encouraged to be "good" and "sweet." Rooted in this tradition, if they successfully negotiate the hazards of the neighborhood street culture, they have a chance to achieve social stability in the ghetto culture.

The Introduction of Crack

One of the worst hazards is crack. If a member of the family begins "hitting the pipe," a process begins that destabilizes an already weak unit and sets the stage for the grandmother to assume her heroic role. It starts with the daughter getting in with the "wrong crowd" or, as the grandmothers say, the "rough" or the "street crowd." She begins to run around at all hours of the day and night, hangs out in the wrong places, goes to bars; that is, she succumbs to the fast life. If she has children, she has less and less time for them. An irony of the situation is that often the grandmother unintentionally aids and abets her daughter's fall into this life by babysitting for the children and helping out financially and in other ways, thus giving the daughter the freedom to pursue a good time. As the daughter becomes increasingly drug-dependent, she becomes a "different person," and the grandmother who was giving so much support becomes aware, sometimes rather precipitously, that she has two or three young children to raise. It is a realization that the amount of responsibility that she has casually been taking for her daughter's children has mushroomed and has suddenly become onerous. Money often becomes a critical problem, as her daughter begs, demands, and cajoles her for it. Ambivalently, she may give in. But then, in time, she finds that she is the only one giving—and receiving little in return. This realization appears to overwhelm all but the strongest grandmothers, but for those who are strong, it is often this realization of the daughter's crack problem that serves to crystallize the whole situation. A litany of events then occurs that "puts things on her mind."

This is when the crisis comes to a head. During this period, for instance, the mother, the daughter, and the daughter's siblings have many fights over what role is to be played by whom. They try to get the daughter in line. They talk to her as though the drug problem is something she got into on her own and something she can get out of on her own, going through a period of denial that the girl is really an addict. Meanwhile, the girl herself is changing. She neglects her appearance, her personal hygiene and health. She becomes increasingly irritable and frustrated. She takes less and less care of her children and may even begin to abuse them. Family members can clearly see this and finally can ignore it no longer. They begin to talk about it, and the girl begins to lose respect in the family. As she becomes cut off from the family, she starts to gravitate ever more completely to the street. The neighbors begin to talk about her. Her reputation becomes sullied, and she is increasingly discredited as a full person in the community. Often people whisper about her, talking about her addiction to crack. Word gets around that she is on the pipe. In the local community, to be on the pipe is a mark of profound deviance, and those who hear about it may react with surprise—depending on the kind of girl she was known to be before "all of this." To end up on the street is to have fallen from putative decency and to be headed nowhere socially, to have fundamentally failed to prevail.

Crack addicts are known to be capable of doing anything to obtain the drug. Women will engage in all forms of prostitution; some formerly outstanding and "decent" girls are known to offer complete strangers a "blow job" for as little as two dollars. Once they are on the pipe, decency and norms of propriety are far from their mind.

At a certain point, the mothers of these women are often forced to disown their daughters, even to put them out. Saying things like, "She ain't doin' nothin'," such a grandmother asserts that her daughter is not functioning as a "real" mother, that she is abdicating her critical mother's role. It is a very damning assessment. In effect, such a grandmother is working to neutralize her affinity to her daughter and thus her maternal responsibilities to her. This is one of the ways in which she begins to sever the connections, culturally making way for herself to take over the child-care responsibilities of her daughter. She does it with a vengeance, coming to grips with her gradual assumption of this new role.

The grandmother's goal in wresting control of the household is to ensure the survival of the family. In contrast to her daughter, she takes a long view of the family and has the moral authority to remind various members of their obligations with regard to generations past and present. An extremely important link, she can rally the rest of the family to deal with the crisis even if they are skeptical of the efficacy or even the wisdom of intervention.

Unemployment, the prevalence of crack, and the increasingly complex social scene all make the grandmother's job more difficult. If her daughter gets on crack, it is never simple for the grandmother to take over the role of mother. Usually she has served as a part-time mother, but the assumption of full-time child-care responsibilities makes her resentful, bitter, and highly frustrated, especially if she has to physically battle her daughter. Moreover, she feels she has already raised her own children and should not have to take responsibility for raising another generation. Frustrated, she may be saddled with a sense a failure. In this situation, tension easily builds and may spill over into fights, violence, and on occasion, even murder.

It is important to note that the grandmother does not always perform the work of primary caretaker by herself. Rather, she calls into action others of her immediate and extended family for help, especially grown siblings of the wayward daughter who until now have been sitting on the sidelines watching and literally wringing their hands. In this regard, she serves as an activator, a facilitator, whose main concern becomes the welfare of the children. To be sure, she does much of the labor-intensive work, but she often does this with the help and moral support of her other children and possibly some of her more extended kin. She and these family members, when they are encouraged, work to reinforce one another.

Often when the grandmother is able to withstand the tension this situation creates, a strong religious component is present. Stepping in for her daughter becomes the grandmother's duty to God. To take care of the children—to serve more fully as their primary caretaker—is to fulfill a religious obligation to Him. It is often from this set of convictions that she is able to carry on, to marshal the sometimes superhuman effort that is required to act in the face of profound adversity—of seeing her own child ravaged by drugs, of dealing with the sometimes knock-down, drag-out fights she has with her daughter over authority over the children or the spending of money.

In these circumstances the grandmother often spiritualizes her situation, taking the whole predicament as a "test" from God. It is a test she must pass, for "God knows the answer if you don't." In meeting the test, she seeks to take care of the children as best she can. Through this interpretation, she feels less of a burden than she otherwise would. She feels that if she prevails, she will be glorifying God. This is where she gets the strength to deal with moral adversity: "I'm not perfect, but I'm trying to be Christ-like." Crack is a test. The devil is constantly working on you, but the Lord works in strange ways. God is love, wisdom, eternal life. Taking care of your grandchildren is part of all this even if your daughter is going to hell. You may not be able to save your daughter, but you can save the grandchildren.

The following first-person account of one decent grandmother, transcribed from a tape-recorded conversation, illuminates both the strength of will of these women and the increasingly dire circumstance with which they must do battle. "Betty Washington" exemplifies many of the traits of the typical inner-city black grandmother, including a strong sense of commitment to family, especially the children, a desire to live an orderly, respectable life despite the personal and social problems that surround her, and a sustaining faith in God.

Betty's Story

I'll be forty in August, and I was born here in Philadelphia, North Philly. When the drugs came in around the corner, everything just went crazy, you know, completely crazy. And even though I lost my house in a fire, I wouldn't want to go back there either. It was really bad there. My oldest daughter, that's where she really had her problems at. It was a mixed neighborhood, Puerto Rican. When I had my first daughter, I was 18. I have two girls. One will be 21 in July, and the oldest one's just turned 22.

I went to Catholic school. Back then it was only $20. I was born Catholic, raised Catholic. I would have liked to have finished it, but at the time money was tight, and I couldn't. Then I went to the public high school, but I didn't graduate. Being that you came from a Catholic school, you learnt more in a Catholic school, then you went to a public school, it was hard to get the teachers to understand that the work that they were giving you, you already knew. You know, the counselors, they didn't really listen to you. So I was really like bored. The best thing I had was geometry. The other classes that I had, the work was too easy. And I wouldn't go to some classes. I'd go to the library, I would sneak over to different churches, stuff like that, and being that this counselor wouldn't listen to me what I was sayin', I was just hangin' out. After that, I started goin' to night school, different programs, stuff like that. I was educatin' myself basically.

When I got pregnant with my first daughter, I was married. I had both my children while I was married, but I haven't been married twenty years. I got divorced. What happened? Well, it was the time the Black Muslims came in. We had a business, everything was goin' fine, he got involved with the Black Muslims. After he got involved with the Black Muslims, he wanted me to convert. I wouldn't do it. Everything just went haywire. Like they told him, "She won't convert, you don't need her." So he was basically going along with everything they said and it got that he wouldn't do for me, he wouldn't do for the kids. I wasn't goin' to fight with him, you go your way, I'll go my way. That's essentially what it was. I had a lot of problems with the Catholic Church. They want you to go to their courts and whatnot. But by that time the man was already seein' somebody. He was already involved and had kids and everything so it didn't make sense for me to go through that. The marriage was gone, you know. I didn't see no sense in it. They didn't actually excommunicate me from the church, but I got a lot of static when it came time to send my kids to Catholic school. There was a lot of trouble with the pay rate. If you was Catholic, you didn't have to pay as much in tuition. So there was a lot of static, but it was necessary so it didn't faze me. I had a tough time in the divorce, you know, raisin' the kids. I still consider myself Catholic. I'm not involved in the Catholic Church as I would like to be because it changed so much, you know, but I did raise my kids Catholic. The only thing is they just didn't go to Catholic school. The oldest one was in there, but they took her out. She was just that bad. They took her out in first grade. But I couldn't afford tuition for them anyway.

I raised my daughters on my own pretty much with the help of my mom. It was not a problem until they got older 'cause she was so attached to them. There was a lot of problems there. I had a boyfriend. That didn't work out either. We had a lot of problems raising Angela. It's hard raising a child and you get the mother interferin', you know. We were younger then. I say she was younger too and set in her ways. So when I started having problems with my daughters, she couldn't see it because she wasn't there every day, you know, and then after everything came to a head and everything got out of hand, she took 'em. *Then* she was able to see what I was talkin' about.

They would run away a lot. They were twelve and eleven. After we had the fire, it was real emotional. I was tryin' to get everything situated with the insurance. I had a lot of problems, you know. I got ripped off with my insurance and the contractors and everything. The house never did get fixed up. And things just wasn't as they were. I hadda go out and work. I had to start doin' things that they wasn't used to. They was used to bein' with me and then I had to start goin' out findin' a job, lookin' for a job, leavin' them with different people. And it just caused a lot of problems with them, and they couldn't adjust. Sometimes they would stay at home, sometimes they'd stay with a neighbor, sometimes they'd stay with my mom. At the time when they really needed me, I couldn't really be there for them. So it was hard. Goin' back to the district attorney, goin' back to the court. It was difficult.

Angela's Problems Become Chronic

And their whole behavior just changed. Angela was twelve years old. She started doin' drugs. Well, at the time it was marijuana. It was the neighborhood. They got kind of wild. They were gettin' more freedom, much more freedom. There was a lot of peer pressure. She used to start doin' things that were so out of place for her. And I guess I was a little strict on her, you know, on account of it was just me. I had to be the mother and the father. And once I started lettin' 'em get out there, they just changed. Well, she has always been a bad, problem child. She got kicked out of first grade. And then the neighborhood started deterioratin' and there was a lot of peer pressure, and she's not the type of person that could stand on their own. She listens to everybody on the outside, no matter what you say.

So everything just started goin' haywire. I had her in counseling for a long time. That didn't work. You know, the counselor couldn't help her much 'cause she was what you call a habitual liar. Her whole attitude just changed. She wanted to fight. She started pullin' knives on me. And this is a young girl. I tried but . . . . She started when she was twelve, and I was at work. There was always some guy, somebody. You know, she's always liked the older men, always having the older men. She was close to her father even though she was two when he left. I can't say she doesn't remember. She was two when he left; after then there was no communication whatsoever. I always say for her wantin' to be with older men, she's looking for her father, you know.

I know I brought her up right, I know I did everything right for her. I might not have been *the best* 'cause I had problems myself. I couldn't do everything, but I did the best I could, but she's—I don't know, she's just a bad seed. My other daughter was a A student. She was one of the first kids they took out of the regular public school and sent to white neighborhoods, takin' the bus. She was good. But then she got on drugs. She was supposed to go to the School for the Performing Arts. She could have went to Cheyney College. She could have done anything she wanted.

But Angela, she's just a bad child. She didn't care what you do to her, if you punish her, how much you talk to her, how much you cry, scream, whatever. She didn't care. Like I say, to me it was a lot of peer pressure. A lot of what she did had to do with bein' that we were livin' in a Puerto Rican neighborhood. Most of the problems I had were with Puerto Rican guys. I had to go out to these people and fight 'em: "Leave my daughter alone." She almost got shot by the cops 'cause she was livin' around the corner in an abandoned house with a whole bunch of those guys. And it was a shock too because I didn't think that she was socializin' with them. The way I had brought her up, it was out of place, completely out of place. The first time I actually had to leave my job and come home because she had ran away was because of marijuana. She was just stoned. She was doin' weird stuff. First I thought it was attention, she wanted a lot of attention. But she really had a problem.

It came to it that she had to be put away. I had to actually put her in a home, and I regret the day I did that because instead of her gettin' better, everything got worse in there. It just got worse. But at the time there was nothin' else I could do. I had myself to think about. I had the youngest one to think about. And this child, she wanted to fight. She pulled knives on me, she said people were gonna blow the house up. This is the type of child that she was. I got her back after about a year. She was doin' the same thing, still wantin' to fight and whatnot. And I didn't think that DHS [Department of Human Services] was really helpin' as much as they could have been.

When she went on crack, her whole attitude changed: "I just don't give a damn" attitude. And she was so—how can I say it—she had no scruples about it, none whatsoever. After I got her back—she was 19—she stayed here for awhile, but at the time I didn't really, really notice she was doin' crack. I knew she smoked marijuana. We started goin' to the same school. I was goin' for the computers and she was goin' for nurse's aid. And she did good, A's and whatnot, but she didn't complete it. And I still didn't really know because at the time she was stayin' with my mother again and she was back and forth here. And she got pregnant. And she was always startin' fightin', and I couldn't deal with that so I had to put her out while she was pregnant. The landlord's daughter lives upstairs. That caused a lot of problems 'cause the landlord would find out what was goin' on. She wanted to bring boys in, she didn't want to do nothin', she wanted to fight all the time, so I had to ask her to leave. And I really didn't connect it to the crack. I knew she was doin' somethin', but I just didn't know she was doin' that. And then after she had the baby, I still didn't know. They didn't really tell me too much. She didn't stay in the hospital too long. I was thinkin' they let her go, but actually she left the hospital.

Betty Becomes "The" Grandmother

Then that's when she said, "You're still my momma." I stayed over with her for a week, and she would go out, and she would not come back. Eventually she went fourteen days and she didn't come back so I wound up bringin' the baby back here with me. And that's when I realized she was on the crack. She was not behavin' like a mother. But she's always been the type of person who eventually lets you know what she's doin'. And she came home, she told me she was doin' whatnot. And by then I had already knew. By me takin' the baby back to the clinic and everythin', the doctors told me. I didn't understand what was goin' on with the baby, the withdrawal symptoms and whatnot. I had already made up my mind, if she wasn't goin' to take care of the baby, if she wasn't goin' to do right, then I would take him. But I tried to give her a chance to take care of her own baby, but that didn't work out. I had to stay here. She wasn't ever here. Jamaicans would come lookin' for her wantin' me to give 'em back their money that she took. I'd give her money to go get Pampers and milk, and she'd take that. I sent her to the laundromat. Someone else would bring the clothes back, she's gone with the money.

What I did was I went with her to court because she knew I was goin' to find out eventually. She went to get custody of her baby, but she didn't have any place to stay. And the address she used, she couldn't stay there because these people was involved in drugs, you know. And we got joint custody. I figured when we had joint custody, everything would work out. That didn't work out. So I had to get full custody. By the time he was ten months, I had full custody.

This is the type of thing this child has always been in. She's always gettin' beat up. She's always gettin' raped and whatnot. She never wanted to press charges, which I didn't understand at the time that this is the way she was livin'. She was livin' doin' these things to take care of her habit. Actually I didn't know that at the time. I didn't understand it. And things just got out of hand, and I couldn't deal with it, you know, fightin', men comin' here lookin' for her. And things just wasn't workin' out. I had the landlord to deal with. I got to have some space to stay. I had to tell her to go. It was like I had to watch over my back, I had to watch everything, I had to hide everything, my food, my silverware. I had to do those kinds of things. And I couldn't live like that. She was takin' things out. Nobody here but me, her, and the baby. I go get something and it's gone. It didn't make sense to me, you know. I couldn't sleep. There was just no peace for me, no peace at all. She became a completely different person, and I couldn't deal with her. So I had to say, "I love you, but you got to go. There is nothin' else I can do for you." I tried to get her into rehab, she wouldn't go.

Even right now, I'm still goin' to counseling. I've been goin' to the center ever since I had trouble with my kids and that's since about 1980. I still go, talk to the counselors. I go to grandparents' support group. I'm not ashamed, you know. If I need help, I'm going to go get it, just talkin' to somebody, the hotline, stuff like that. I do those things. I worry about her a lot, but there's nothing else I can do for her. She got to start doin' things for herself. It's hard. It's a good support group. You find out you're not by yourself. There's a lot of people like that.

Now I have the little baby. She's 13 months now. I got custody of the oldest boy. I went to court. That's a lot of money goin' back and forth to court. You know, I had to do that. Then the father, he decided he wants to get upset because I won't let him see them when he wants to see them. You know, he had a set time to come and see 'em. He never showed up, but he took me to court. I had to wind up payin' the money, altogether about $700, and still to this day we have four court orders for him to come and see his son on Sunday from one to three; he has not once showed up, not once, not one time.

When you have a crack baby, it's always some problem. It can be physical. You don't really understand the babies, what the babies want from you, you know, the crying, the anger. The babies get hyper, you know, they get really upset, and that's a lot to deal with, a lot to deal with. So you take them back and forth to the clinic. And there's always somethin' wrong with these children. What really happened with this baby, the little boy, he wound up with some kind of infection. I knew she had herpes, but I didn't know she had syphilis. The baby got sick, and they thought he had meningitis. Well, if I didn't have custody of him, there was no way that I could have had him treated without the mother. Where was I supposed to find her at? Where was I supposed to look for her at? And I didn't know at the time, but I found out two months later she had syphilis, second stage, secondary syphilis. And that's hard, that's really hard.

She fades in and out of my life. If she's not at the hospital right now, I couldn't tell you where she is. She just had another baby, only weighed two pounds, it's still in the hospital. Right now, the little baby, I'm trying to get custody of her. I filed a petition to get custody of her. What they're telling me now is you've got to have an address for the father and the mother. I don't have the address. I don't know where they are. They say I have to go find 'em. Where am I supposed to look for them at? I know nothin' about the father. I don't know where to find the mother unless she's in the hospital. She might be there two days, then she's gone. To get custody of her, you have to get involved with DHS. It's so different from last year because once she got tested for cocaine and they knew she didn't have a place to stay, the baby was automatically turned over to DHS. All she had to do was agree to let me have her, which she did. Like I say, I have her now for 13 months. The new baby, I don't know what they're goin' to do with, I really don't. She still don't have a place to stay. She still tests cocaine. What the social worker tells me now is just because she's doin' cocaine doesn't mean you can take the baby from her, which is so different from last year, you know.

From the World of Work to the World of Welfare

But you have to step in and take the responsibility. You have no other choice. I don't want to see him in a foster home, and I would hate to see right now for them to be split up like that. But it's hard. Yeah, everything is in God's hands. He shows you what you have to do and what you don't have to do. The only problem I have is that there's no man in my life. I don't have time for those things no more. Everything is those children. Everything is a circle around those kids. You have to have a place to stay, you have to get food, you have to do these things. So it's hard.

I haven't worked since I got the oldest boy. I live off aid. You have a court order where the father pays the court. No matter how much he pays, you only goin' to get $50 of it. He does that, but he's just not involved with the babies. He's a security guard.

You're takin' care of those babies from the time they come home from the hospital. You know, the mother's doin' nothin' for 'em. You're doin' everything for that baby. If I let her take that baby out of here and take him to a crack house, I'm responsible 'cause I know what's goin' on. So it was a lot of conflict. I couldn't let her take the baby. I had to watch him. This is somethin' I had to do. There's nothin' else you can do except let the baby go be put in a foster home, and I'm not about to let that happen. So I did it for the first one. I didn't never expect to have another one and I didn't never expect to have another one, you know. With the first one they see that you mean business, that you goin' to do what you say you goin' to do. But that don't faze them, that don't faze them.

My mom's been real good. She's been real good about helping me with the first one and then the second one, but this time she's like, "If you do that, you won't never come out of it. I don't think you should go ahead and keep on takin' her babies for her." Which I can understand in a way, you know, because I don't have the space for 'em. I'm lookin' for a place now. I really don't have the room for 'em. And these babies take up a lot of time, you know, they take up a lot of your time. The youngest one is in this program for slowly developed children. Her teacher comes now on Tuesdays and Thursdays, comes down and teaches her. You know, you go to the clinic every week, the special baby clinic, the neurology clinic. The first thing they say in the hospital is it has to do with the cocaine because she was exposed to cocaine. And that's hard. And I hate that labelin' them children like that, but it's the truth.

I don't feel so much angry. I feel as though even if she was to get herself straightened out, it would be hard for me to give them children up, you know, 'cause I feel as though they've been neglected, something's been taken away from them. The mother has been taken away from them. They don't know her, and if you just take these kids and give them back to her, that's goin' to be hard on the children. How are you goin' to explain—you know, the children don't understand what's goin' on. They know that the grandmother right now is the mother, and it would be hard for 'em. They don't have no contact with her, don't see her. That's goin' to be hard on them, and I couldn't do that. I would rather raise them 'til they get of age, you know. Right now, there's nothin' much I can say to them. I can't say, "Well, this is your mother," 'cause I don't see her. She's supposed to come see 'em, and she never shows up. So I feel for the children more than I feel for the mother right now. I really do.

There's no sense gettin' upset. This is what you have to do. If you didn't see any sense in it, you wouldn't be doin' it. That's the way I look at it. These kids are special. They're special kids because they have been exposed to crack. So it's a lot of time, a lot of patience, and a lot of love. You've got to give it to 'em. So I enjoy it. I really do. I do it. I get tired sometimes. Sometimes I get frustrated, but I don't dwell on it, you know. I don't dwell on it. Right now the most important thing is these children. That's most important. Yeah, some people say that God is testing them and good things is goin' to come out of it.

Right now financially it's hard. I really need a place, I need a place of my own. Livin' in this apartment is not good for the kids. It's a problem all the time, problems with the neighbors, problems with the landlord. They come and use my phone when I'm not here. I have to keep it locked in my bedroom and then I can't hear it. At the time I took this place, it was just me, and I was workin'. I thought once I earn some money, I'll get out of here. Once I got the grandbabies, all that stopped, you know. Life is hard, it's really hard. It's always somethin', always, always somethin'.

Life of a Black Grandmother in the 1990s

And even though I don't see their mother, when we do hear from her, it's so much confusion and turmoil. I get so upset with her. I wish she'd just go and stay away, just stay away completely. It got to the point where I wouldn't even stay in here because she would come here and she'd want to fight, you know, arm fight. I was often worn out. So now I get up and I go every day. You know, you say things for their own benefit, they don't want to hear that. And the main thing is these kids are in my custody. *I'm* takin' care of these kids. *I've* got to do what's best for the children, not you. Regardless of whether you're their mother or not, I don't want to hear that. You're not doin' anything for them, and I can't let her take these children knowin' the lifestyle she lives, you know. That's the main thing right there. I can't do that. They could wind up anywhere. So this is what I had to stipulate. Like the judge told me, "You're responsible for these children. The mother or the father comes for 'em, they are not to have 'em." That's the number one rule. That's what I have to live by. And my rules are, I'm goin' to do what I have to do. If I wanna go out, I go out. I'm not goin' to stop what I'm doin' to let you come and go when you please. You know, I can't do that. And most of the time when I wait for her, she never shows up anyway. It didn't make sense for me to sit here all the time just waitin' and waitin' and waitin'. She never shows up.

Just like the father, you know. I sit every Sunday, and he never comes. I got so I'm not doin' that anymore. Let the court say what they wanta say. It doesn't make sense, you know, to get this child all geared up to go, even without sayin' anything to him, to get him all ready to go to see his father, he never shows up. So I stopped. I just stopped. It's too much. It's too much. This boy is three years old, and he hasn't made a effort to show up. This is Robert. And Carla's the youngest one. T.J. is my youngest daughter's boy, but he's not in my custody.

Carla's not really in my custody; she's just turned over to me by DHS. I have to get like what they call a confirmation of custody, and that's like $200, $350. Unless I know the address for the father and the mother, they won't go ahead and file the petition. I don't know what I'm goin' to do there. I really don't know. I don't know where the girl is. She's livin' in a abandoned house somewhere, where I don't know. I have no address for her, you know, none at all. I was up at the hospital on Monday. I had an appointment with the social worker, talkin' to her, and she was askin' me, "What are you goin' to do? She needs help." The only thing I could tell her was, I can't come up there every day because I don't have the carfare and I have a list of houses I'm supposed to be lookin' at. I'm tryin' to do that every day.

Mothers, Crack, the Law, and God's Test

They really need to pass a law—in fact, I thought they had did this—any mother that has a baby that's exposed to crack, they was supposed to put 'em in jail. They haven't done that. And I think that instead of waitin' thirty days after they get out of the hospital to have their tubes tied, they should do it while they've got them in the hospital right then and there, tie their tubes.

Until they do something, these women are goin' to keep on havin' these babies. They're goin' to keep right on doin' it. And it's rough on grandparents 'cause you know the grandparents are the ones who are goin' to take these children. A lot of them are goin' to do it. Some of them they just won't do it. But a lot of them are goin' to do it, you know, 'cause it's bad puttin' these kids in foster homes. You hear so much bad things about foster care. All the things that's goin' on, a lot of bad and whatnot. So it's rough. So you take 'em. You take 'em and you raise 'em.

I don't go to church that much. Somebody might invite me to a church, I might go. Most of the times, like I said, I do a lot of talking, friends. I have a lot of support from friends, my mom. I still go to counseling and I talk things out. I pray a lot too. You know, you pray a lot . . . and just hope for the best and hope that you're doing the right thing. It's hard. You know, every day it's always somethin'. And then when you get to thinkin' everything goes all right and you're feelin' good and whatnot, somethin' happens. So you just take it one thing at a time, one thing at a time. I feel like I'm bein' tested 'cause there's a lot goin' on right now that I really don't have no control over. So it's hard.

Can Adult Daughters Return to the Nest?

My youngest daughter, she wants to stay here. She was leavin' T.J. here on a regular basis, but I stopped that 'cause he was upset bein' away from his mother. I was keepin' him while she was workin', and then when she stopped workin' she started smokin' more marijuana. She has this old man, he was doin' drugs unbelievable. He had a roofin' business and he was doin' good, bringin' the money home, and she was savin' it. But now they got thrown out of their apartment. It was his mother's company, but he was runnin' it for her so he just messed up all the way round. If it was just her, I would be glad to let her come back here. But with the two of them, I couldn't afford for my rent to get raised. It just wouldn't work out. She's at that lazy point right now, a little lazy right now. And I just couldn't see it. She hasn't seen her father in twenty years, and all of a sudden he pops up out of nowhere. Now she wants to go and live off of him. So I don't know what she's goin' to do. She's kind of upset with me right now, but I can't have her here when I'm plannin' on takin' my baby.

She smokes marijuana. When you come and tell me you're doin' somethin', O.K., fine. She's not doin' it to the point where I got to tell her don't do that around your baby. But when you come and tell me you're doin' this heavily 'cause you got so many problems, and I can't talk to you and try to make you see what you're doin' wrong, then, you know, what's the point? If you come and ask me to give you advice, and I tell you how I feel about it and yet it upsets you, well then, what else can I say? You don't need to do it. I'm not goin' to tell you not to do it because you're goin' to do it anyway. But that's what's happenin' with her. She gettin' worse with it. But she's not a dumb child. She could have gone on to college, gave it up for this nigger to get stoned. Don't mean her no good. And when I was tryin' to tell her this, she didn't want to hear it. Now that I don't have nothing to say about it and she gets upset, I say why. I did everything I could do. All I can do is pray for her. And she was good to me, she was really good to me, but in the last three months she's just . . . . She's smokin' that stuff, and people got to understand that that stuff messes you up, really messes you up so she's not herself. So all I can do is pray for you. I'll talk to you. If you want to talk to me, come talk to me and I'll tell you how I feel, but I don't press the issue. I don't do that any more. I think she's kind of upset with me right now because I won't let her come back here and stay with us. It's really no room. We can't afford to have our rent go up. I'm trying to get out of here myself. I'm not goin' to deal with the boyfriend, you know. You come by yourself, you and the baby, fine, but the boyfriend can't come. Especially someone who's doing drugs like he's doin'. I said no. I didn't put up with that with your sister, I'm not goin' to put up with your boyfriend, you know what I mean?

I can always tell when she's high, always. Like I say, my children have never really been able to hide anything from me, and they will—I can say that much—they will tell you. Even when I don't see Angela, whatever is goin' on in her life, when I do hear from her she tells me everything. I may not want to hear it, but she tells me everything that's goin' on in her life, whether she's been in jail, how many times she got beat up, what, who, everything. So that's one thing I can say.

The Final Reality: Betty Accepts Her Heroic Role

She says to me, "If I tell 'em I'm goin' to straighten myself up, would you let me have my kids back?" If I saw it, it would be a completely different thing, but just by you comin' and tell' me, uh-uh, because I would know better. I've heard it so many times: "Ma, I'm goin' to do this. Ma, I goin' to do that." And it never get done. Never. And there's always the hope. You know, I pray for you. I'm lookin' forward to seein' it happenin'. It just never does. It never does. It just goes in one ear and out the other ear. She called my Aunt Esther. It was Angela's birthday. See, I know my kids so well. It was her birthday. I had called the hospital. They hadn't heard from her in about three days. It's not like she's goin' there every day to see the baby, which I already knew she wasn't goin' to be doin'. And it was her birthday. She called about 9:30. I knew who it was. She called cryin'. She and her boyfriend got in a great big fight. I didn't want to hear it. I did not talk to her. I did not. I let my aunt talk to her because I'm out, I'm havin' a good time, I was enjoyin' myself. I didn't want to be bothered 'cause then that would just bring me down. You know, if I had to come home, stay up all night worryin' if this girl is goin' to get killed or whatnot. I let my aunt talk to her. Like my aunt was sayin', you've got to not let yourself get upset. 'Cause soon as I hear her name—they say, "Angela's on the phone"—I just get all "what is goin' on?" And that's no good. That is no good, no good at all.

Betty feels keenly the pressures of her situation—internally from within her family and externally from the streets and institutional bureaucracy—but she is determined to endure in spite of them because she feels her responsibility is to future generations. Despite her own responsible behavior, however, her situation is becoming more and more difficult—possibly even untenable—because of her daughter's actions. It is Betty's daughter who persists, for complicated reasons of her own, in bringing into the world children she is completely unable to care for. Angela has gotten caught up in the drug culture that has so pervaded the black inner-city community, in part as an indirect result of deindustrialization and the consequent loss of blue-collar jobs (see Perrucci et al. 1988; Bluestone and Harrison 1982). As noted above, men with no prospects of legitimate jobs turn to the underground economy, particularly the drug trade. Getting women hooked on crack is one way of developing a customer base—and also a "supply" of easily manipulated women. But when Angela falls into this social trap, her entire social network is affected.

At the same time, the details of Betty's struggle reveal how the society has stacked the deck against her. In order to receive welfare support, Betty was forced to quit her job as a nurse's aide, even though she enjoyed working. There is also the issue of caring for the children, especially the crack baby, who required special attention. The lack of good, affordable day care in conjunction with the rules of welfare eligibility left Betty with only one responsible course of action: to leave her job in the private sector in order, in effect, to become employed by the state to raise her grandchildren.

The Grandmother as Old Head

Many inner-city black people have raised children not their own and many others have "fictive" grandchildren: children who are not their grandchildren but for whom they play the grandparent role (Bengtson 1985). Some grandmothers expand their role even further by becoming in a sense community grandmothers, taking it upon themselves to act as the wise, responsible "oldest head" of the neighborhood. In this capacity they are an important source of social control and organization, offering concern, support, and advice to local children but also doling out discipline, including corporal punishment. One such elderly woman described her role as old head as follows:

> They call her just a mother, a real mother, not a mother who don't care for children from the bottom. The way I feel about it, the way I tell these children, is "I love all children: If you don't love somebody else children, you really don't love yo' own."
>
> This is when you see any child out there doing wrong, you goes to him and you corrects him, just like he is yo' child. And that's what I do. I don't care what I'm doing, if I see somebody fighting, arguing, or whatever. I have taken care of all the kids in this street going backwards and forwards to school. They come through here, get in a fight, I get out there and stop it.
>
> And if they wanta be strong with me, I get stronger. I let them know that they not gon' outdo me. I tell 'em, "If you want me to take you in the house and give you a good spankin', I will do it."

Today, however, people are increasingly reticent about playing the role of old head due to the changes in the community, especially the rise of the drug culture. Part of it has to do with how rough the streets have become, part of it with the way people now move in and out. This is not to say that the old heads are gone, but they seem to be on the decline in terms of authority and ability and willingness to play these roles. This is another factor leading to the diminished resilience of the community.

Conclusion and Implications

The context that accounts for the difference between what is happening in poor black urban communities now and what happened in the past is the economic and social changes that have swept urban America. Blacks have always been apart from the dominant society, and they have always been segregated and beset by the problems that come with segregation. In the past thirty years, there has been a change for the greater inclusion of blacks in American society and the sharing of its fruits, but these changes have most often helped those blacks who were ready to take advantage of them—the middle classes, the educated people. The poor, who lack the skills, the education, as well as the outlook to take advantage of this opportunity, have not been beneficiaries but more often victims of the changes (see Wilson 1980, 1987).

All this has implications for the way poor black families operate (see Edelman 1987; Jencks and Peterson 1991). There has been a rise in the underground economy, which is, for the most desperate people, an alternative to the regular economy that very often does not support their basic human needs. But at the same time the underground economy offers an alternative, it has a socially deleterious effect on the rest of the community, undermining it in a very basic way. Those who are involved in the underground economy exploit the community, and so even the "decent" people among the black lower classes sometimes become ensnared in their schemes. This engenders increasing alienation on the part of some of these people, and they begin to distrust the wider culture's conventionality. Inner-city residents, particularly young men, want many of the things that middle-class white people have—nice cars, nice clothes—but because the wider system is so bankrupt in their minds, it becomes very important for them to combine these items with a marked unconventionality of dress and behavior. A counterculture thus becomes elaborated with the purpose of making a cultural statement against a dominant society that many young inner-city blacks feel "disrespects" them. In effect, these young people are saying, "While I want what the white people have in terms of money and privilege, I don't want those pin-striped suits. I don't want to look like that. I want to do my own thing. I want to be my own person." Flashy jewelry is very far away from the pin-striped suit. So are the untied shoelaces and the coveralls with their suspenders hanging down at the sides that characterize the latest style of the urban hip. In contrast, for the white kids who mimic them, these styles may just be a lark that they easily give up when they realize it is time to become serious about life.

Probably the most worrisome development of all is the emergence and proliferation of what I would call a crack culture, which is to be distinguished from the ordinary underground economy and drug culture. Crack is special and leaves in its wake great numbers of casualties. Seen indirectly by most other people, victims of crack in inner-city poor communities suffer acutely.

The primary victim of the present situation is the poor black family, which is experiencing a profound crisis. The crisis spreads through combinations and permutations of this problem because for survival, people, particularly the young, are drawn to the underground economy. The metaphor of a raging fire or a cancer comes to mind. It leads to death, to illness, to the proliferation of homeless children, crack babies, teenage pregnancy, and other social problems.

As indicated above, in the inner-city community, there is the social distinction between decency and "the street"; people with a positive sense of the future are associated with decency and those headed nowhere socially are associated with the street. In the community, "the street" has a kind of magical magnetic quality; it pulls those who are not well anchored to more conventional social forms. It is a seductive thing, and those of the community who would be decent must resist its draw. To be unsuccessful is to fall socially or to be "out there in the streets." To prevail is to have resisted the streets and to have done so in a manner that is praiseworthy in the minds of many who see themselves as decent. In this respect, decency and the street represent polarities around which social identity may be worked out and formed.

This is the context in which the grandmother must be seen. The traditional role of the grandmother, who serves as an anchor, a cornerstone, or even a lifeboat of the black ghetto family, emerges and crystallizes in this context. In this context she becomes heroic, saving people, assisting people who are receptive in some way. She cannot be fully understood independent of this social context. The role is not that different from the role she has played in the past. Without her presence, the breakdown and disorganization would be even more profound in its implications and consequences for community life.

Standing firmly against the counterculture, the black grandmother believes in the wider system, emphasizing a strong commitment to decency and propriety. She dismisses structural arguments of the various social ills besetting the community, believing that if you just clean yourself up and act right, you will be rewarded; if you are civil, if you are decent, you can make it. She stands at the spot where personal responsibility begins to mesh with the structural problems. The grandmother who successfully plays her role tries to transmit her orientation to the young. But to prevail she must do battle with the increasingly pervasive street culture, and even the strongest of these indefatigable women sometimes despair of what the future holds for those they are trying so desperately to save. The grandmother's resilience through the generations has been extraordinary, but many now feel the negative social forces tearing at their community are stretching her considerable personal resources to the limit, if not beyond it. As the grandmothers get older, they become increasingly less able to control volatile adolescents, especially when they must compete for influence with the lure of the street. Since they are not in the work force, they are not role models and, though generally loved and respected even when disobeyed, they may come to seem irrelevant, particularly to their grandsons.

At the same time as the grandmothers are losing clout and energy, few of them are being replaced. Crack, unemployment, and other social problems that follow in the wake of deindustrialization work to dispel the human capital of grandmothers, so fewer women have the capacity to undertake the role. It is unlikely that Angela will ever follow in her mother's footsteps. As the grandmothers become less effective, the multiplier effects grow, and the black inner-city community moves close to social disintegration.

References

Anderson, Elijah. 1978. *A Place on the Corner.* Chicago: University of Chicago Press.

Anderson, Elijah. 1989. "Sex Codes and Family Life among Poor Inner-City Youths." *Annals of the American Academy of Political and Social Science* 501: 59–78.

Anderson, Elijah. 1990. *Streetwise: Race, Class, and Change in an Urban Community.* Chicago: University of Chicago Press.

Anderson, Elijah. 1991. "Neighborhood Effects on Teenage Pregnancy." In *The Urban Underclass,* edited by Christopher Jencks and Paul E. Peterson. Washington, D.C.: The Brookings Institution.

Anderson, Elijah. 1994. "The Code of the Streets." *The Atlantic Monthly,* May.

Becker, Howard S. 1958. "Problems of Inference and Proof in Participant Observation." *American Sociological Review* 23: 652–660.

Becker, Howard S. 1970. *Sociological Work.* Chicago: Aldine.

Bengtson, Vern L. 1985. "Diversity and Symbolism in Grandparental Roles." In *Grandparenthood,* edited by Vern L. Bengtson and Joan F. Robertson. Beverly Hills: Sage Publications.

Blassingame, John. 1972. *The Slave Community.* New York: Oxford University Press.

Bluestone, Barry, and Bennett Harrison. 1982. *The Deindustrialization of America: Plant Closings, Community Abandonment, and the Dismantling of Basic Industry.* New York: Basic Books.

Burton, Linda M., and Vern L. Bengtson. 1985. "Black Grandmothers: Issues of Timing and Continuity of Roles." In *Grandparenthood,* edited by Vern L. Bengtson and Joan F. Robertson. Beverly Hills: Sage Publications.

Cherlin, Andrew J., and Frank F. Furstenberg, Jr. 1986. *The New American Grandparent.* New York: Basic Books.

Drake, St. Clair, and Horace R. Cayton. 1962. *Black Metropolis: A Study of Negro Life in a Northern City.* New York: Harper and Row.

Dunston, Patricia J., et al. 1987. "Black Adolescent Mothers and Their Families: Extending Services." In *The Black Adolescent Parent,* edited by Stanley F. Battle. New York: Haworth Press.

Edelman, Marian Wright. 1987. *Families in Peril: An Agenda for Social Change.* Cambridge, Mass.: Harvard University Press.

Frazier, E. Franklin. 1939. *The Negro Family in the United States.* Chicago: University of Chicago Press.

Furstenberg, Frank F., Jr., Theodore Hershberg, and John Modell. 1981. "The Origins of the Female-Headed Black Family: The Impact of the Urban Experience." In *Philadelphia: Work, Space, Family and Group Experience in the Nineteenth Century,* edited by Theodore Hershberg. Oxford: Oxford University Press.

Geertz, Clifford. 1983. *Local Knowledge: Further Essays in Interpretive Anthropology.* New York: Basic Books.

Gutman, Herbert. 1976. *The Black Family in Slavery and Freedom.* New York: Vintage Books.

Hays, William C., and Charles H. Mindel. 1973. "Extended Kinship Relations in Black and White Families." *Journal of Marriage and the Family* 35: 51–57.

Heiss, Jerold. 1975. *The Case of the Black Family.* New York: Columbia University Press.

Hershberg, Theodore. 1973. "Free Blacks in Ante-bellum Philadelphia." In *The Peoples of Philadelphia: A History of Ethnic Groups and Lower-Class Life, 1790–1940*, edited by Allen F. Davis and Mark H. Haller. Philadelphia: Temple University Press.

Jackson, Jacquelyne J. 1971a. "The Blacklands of Gerontology." *Aging and Human Development* 2: 156–171.

Jackson, Jacquelyne J. 1971b. "Aged Blacks: A Potpourri in the Direction of the Reduction of Inequities." *Phylon* 32: 260–280.

Jaynes, Gerald David. 1986. *Branches without Roots: Genesis of the Black Working Class in the American South, 1862–1882.* New York: Oxford University Press.

Jencks, Christopher, and Paul E. Peterson, eds. 1991. *The Urban Underclass.* Washington, D.C.: The Brookings Institution.

Jones, Faustine C. 1973. "The Lofty Role of the Black Grandmother." *The Crisis* 80 (no. 1): 41–56.

Katz, Michael B. 1989. *The Undeserving Poor: From the War on Poverty to the War on Welfare.* New York: Pantheon Books.

Kornhaber, Arthur, and Kenneth L. Woodward. 1981. *Grandparents/ Grandchildren: The Vital Connection.* Garden City, N.Y.: Anchor Press, Doubleday.

Lemann, Nicholas. 1991. *The Promised Land: The Great Black Migration and How It Changed America.* New York: Alfred A. Knopf.

Perrucci, Carolyn C., et al. 1988. *Plant Closings: International Context and Social Class.* New York: Aldine de Gruyter.

Presser, Harriet B. 1980. "Sally's Corner: Coping with Unmarried Motherhood." *Journal of Social Issues* 36 (no. 1): 107–129.

Register, Jasper C., and Jim Mitchell. 1982. "Black-White Differences in Attitudes toward the Elderly." *Journal of Minority Aging* 7 (nos. 3–4): 34–46.

Rickel, Annette U. 1989. *Teen Pregnancy and Parenting.* New York: Hemisphere.

Smith, E. W. 1975. "The Role of the Grandmother in Adolescent Pregnancy and Parenthood." *Journal of School Health* 45 (no. 5): 278–283.

Stack, Carole. 1974. *All Our Kin.* New York: Harper and Row.

Stampp, Kenneth M. 1989. *The Peculiar Institution: Slavery in the Ante-Bellum South.* New York: Vintage Books. (1956).

Troll, Lillian E. 1971. "The Family in Later Life: A Decade Review." *Journal of Marriage and the Family* 33: 263–290.

Walker, Alice. 1982. *The Color Purple.* New York: Pocket Books.

Williams, Constance W. 1991. *Black Teenage Mothers: Pregnancy and Child Rearing from Their Perspective.* Lexington, Mass.: Lexington Books, D. C. Heath.

Wilson, William Julius. 1980. *The Declining Significance of Race.* Second edition. Chicago: University of Chicago Press.

Wilson, William Julius. 1987. *The Truly Disadvantaged: The Inner City, the Underclass, and Public Policy.* Chicago: University of Chicago Press.

Wilson, William Julius. 1995. From Poverty to Joblessness: The Inner-City since Myrdal's *An American Dilemma.* Paper delivered at the Harvard Conference on the 50th Anniversary of Gunnar Myrdal's *An American Dilemma*, Harvard University, Cambridge, Mass., September 28–30.

3

America's Working Poor: 1980–1990

JOHN D. KASARDA

Concerns about the polarization of wages in the United States have generated increased scholarly interest in a purportedly growing segment of the labor force known as the working poor (Bradbury 1986; Craypo 1991; Danziger and Gottschalk 1986; Gardner and Herz 1992; Harrison and Bluestone 1988; Klein and Rones 1989; Kosters, Levitan, Gallo, and Shapiro 1990). These concerns are derived, in part, from the "good jobs vs. bad jobs" debate in which it is contended that the majority of jobs created in the U.S. after 1979 have been of low-wage and dubious quality (Bluestone 1990).

Such "poverty-level" work, it is argued, has been increasingly taken by women and minorities as well as by white males displaced from higher-paying unionized jobs in the manufacturing sector (Burtless 1990; Harrison and Bluestone 1988). With low-wage work on the rise, the discussion surrounding work requirements in welfare reform questions whether working (even full-time) will be enough to lift many families out of poverty (Danziger 1991; Elwood 1993).

In this essay, I look at the relationship of work and poverty in the United States from 1980 to 1990 using the most comprehensive data sources available: the 5 Percent Public Use Microdata Sample (PUMS) from the 1980 and 1990 Censuses of Population. This database enables us to obtain more detailed and reliable demographic and geographic information about the working poor than the Current Population Survey, which has served as the basis for most of the research on the working poor to date.

Fundamental questions will be answered regarding the changing size, composition, and location of America's working poor. How large is the working poor population? What changes took place between 1980 and 1990 in the racial, ethnic, and gender makeup? Which regions and states have experienced the highest rates of working poor and how do these rates vary across their central-city, suburban, and non-metropolitan areas? To what extent are such factors as education, age, and gender associated with the prospects of working and being poor? Which industries and occupations have the highest concentrations of poverty-wage workers?

My primary purpose herein is not to explain these phenomena, but rather to establish a descriptive framework for further analysis. I begin with an overview of measurement issues and my methodology. Next, descriptive data are presented on the working poor in terms of their size, composition, and spatial distribution, and how these have changed between 1980 and 1990. I then look at relationships of race, gender, education, age, and location to working-poor status. The chapter concludes with an assessment of the industries and occupations with the highest concentration of poverty-wage workers.

Measurement Issues

Counting the working poor is neither simple nor clean. This is because working is an attribute of an individual while poverty is defined in terms of the total income of the family to which the individual worker belongs. Total family income, in turn, refers to considerably more than the sum of wages and salaries of related individuals in a household. It also encompasses self-employment income; interest, dividend, rent, and royalty income; social security and retirement income; and public assistance and disability income.

Poverty thresholds, established by total family income cut-points, are likewise multifaceted and, to some extent, arbitrary. The Office of Management and the Budget's poverty thresholds used by federal agencies are composed of forty-eight cut-points arranged in a two-dimensional matrix consisting of family size (from one person to nine persons) cross-classified by presence and number of family members under 18 years of age. Unrelated individuals and two-person families are further differentiated by whether the householder is under 65 years of age or not.

Appendix A presents the matrix for 1989 income poverty thresholds (utilized for 1990 census data analysis). These thresholds range from $5,947 for one-person households to $26,921 for nine or more person families with three related children under age 18. When determining which income threshold to apply, the Bureau of the Census cross-classifies the previous year's family income with the current year's family size.

Poverty thresholds are based on a definition originated by the Social Security Administration (SSA) in 1964 and derived from the least costly nutritionally adequate food plan designed by the Department of Agriculture in 1961. To determine the poverty level, the SSA simply multiplied the cost of this food plan by three, since a 1955 survey of food consumption conducted by the Department of Agriculture found that families of three or more persons spend approximately one-third of their income on food. For smaller families, the cost of the food plan was multiplied by factors slightly higher to compensate for the relatively greater fixed expense for these households (U.S. Bureau of the Census 1993).

With the exception of relatively minor modifications by federal interagency committees in 1969 and 1980, the poverty thresholds were revised annually after 1964 by adjusting them by the consumer price index. These poverty thresholds are applied to all families and unrelated individuals on a national basis and have never been adjusted for regional, state, or local differences in cost of living. This is an important limitation that will be highlighted when we present regional and state figures on the working poor.

Definitions of the Working Poor

A variety of studies of the working poor have applied a variety of definitions. Danziger and Gottschalk (1986), for example, defined the working poor as heads of households who earned less than $204 a week in 1984 dollars. Such a person would remain below the poverty level even if he or she worked 52 weeks a year. Levitan, Gallo, and Shapiro (1993) define the working poor as persons whose earnings are not sufficient to lift them or their families out of poverty.

Until 1989, the Bureau of Labor Statistics (BLS) measured the working poor using hourly paid workers whose wages were at or below the minimum wage. In 1989, BLS researchers Klein and Rones defined the working poor as "persons who devote more than half a year working or looking for work and who lived in families below the poverty level." A follow-up study by BLS researchers Gardner and Herz (1992) used the same definition, that is, persons in poverty who either worked or looked for work for at least 27 weeks during the previous year. In 1993, BLS continued to employ the Klein-Rones definition in their new series of reports profiling the relationship between work and poverty (U.S. Department of Labor 1993).

Under the most recent BLS definition, people who look for work for at least 27 weeks, even if they do not obtain any employment, are classified as "working poor." In my opinion, one should actually work in order to be classified as "working poor;" seeking employment should qualify one to be a member of the labor force but not the *working* labor force, unless one actually obtains work. Therefore, in this chapter, I will apply the following more restrictive definition that I suggest more validly captures the concept of "working poor."

Working Poor

Working poor are those persons age 16 and older who have worked for at least 27 weeks the previous year, usually for at least 20 hours a week, and who lived in families with incomes below the official poverty threshold.

Because family income is affected by family size, number of family workers, and other income sources besides earnings, it may be argued that total family income is not a good criterion to distinguish the working poor. For example, a young adult male who works full time at the minimum wage but lives with one of his working parents because he cannot afford to live alone or marry the mother of his child is unlikely to be classified as working poor under either the BLS definition or the revised definition above. In order to measure the working poor more as a labor force concept that influences poverty than as basically a family income concept, the following definition will be used.

Poverty-wage Workers

Poverty-wage workers are those persons 16 and over who work full time (50 or more weeks per year, including paid vacation, usually for 35 hours or more per week) and who do not earn enough to lift a family of four out of poverty. In 1989, a worker had to earn at least $12,674 to support a family of four above the poverty threshold. In 1979, the earnings had to be at least $7,412.[1]

The poverty-wage worker definition allows us to get much closer to the concept of working poor as affected by low earnings than do the definitions of working poor based primarily on family income. It also allows a crisper assessment of the roles that education, gender, race, age, and location play in the likelihood of having a full-time job that cannot lift a family of four out of poverty.

The databases which will be used to count working poor and poverty-wage workers are the 1980 and 1990 Census of Population Public Use Microdata Sample (PUMS) 5 percent sample machine readable files. The 5 percent PUMS files, containing records on over 10 million individuals, are the largest and most reliable database for assessing individual and locational characteristics of the working poor. The large sample enables considerable cross-classification of individual records and reliable estimates of rates by race and gender down to metropolitan central-city and suburban-ring levels. No other database comes close to the PUMS files in terms of reliability of sample estimates.

Table 3.1

Number and Rate of Working Poor (27 weeks, 20 hours) in the U.S. 1990 and Change 1980–1990 (in thousands)

Race	All Workers		Males		Females	
	1990	Change 1980–90	1990	Change 1980–90	1990	Change 1980–90
Total	3,752	404	1,888	-5	1,863	408
White	2,295	59	1,167	-141	1,128	201
Black	682	11	244	-56	438	67
Hispanic	626	272	392	159	234	113
Asian & Other	149	61	86	34	63	27

Race	All Persons		Rate Males		Females	
	1980	1990	1980	1990	1980	1990
Total	3.8	3.6	3.6	3.2	4.2	4.1
White	3.1	2.7	2.9	2.4	3.3	3.1
Black	8.4	6.8	7.2	5.0	9.8	8.4
Hispanic	7.6	8.0	8.0	8.3	7.0	7.6
Asian & Other	4.6	4.2	4.8	4.4	4.4	4.0

Source: Bureau of the Census, *1980 and 1990 Public Use Microdata Sample,* 5 percent sample, machine-readable files.

Size, Composition, and Distribution of the Working Poor

The top panel of Table 3.1 provides a count of the working poor in America in 1990, cross-classified by race and gender, along with changes in these numbers between 1980 and 1990. In 1990, approximately 3.8 million Americans worked for at least 27 weeks for 20 hours per week and were in families below the poverty line. This represents a growth of slightly more than 400,000 since 1980, all of which were accounted for by the growth of female working poor.[2] Over two-thirds of the increase in working poor were Hispanics. In sharp contrast to whites and blacks, where male working poor showed considerable declines, the growth in Hispanic working poor was led by males. Note, as well, that whereas whites and blacks together constituted 80 percent of the working poor in 1990, because of declines in their working poor males, whites and blacks constituted only 17 percent of the overall growth (70,000 of 404,000).

The bottom panel presents the poverty rates for each subgroup of workers. These rates measure the percent in poverty of persons within the racial/gender subgroups who worked at least 27 weeks for 20 hours a week during the previous year. The 1990 percentages range from 2.4 for white males to 8.4 for black females, with Hispanic workers having the overall highest racial/ethnic group poverty rate (8.0). Interestingly, with the exception of Hispanics, all racial/ethnic and gender groups declined in rates of working poor between 1980 and 1990.

Cross-classification by education (table not shown here) revealed sharp gradients. Rates of working poor in 1990 were 8.7 for those not completing high school, 3.8 for high school graduates only, 3.2 for those with some college, and 1.2 percent for college graduates. Between 1980 and 1990 rates declined for college graduates and for those with some college but rose for those with only a high school education or less. Highest rates in 1990 were for Hispanics with less than a high school degree (13.9), followed by blacks without a high school degree (12.5). Among major racial/ethnic groups with some college, all had rates under 5.0. Among those with college degrees, no racial/ethnic group had rates of 2.5 or more. In fact, with the exception of Hispanic college graduates (2.3), all other college-educated racial/ethnic groups had rates under 2.0 in 1990.

Further cross-classification of working poor in 1990 by region showed that the Northeast had the lowest rate (2.0) and the South had the highest (4.5). The highest intraregional rates of working poor categorized by race/ethnicity were among southern Hispanics (10.3), followed by southern blacks (8.4), and Hispanics in the West (8.0). The lowest intraregional rate was 1.7 for whites in the Northeast.

Between 1980 and 1990 rates of working poor went down in every region but the Midwest. Within the Midwest, rates increased for all major racial/ethnic groups with the exception of whites whose rate remained constant at 3.1. Each racial/ethnic group within each of the other three regions exhibited declines in their rates of working poor between 1980 and 1990, with the exception of Hispanics in the West, whose rate rose from 7.1 to 8.0.

Comparing states in 1990, Mississippi had the highest rate of working poor (7.8) followed by New Mexico (7.4) and Louisiana (7.0). The lowest rates of working poor are found in Connecticut (1.0), New Jersey (1.3), and Massachusetts (1.4). A complete ranking of the fifty states reveals that almost all of the states with the highest rates of working poor are either in the South or are less urbanized states, while the states with the lowest percentage of workers in poverty are concentrated in the urbanized Northeast.

The relatively high poverty rates among workers in the South and predominantly rural states compared to the Northeast and predominantly urban states highlight two problems with family income measures of the working poor. First, poverty is assigned based on nationally standardized family income cut-points, regardless of location. Thus, a family of four in Boston or New York City has the same poverty cut-point as a family of four in rural Mississippi ($12,674), despite the fact that living costs in rural Mississippi are considerably less than those of the metropolitan Northeast. Second, public assistance income, which is counted in total family income for poverty classification purposes, tends to be much higher in the urban North than the rural South. Thus, the numbers and rates of working poor are no doubt larger in real terms in the North and lower in the South than are described herein using nationally standardized, poverty-income cut-points.

An even more fundamental shortcoming of total family income–based measures of the working poor was noted initially. That is, using family income and family composition as determining criteria misses much of what is supposed to be labor market and worker attributes. For this reason, I will examine patterns and trends of full-time workers whose jobs do not provide sufficient income to lift a family of four out of poverty. Using these criteria, persons who worked at least 50 weeks (including paid vacations) for at least 35 hours per week and earned less than $7,412 in 1979 and $12,674 in 1989 are classified as poverty-wage workers in 1980 and 1990, respectively.

Table 3.2 provides the number of poverty-wage workers in 1990, their change from 1980 to 1990, and rates (percentage of full-time workers earning poverty wages) by race/ethnicity and gender. In 1990 there were a total of 12 million poverty-wage workers, a nearly 3 million increase since 1980. The percentage of all full-time workers earning poverty wages increased from 15.2 to 16.3 between 1980 and 1990.

Despite a rise in male poverty-wage workers between 1980 and 1990 and a decline in female rates, rates of female poverty workers in 1990 were twice that of males (23.8 vs. 11.5). The largest gender gap was for whites where females had a poverty-wage worker rate of 22.4 compared to 9.7 for males. Moreover, even though the white female rate declined from 24.7 to 22.4 during the 1980s, there were 933,000 more female poverty-wage workers in 1990 than in 1980. The highest rates of poverty-wage workers in 1990 were found among Hispanic females (35.3) and black females (27.3).

Table 3.3 presents the racial/gender composition of poverty-wage workers and how this compares to all full-time workers. A complete flip in the gender distribution can be seen in the all full-time workers vs. the poverty-wage

Table 3.2

Poverty-Wage Workers (full-time workers unable to support family of four) in the U.S.1990 and Change 1980–1990 (in thousands)

	Poverty-Wage Workers		Males		Females	
Race	**1990**	**Change 1980–90**	**1990**	**Change 1980–90**	**1990**	**Change 1980–90**
Total	12,034	2,875	5,232	1,358	6,802	1,517
White	8,606	1,661	3,610	728	4,996	933
Black	1,593	302	662	113	931	189
Hispanic	1,417	704	772	420	645	284
Asian & Other	418	208	188	97	229	111

	Poverty-Wage Workers		Rate Males		Females	
Race	**1980**	**1990**	**1980**	**1990**	**1980**	**1990**
Total	15.2	16.3	9.7	11.5	26.1	23.8
White	13.7	14.5	8.4	9.7	24.7	22.4
Black	24.5	22.8	18.7	18.6	32.0	27.3
Hispanic	23.6	28.2	17.4	24.1	36.5	35.3
Asian & Other	16.7	17.3	11.8	13.5	24.4	22.5

Source: Bureau of the Census, *1980 and 1990 Public Use Microdata Sample,* 5 percent sample, machine-readable files.

workers distributions in 1990. While females constitute only 38.7 percent of all full-time workers, they constitute 56.5 percent of poverty-wage workers. White males constitute just over half of all full-time workers, but only 30 percent of the nation's poverty-wage workers. Conversely, white females constitute 30 percent of all full-time workers, but 41.5 percent of poverty-wage workers. Blacks and Hispanics, regardless of gender, have higher percentages of poverty-wage workers than of all full-time workers.

Regional distributions of poverty-wage workers by race/ethnicity are shown in Table 3.4. In 1990, the South accounted for 43 percent of the nation's poverty-wage workers compared to 34 percent of all full-time workers. Conversely, the Northeast contains just 14 percent of the nation's poverty-wage workers, compared to 21 percent of all full-time workers. The poverty-wage worker rate in the South is nearly twice that in the Northeast (20.1 vs. 11.0).

Table 3.3
Percent Distribution and Intragroup Rate of Poverty Wage Workers by Race/Ethnicity and Gender, 1980 and 1990

Race/ Ethnicity & Gender	1980 All Workers* %	1980 Pov.-Wage Workers %	1980 Pov.-Wage Workers Rate	1990 All Workers* %	1990 Pov.-Wage Workers %	1990 Pov.-Wage Workers Rate
Total	100.0	100.0	15.2	100.0	100.0	16.3
Male	66.3	42.3	9.7	61.3	43.5	11.5
Female	33.7	57.7	26.1	38.7	56.5	23.8
White	84.2	75.8	13.7	80.5	71.5	14.5
Male	56.8	31.5	8.4	50.3	30.0	9.7
Female	27.4	44.4	24.7	30.2	41.5	22.4
Black	8.7	14.1	24.5	9.4	13.2	22.8
Male	4.9	6.0	18.7	4.8	5.5	18.6
Female	3.9	8.1	32.0	4.6	7.7	27.3
Hispanic	5.0	7.8	23.6	6.8	11.8	28.2
Male	3.4	3.8	17.4	4.3	6.4	24.1
Female	1.6	3.9	36.5	2.5	5.4	35.3
Asian and Other	2.1	2.3	16.7	3.3	3.5	17.3
Male	1.3	1.0	11.8	1.9	1.6	13.5
Female	0.8	1.3	24.4	1.4	1.9	22.5

* All workers who worked 50 weeks or more and usually worked 35 hours or more per week in the previous year.

Source: Bureau of the Census, *1980 and 1990 Public Use Microdata Sample,* 5 percent sample, machine-readable files.

Again, however, it should be noted that these rates do not adjust for regional differences in cost of living.

Between 1980 and 1990 poverty-wage worker rates rose in all regions but the Northeast. The Midwest experienced the greatest rise in rates over the decade. Blacks in the Northeast experienced the largest drop during the 1980s (16.6 to 12.9) with their 1990 rate falling lower than that of whites in each of the other census regions. Hispanics in the West saw their poverty-worker rate climb considerably during the 1980s such that their 28.6 rate in 1990 was nearly as high as that for southern blacks (29.4) and southern Hispanics (32.9).

The states with the highest and lowest rates of poverty-wage workers in 1990 are shown in Table 3.5. South Dakota fares the worst where nearly one-

Table 3.4

Percent Distribution and Intragroup Rate of Poverty-Wage Workers by Region and Race/Ethnicity, 1980 and 1990

Region and Race/Ethnicity	1980 All Workers* %	1980 Pov.-Wage Workers %	1980 Pov.-Wage Workers Rate	1990 All Workers* %	1990 Pov.-Wage Workers %	1990 Pov.-Wage Workers Rate
Northeast	22.1	18.0	12.4	21.2	14.4	11.0
White	19.2	14.6	11.6	17.6	10.8	10.0
Black	1.7	1.8	16.6	1.9	1.5	12.9
Hispanic	0.9	1.2	21.9	1.2	1.5	20.6
Asian & Other	0.3	0.3	17.1	0.6	0.6	16.3
Midwest	26.2	23.5	13.7	24.0	24.5	16.6
White	23.8	21.0	13.4	21.5	21.3	16.2
Black	1.7	1.8	16.2	1.6	1.9	19.2
Hispanic	0.4	0.5	16.3	0.5	0.8	24.6
Asian & Other	0.3	0.3	15.4	0.3	0.4	19.2
South	33.1	42.3	19.4	34.4	42.6	20.1
White	26.6	29.2	16.7	26.6	28.4	17.3
Black	4.6	9.6	32.1	5.0	9.1	29.4
Hispanic	1.6	3.0	28.4	2.1	4.3	32.9
Asian & Other	0.4	0.5	21.8	0.6	0.8	22.3
West	18.6	16.2	13.2	20.3	18.6	14.9
White	14.5	11.1	11.6	14.7	11.0	12.2
Black	0.8	0.8	16.0	0.9	0.7	13.3
Hispanic	2.1	3.1	22.3	3.0	5.2	28.6
Asian & Other	1.2	1.2	15.3	1.7	1.6	15.5

* All workers who worked 50 weeks or more and usually worked 35 hours or more per week in the previous year.

Source: Bureau of the Census, *1980 and 1990 Public Use Microdata Sample,* 5 percent sample, machine-readable files.

third of its full-time workers earned poverty wages, followed closely by Mississippi and Arkansas. Faring best were workers in Connecticut where under 7 percent of all full-time workers earned poverty wages. Also coming in at under 10 percent poverty-wage workers were Massachusetts, New Jersey, and New Hampshire. The list reveals the much greater percentages of poverty-wage workers in predominantly rural states and lower percentages in the predominantly urban states of the Northeast.

Some of the data presented in Tables 3.4 and 3.5 might seem inconsistent

Table 3.5
States Ranked on Rate of Poverty-Wage Workers, 1990

Highest Rate States

		Poverty-Wage Workers	
Rank	**State**	**Rate**	**(1000s)**
1	South Dakota	30.8	62
2	Mississippi	29.1	185
3	Arkansas	28.6	181
4	North Dakota	28.1	49
5	Montana	26.5	55
6	West Virginia	24.5	100
7	Louisiana	24.4	247
8	New Mexico	24.0	92
9	Kentucky	24.0	238
10	Nebraska	23.7	119

Lowest Rate States

		Poverty-Wage Workers	
Rank	**State**	**Rate**	**(1000s)**
1	Connecticut	6.8	76
2	Massachusetts	7.4	141
3	New Jersey	8.3	213
4	New Hampshire	9.9	37
5	Alaska	10.0	15
6	Maryland	10.0	171
7	New York	11.4	611
8	Rhode Island	12.3	38
9	Washington	13.0	180
10	Delaware	13.1	30

Source: Bureau of the Census, *1990 Public Use Microdata Sample,* 5 percent sample, machine-readable files.

with the literature on industrial restructuring and urban poverty which documents that metropolitan areas in the Northeast and Midwest experienced the greatest loss in better paying blue-collar jobs during the 1980s. For example, metropolitan areas in these two Frostbelt regions lost 1.5 million manufacturing jobs between 1980 and 1990. Of this loss, more than 1.3 million occurred in their central cities (Kasarda 1995).

Associated with this job loss, aggregate earnings of persons employed in manufacturing establishments in the twenty-eight largest metropolitan centers of the Frostbelt declined by $26 billion between 1980 and 1990 (in constant 1987 dollars). During the same period, aggregate manufacturing earnings declined by another $10 billion in the sixty-five mid-sized metropolitan centers of the Frostbelt (Kasarda 1995). Plummeting most precipitously were Chicago (Cook County) where workers in manufacturing earned an aggregate of $4.9 billion less in 1990 than in 1980; Detroit (Wayne County) where aggregate manufacturing earnings declined by $4.3 billion; New York City and Pittsburgh (Allegheny County), each declining by $2.9 billion; and Milwaukee where manufacturing workers earned $1.6 billion less in 1990 compared to 1980 (again, in constant 1987 dollars.)

The highest concentrations of people in poverty are also found in the largest metropolitan centers in the Northeast and Midwest, with approximately one out of every five central-city residents in each region living in poverty. This locational correspondence between manufacturing job loss and concentrated urban poverty is central to labor market interpretations of the latter by Kasarda (1985), Wilson (1987), Harrison and Bluestone (1990) and Johnson and Oliver (1992), among others. They argue that while service-sector job growth may have compensated for manufacturing job losses in many northern cities, the newer service-sector jobs were either low paying or had higher skill requisites that excluded most lesser-educated labor. The upshot was a simultaneous growth in poverty-wage work and joblessness among central-city residents, especially poorly educated minorities residentially confined to inner-city areas of greatest blue-collar job loss.

Table 3.6 describes concentrations (rates) of poverty-wage workers by race and ethnicity for central cities, suburban rings, and nonmetropolitan areas within the four census regions in 1990. As might be expected, given their job growth and income selectivity, suburban areas have the lowest poverty-wage worker rates for every racial/ethnic group. Nonmetropolitan areas have considerably higher poverty-wage worker rates than the central cities for full-time workers as a whole in every region. Detailed breakdowns by race and ethnicity show that the only exceptions are higher rates for central-city Hispanics in the Northeast and the West and for Asians residing in the central cities of the Northeast.

Central cities in the Northeast fare the best by a wide margin with all but Asians exhibiting substantially lower rates of poverty-wage workers than their racial/ethnic counterparts in central cities in the other census regions. This is consistent with findings presented elsewhere showing that, in contrast to cities in other regions, Northeastern cities exhibited declines in residents in poverty between 1980 and 1990 (Kasarda 1993).

Table 3.6
Rates of Poverty-Wage Workers
by Region, Residence, and Race/Ethnicity, 1990

Region and Race/Ethnicity	Central City	Suburban	NonMetro
Northeast	12.3	8.6	18.8
White	8.5	8.2	18.7
Black	12.8	10.2	23.9
Hispanic	22.4	15.4	18.6
Asian & Other	23.7	10.2	23.5
Midwest	16.4	10.8	25.3
White	13.4	10.4	25.1
Black	18.9	14.5	30.4
Hispanic	27.3	19.4	34.2
Asian & Other	24.3	10.9	28.3
South	20.0	14.2	28.9
White	13.1	12.4	26.0
Black	27.2	18.8	44.2
Hispanic	35.7	25.7	42.3
Asian & Other	22.8	16.5	29.0
West	16.3	12.6	21.7
White	10.7	9.9	20.3
Black	15.1	13.2	32.2
Hispanic	34.7	24.9	32.3
Asian & Other	16.1	12.7	23.3

Note: These calculations are based on the 1% sample records which could be identified by the state and metropolitan status of residence (in other words, Area 99 and Mixed areas where excluded). These records include approximately 70 percent of all 1% sample records.

Source: Bureau of the Census, *1990 Public Use Microdata Sample,* 1 percent sample, machine-readable files.

Attributes of the Working Poor

The variable that has been demonstrated time and again to be most clearly related to poverty earnings is education. Table 3.7 provides further clear evidence of this association. It also demonstrates how the association has strengthened over time. In 1980, 25 percent of full-time workers who lacked a high school degree were earning poverty wages. By 1990 the rate had risen to 34 percent. Of those only completing high school the rate rose from 17 percent to 21 percent between 1980 and 1990, while for those with some college it

Table 3.7
Percent Distribution and Intragroup Rate of Poverty-Wage Workers by Education and Race/Ethnicity, 1980 and 1990

	1980			1990		
Region and	**All Workers***	**Pov.-Wage Workers**		**All Workers***	**Pov.-Wage Workers**	
Race/Ethnicity	**%**	**%**	**Rate**	**%**	**%**	**Rate**
Less Than High School	22.4	33.9	25.2	10.5	29.6	33.9
White	15.1	22.0	22.2	6.7	13.3	28.9
Black	2.8	6.4	35.3	1.4	5.3	39.3
Hispanic	2.1	4.6	32.6	2.1	9.9	44.8
Asian & Other	0.4	0.8	34.0	0.3	1.1	40.7
High School Graduate	40.5	44.6	16.7	33.9	35.7	21.4
White	35.0	36.1	15.7	27.3	22.1	19.8
Black	3.4	5.5	24.5	3.6	8.1	28.7
Hispanic	1.6	2.2	21.2	2.1	4.1	28.4
Asian & Other	0.6	0.8	20.6	0.8	1.3	26.6
Some College	19.6	14.7	11.4	30.7	26.6	13.6
White	16.6	11.7	10.7	25.0	19.4	13.0
Black	1.7	1.8	16.1	3.0	4.0	16.7
Hispanic	0.8	0.8	14.0	1.8	2.1	16.9
Asian & Other	0.4	0.4	13.1	0.9	1.0	14.9
College Graduate	19.5	6.9	5.4	24.2	8.2	5.2
White	17.5	5.9	5.2	21.4	6.4	5.0
Black	0.9	0.4	7.2	1.5	0.7	5.7
Hispanic	0.5	0.2	8.0	0.8	0.5	7.7
Asian & Other	0.7	0.3	6.2	1.3	0.6	6.6

* All workers who worked 50 weeks or more and usually worked 35 hours or more per week in the previous year.

Source: Bureau of the Census, *1980 and 1990 Public Use Microdata Sample,* 5 percent sample, machine-readable files.

rose from 11 percent to 14 percent. Only for college graduates was there a decline during the 1980s in the percentage of workers who had poverty earnings, from 5.4 to 5.2.

The largest discrepancy in all full-time workers vs. poverty-wage workers distributions is also found at the lowest education levels. Those without a

Table 3.8
Percent Distribution and Intragroup Rate of Poverty-Wage Workers by Age and Race/Ethnicity, 1980 and 1990

	1980			1990		
Region and Race/Ethnicity	All Workers* %	Pov.-Wage Workers %	Pov.-Wage Workers Rate	All Workers* %	Pov.-Wage Workers %	Pov.-Wage Workers Rate
Aged 16–34	43.3	51.2	18.0	39.8	51.4	21.0
White	35.6	38.2	16.3	31.2	35.6	18.6
Black	4.1	7.3	27.0	4.0	7.1	29.4
Hispanic	2.6	4.6	26.8	3.4	7.2	33.8
Asian & Other	0.9	1.2	18.8	1.2	1.6	20.5
Aged 35–59	49.4	39.5	12.1	54.0	40.6	12.2
White	42.0	29.9	10.8	44.0	29.5	10.9
Black	4.1	5.8	21.1	5.0	5.3	17.2
Hispanic	2.2	2.8	19.5	3.1	4.1	21.9
Asian & Other	1.1	1.0	13.9	1.9	1.7	14.6
Aged 60 and Over	7.3	9.3	19.4	6.2	8.0	21.1
White	6.5	7.7	18.0	5.3	6.5	20.0
Black	0.5	1.1	33.2	0.5	0.8	28.8
Hispanic	0.2	0.4	27.9	0.3	0.5	28.7
Asian & Other	0.1	0.2	26.2	0.1	0.2	24.9

* All workers who worked 50 weeks or more and usually worked 35 hours or more per week in the previous year.

Source: Bureau of the Census, *1980 and 1990 Public Use Microdata Sample,* 5 percent sample, machine-readable files.

high school degree made up just 11 percent of the nation's full-time workers in 1990 but 30 percent of the nation's poverty-wage workers. At the other end of the continuum, college graduates comprised 24 percent of the nation's full-time workers, but just 8 percent of the poverty workers. On the whole, those full-time workers without a high school degree are six times more likely to have poverty earnings than are college graduates.

Full-time workers under age 35 and those aged 60 and over are also at considerably more risk of poverty earnings than are those aged 35 to 59, as Table 3.8 shows. This table further reveals that, while poverty earnings rates held essentially constant between 1980 and 1990 for middle-age workers, they rose for both younger and older workers. In terms of discordant distributions, workers aged 16 to 34 made up slightly less than 40 percent of full-time workers in 1990 but 51 percent of poverty-wage workers, while those aged 35 to 59 made up 54 percent of all full-time workers but 41 percent of poverty-wage workers. Both gaps widened during the 1980s.

Considerable attention has been given to the proliferation of poverty work as reflected in the changing structure of U.S. employment and wages (Burtless 1990; Levitan, Gallo, and Shapiro 1993; Levy 1995; Wetzel 1995.) While the U.S. economy churned out nearly 20 million jobs between 1980 and 1990, a large percentage of these jobs, it is argued, had little or no chance of lifting a worker out of poverty even if the worker was employed full time.

I now describe the leading industries and occupations where these poverty-earnings jobs were concentrated in 1990. The focus is on industries and occupations employing at least 100,000 nationwide. Standardized 3-digit SIC and SOC classifications are used for numerical comparisons between 1980 and 1990.[3]

Poverty-wage industries and occupations are ranked in terms of percent of their full-time workers who earned less than the poverty threshold for a family of four in 1989. Along with the rankings of the twenty industries and occupations with the highest concentration of poverty-wage workers, I will show the following for each industry and occupation: 1) their number of full-time poverty-wage workers in 1990 and 1980; 2) the proportion of workers earning poverty wages at each date; 3) the average earnings of workers in 1990; 4) the percent of female workers earning poverty wages; and 5) the percent of male workers earning poverty wages. To assess gender distribution, I will also show the percent of full-time poverty workers in each industry and occupation who are female.

Table 3.9 ranks concentrations (proportion) of full-time poverty-wage workers by industry. Two industries (private household personal services and child day-care services) have more than two-thirds of their full-time workers with annual earnings below the poverty threshold in 1990. Both of these industries are composed almost entirely of female workers (private household personal services at 94 percent female and child day-care services at 98 percent female). The child day-care industry, which also has the lowest average annual full-time worker earnings ($11,617), more than quadrupled in the number of poverty-wage workers between 1980 and 1990 (60,480 to 268,584). At the same time, the proportion of all full-time workers earning below the poverty threshold rose from 58 percent to 68 percent.

The next two highest concentrated poverty-earnings industries are apparel and accessories and beauty shops. Each has approximately half of their full-time workers earning less than the poverty standard, and they also are almost entirely dominated by females (87 percent and 91 percent, respectively).

Table 3.9
Poverty-Wage Workers by Industry1990 and 1980

	1990						1980	
Industries	**Poverty-wage workers**	**% with poverty wage**	**Average earnings**	**% Female poverty wage**	**% Male poverty wage**	**% Female in industry**	**Poverty-wage workers**	**% with poverty wage**
Private households personal services	128,026	67.9	12,471	71.2	39.9	93.8	123,040	74.4
Child day-care services	268,584	67.6	11,617	68.8	35.5	98.0	60,480	58.0
Apparel and accessories manufacturing	282,175	50.2	18,359	58.9	25.0	87.1	289,880	45.7
Beauty shops	157,831	47.0	16,358	50.9	26.4	91.1	96,300	42.3
Eating and drinking places	927,126	45.6	18,242	56.7	35.5	59.3	582,740	43.9
Agricultural production, livestock	226,460	44.1	19,534	64.6	40.4	22.7	268,760	43.5
Agricultural production, crops	316,510	44.8	21,099	54.7	39.9	17.2	345,420	40.0
Laundry, cleaning, and garment services	105,112	41.7	19,579	59.4	22.9	73.4	82,160	38.8
Nursing and personal care facilities	305,644	41.6	17,562	43.8	28.8	90.1	224,600	45.0
Services to dwellings and other buildings	119,181	35.5	20,042	53.1	26.3	51.2	37,820	25.4
Hotels and motels personal services	229,448	35.4	19,760	43.6	27.0	62.4	150,060	37.6
Gasoline service stations	100,231	33.9	21,680	50.6	28.2	38.0	84,320	24.7
Department stores	279,716	33.5	20,330	41.2	20.0	78.3	239,420	28.8
Sporting goods, bicycles, and hobby stores	45,490	32.9	21,585	46.7	23.8	56.5	27,060	29.4
Knitting mills	32,720	32.5	19,096	42.3	15.3	82.9	36,520	32.7
Apparel and accessory stores, except shoe	115,670	31.5	22,062	38.2	16.3	84.1	103,020	32.7
Agricultural services	131,106	31.4	24,011	40.0	28.9	28.4	55,100	26.5
Miscellaneous personal services	42,062	29.7	23,202	36.5	21.5	67.6	17,100	29.5
Retail bakeries	31,388	29.3	21,529	48.8	17.0	64.4	20,200	30.3
Hardware stores	32,542	29.1	22,540	48.5	21.2	48.0	25,900	23.6
All civilian industries	11,891,774	16.3	29,489	23.8	11.5	57.0	8,974,680	15.1

Notes: Includes all workers who worked 50 weeks and 35 hours per week in the previous year. Industries included if they had at least 100,000 total employees. Persons who listed their industry of employment as Active Duty Military are excluded.
Source: Bureau of the Census, *1980 and 1990 Public Use Microdata Sample,* 5 percent sample, machine-readable files.

Excluding the agricultural sector, most of the remaining highly concentrated poverty-wage worker industries are dominated by females.

Of special note, observe that in all of the industries with the highest concentration of poverty workers that women are much more likely to receive poverty wages than men. For example, 71 percent of the female workers employed in private household personal services do not earn enough to lift a family of four out of poverty compared to 40 percent of the men employed in this industry. In many of the remaining concentrated poverty-wage industries, women are more than twice as likely as men to be receiving below poverty wages. Thus, while 59 percent of women workers employed in apparel and accessories factories earn less than the poverty threshold, only 25 percent of the men working in these factories do so. Likewise, whereas 49 percent of women working in retail bakeries have poverty earnings, just 17 percent of the men working in this industry earn below the poverty threshold.

Table 3.10 describes the twenty occupations with the highest concentrations of poverty-wage workers. Child-care workers, with 72 percent earning less than the poverty threshold, top the list. The average annual earnings of all full-time workers in this occupation are $10,472, approximately one-third of the average earnings of all full-time workers ($29,426.) Virtually all child-care workers are female (98 percent). Of those males who are employed as child-care workers, 34 percent earn poverty wages compared to 74 percent of female child-care workers.

Between 1980 and 1990, the number of child-care poverty-wage workers almost tripled (from 79,900 to 223,327.) Poverty-wage worker concentration in child-care occupations also increased (from 67 percent of all full-time child-care workers to 72 percent.) This mirrors the increase in poverty-wage worker concentration in the child-care industry shown in Table 3.10.

Of the twenty most highly concentrated poverty-wage occupations, only five showed declines in the degree of concentration (waiters and waitresses, miscellaneous food preparation, apparel sales workers, nursing aids and orderlies, and sales workers not elsewhere classified). Some of the occupations exhibited considerable increases in poverty-wage worker concentration between 1980 and 1990. These include cashiers (42 percent to 52 percent), bartenders (40 percent to 49 percent), bank tellers (35 percent to 41 percent), packagers (28 percent to 38 percent), groundskeepers (27 percent to 37 percent), and stock handlers (29 percent to 37 percent.)

Comparing gender-specific concentrations, females have much higher proportions of poverty-wage workers for all occupations except miscellaneous food preparation. In addition to child-care workers, female concentra-

Table 3.10

Poverty-Wage Workers by Occupation
1980 and 1990

	1990						1980	
Occupations	**Poverty-wage workers**	**% with poverty wage**	**Average earnings**	**% Female poverty wage**	**% Male poverty wage**	**% Female in occupation**	**Poverty-wage workers**	**% with poverty wage**
Child-care workers, except private household	223,327	71.5	10,472	73.5	33.5	97.6	79,900	67.3
Textile sewing machine operators	256,059	60.2	12,951	64.5	32.0	93.0	233,980	57.6
Waiters and waitresses	223,556	60.0	13,072	65.9	41.2	83.5	200,220	66.1
Miscellaneous food preparation	99,687	59.4	13,250	59.0	59.8	48.0	71,080	60.2
Farm workers	164,407	55.7	13,568	74.5	52.7	18.8	183,800	51.8
Cooks	382,086	55.1	14,149	67.1	45.6	53.8	208,060	50.6
Maids and housemen	160,833	54.9	13,476	62.1	34.5	83.7	135,460	51.6
Cashiers	380,129	52.1	15,578	58.1	34.9	82.7	213,740	41.9
Laundering, dry cleaning machine operators	54,760	51.8	15,528	63.8	33.7	73.9	43,500	48.6
Bartenders	66,618	48.9	15,059	61.5	38.5	56.7	51,420	40.1
Hairdressers and cosmetologists	159,816	48.1	16,050	51.7	27.5	91.5	93,560	42.5
Farmers, except horticultural	260,893	45.8	20,851	69.9	43.0	15.9	368,460	42.1
Sales workers, apparel	49,109	43.7	18,454	52.3	22.4	85.3	55,080	46.4
Nursing aids, orderlies, and attendants	381,189	42.6	16,423	45.4	26.8	90.4	273,120	43.0
Bank tellers	108,607	41.3	14,850	42.6	27.8	94.3	97,620	34.8
Garage and service station related	45,947	40.0	17,934	52.8	38.5	13.7	42,000	37.4
Hand packers and packagers	63,370	37.6	16,603	41.5	30.7	70.9	80,120	27.9
Groundskeepers and gardeners, except farm	109,617	37.3	17,591	53.7	36.3	8.8	12,380	26.5
Stock handlers and baggers	118,040	36.8	17,781	47.2	31.8	41.7	53,840	28.6
Sales workers, other commodities	245,083	36.1	21,871	48.2	21.8	72.4	226,120	40.6
All occupations	11,997,219	16.3	29,426	23.8	11.5	56.7	8,974,680	15.1

Notes: Includes all workers who worked 50 weeks and 35 hours per week in the previous year. Occupations included if they had at least 100,000 total civilian employees. Persons who listed their occupation as Military are excluded

Source: Bureau of the Census, *1980 and 1990 Public Use Microdata Sample,* 5 percent sample, machine-readable files.

tions exceed male concentrations by at least a two-to-one margin for textile sewing machine operators (65 percent vs. 32 percent), apparel sales workers (52 percent vs. 22 percent), and salesworkers not elsewhere classified (48 percent vs. 22 percent). For all occupations, the poverty-wage worker concentration is 24 percent for females and 12 percent for males, providing striking testimony to gender inequity arguments.

This chapter discussed definitions and measurement issues apropos America's working poor and provided an empirical snapshot of its changing size, composition, and spatial distribution. An overview of research to date shows that the definitions and measurements of the working poor vary markedly and sometimes miss central elements of the concept. For example, the Bureau of Labor Statistics definition that treats the working poor as persons who devoted more than half a year working or looking for work and who lived in families whose total income falls below the poverty line counts many people who do not work at all as working poor. It also categorizes working poor on the basis of the combined incomes of all family members rather than on the earnings derived from the worker's job. Thus, if a young woman works full time, earning just $8,800 a year but lives with her mother who receives $3,900 in public assistance income, that young woman would *not* be classified as working poor.

A sound argument can be made that poverty status is indeed a combined family income factor since most expenses in a household such as rent, utilities, taxes, and to some extent food, are typically shared expenses paid through pooled family resources. For instance, there are many individuals who do not work or who work for quite low wages who would hardly be characterized as poor because they live with parents or other close relatives who have substantial incomes. These individuals experience quite different living standards than those poorly paid workers who do not live with other relatives whose combined incomes fail to lift them out of poverty.

Nevertheless, it seems essential that to be classified as "working poor" or "working and poor" one needs to actually work, even if part time. "Looking for work" is fundamentally different from "working." For this reason, I modified the BLS definition using family poverty criteria and including as working poor only those who worked for at least half a year.

Under this definition there were approximately 3.8 million Americans who would be classified as "working poor" in 1990, up from 3.4 million in 1980. Minorities constitute 83 percent of the overall growth during the 1980s in "working poor" with Hispanics alone accounting for slightly over two-thirds of this growth. Hispanics also exhibited the highest racial/ethnic percentage of full-time working poor (8.0) in 1990. Cross-classification by race and gender showed the percentage of working poor ranged from 2.4 for white males to 8.4 for black females. Cross-classification by race and education revealed steep downward gradients as education improved, with the highest rates found among Hispanics without a high school degree (13.9) and blacks without a high school degree (12.5). Among the college educated, Hispanics with 2.3 percent working poor were the only racial/ethnic group above 2.0. Within regions, the highest rates were found among southern Hispanics (10.3 percent) and southern blacks (8.4 percent), while the lowest poverty rate (1.7 percent) was for whites residing in the Northeast. Between 1980 and 1990, poverty rates among persons who worked for at least half a year declined in all regions but the Midwest.

Patterns and trends in full-time workers whose annual earnings are not sufficient to lift a family of four out of poverty were also examined. These workers, labeled poverty-wage workers, exhibited considerably higher numbers and rates than the working poor defined in terms of total family income. In 1990, there were more than 12 million poverty-wage workers constituting 16 percent of all full-time workers. Whereas poverty-wage worker rates went up for males and down for females between 1980 and 1990, at the latter date full-time female workers were still more than twice as likely as full-time male workers to have below poverty-level earnings. Percentages of poverty-wage workers range from 9.7 for white males to 35.3 for Hispanic females, with at least 20 percent of full-time female workers in every major racial/ethnic group earning poverty wages.

States in the urbanized Northeast had the lowest poverty-wage worker rates while rural and Southeast states had the highest rates within each census region; nonmetropolitan areas had the highest poverty-wage worker rates and suburban areas the lowest ratio with central cities in between. These rates are not standardized for local cost of living differences, however, which is an important limiting factor.

Powerful negative associations across all major racial/ethnic groups were shown between education and poverty-wage earnings with the associations strengthening over time. Among full-time workers with only a high school education or less, percentages earning less than the poverty threshold for a family of four rose substantially between 1980 and 1990. While only one out of ten full-time workers in the United States had not completed high school in 1990, this educational group accounted for one-third of the nation's poverty-wage workers.

Industries and occupations with the highest percentages of full-time poverty-wage workers in 1990 were also described. These industries and occupations tended to be dominated by women. The child-care service industry and child-care worker occupations, each with over two-thirds of their workers with poverty earnings, are 98 percent female. Not only did the number of child-care poverty-wage workers quadruple during the 1980s, but their concentration (proportion of all child-care workers) increased as well.

Cross-classification of concentrated poverty-wage industries and occupations by gender of workers revealed that women are much more likely to be earning less than the poverty threshold across virtually all industries and occupations. For example, among textile sewing machine operators, 65 percent of the female full-time workers have below poverty earnings compared to 32 percent of the male full-time workers.

The results summarized above show that poverty-wage work is increasing in America and that it is highly uneven in its demographic and locational mix. Patterns and trends presented were broad based and descriptive. They are meant to serve as a point of departure for more detailed analysis of characteristics of the working poor as well as antecedent conditions. In conducting this more sophisticated work, sensitivity to measurement issues, such as those discussed above, must be exhibited if researchers are to capture more precisely the number, nature, and causes of America's working poor.

Notes

I wish to thank Sheldon Danzinger and Thomas R. Swartz for their comments on an earlier draft of this essay and Andrea Bohbig and Kwok Fai Tuig for excellent computer assistance.

1. Since the workers are enumerated in 1980 and 1990, we will refer to poverty-wage workers as of those dates.

2. Applying the broader BLS definition of working poor to current population survey data yields 6.6 million working poor in 1990, up from 6.3 million in 1989, with the rate rising from 5.3 percent in 1989 to 5.5 percent in 1990 (U.S. Department of Labor 1993).

3. The census industrial classification system consists of 231 categories in 1980 based on the 1972 Standard Industrial Classification (SIC) Manual and its 1977 supplement, and 235 categories developed from the 1987 SIC Manual. The census occupational classification system has 502 categories in 1980 and 500 categories in 1990, both of which are based on the 1980 Standard Occupational Classification (SOC) Manual. The census system reclassified the SIC and SOC 3-digit and 4-digit industrial and occupational categories because responses given on the census questionnaire are not specific enough to identify detailed SIC and SOC categories. The 1980 and 1990 census industrial and occupational systems are similar to each other. A few industrial and occupational categories in the 1980 systems were combined in 1990; and a few categories in the 1980 systems are split into several more categories.

To allow comparability of the 1980 and 1990 census, we combined categories that were split in either census year. As a result, we obtained 220 comparable industrial categories and 497 occupational categories for both years.

References

Bluestone, Barry. 1990. "The Great U-Turn Revisited: Economic Restructuring, Jobs, and the Redistribution of Earnings." In *Jobs, Earnings, and Employment Growth Policies in the United States*, edited by John D. Kasarda. Boston: Kluwer Academic Publishers.

Bradbury, Katharine. 1986. "The Shrinking Middle Class." *New England Economic Review* (September-October): 41–55.

Burtless, Gary. Ed. 1990. *A Future of Lousy Jobs: The Changing Structure of U.S. Wages.* Washington, D.C.: Brookings Institution.

Craypo, Charles. 1991. "Industrial Restructuring and the Working Poor in a Midwestern US Factory Town." *Labour and Society* 16 (no. 2): 153–173.

Danziger, Sheldon. 1991. "The Poor." In *Human Capital and America's Future: An Economic Strategy for the Nineties*, edited by David W. Hornbeck and Lester M. Salamon. Baltimore: Johns Hopkins University Press,.

Danziger, Sheldon, and Peter Gottschalk. 1986. "Work, Poverty and the Working Poor: A Multifaceted Problem." *Monthly Labor Review* 9 (no. 9): 17–21.

Ellwood, David T. 1989. "If You Work, You Shouldn't Be Poor." *The Washington Post* (April 4): A25.

Ellwood, David T. 1993. "The Changing Structure of American Families: The Bigger Family Planning Issue." *Journal of the American Planning Association* 59 (no. 1): 3–8.

Gardner, Jennifer M., and Diane E. Herz. 1992. "Working and Poor in 1990." *Monthly Labor Review* 115 (no. 2): 20–28.

Harrison, Bennett, and Barry Bluestone. 1990. *The Great U-Turn: Corporate Restructuring and the Polarizing of America.* New York: Basic Books.

Johnson, James H., and M. L. Oliver. 1992. "Economic Restructuring and Black Male Joblessness: A Reassessment." In *Urban Labor Markets and Job Opportunity*, edited by George Peterson and Wayne Vrohman. Washington, D.C.: Urban Institute Press.

Kasarda, John D. 1985. "Urban Change and Minority Opportunities." In *The New Urban Reality*, edited by Paul E. Peterson. Washington, D.C.: Brookings Institution.

Kasarda, John D. 1993. "Inner-City Concentrated Poverty and Neighborhood Distress: 1970 to 1990." *Housing Policy Debate* 4, issue 3. Washington, D.C. Fannie Mae.

Kasarda, John D. 1995. "Industrial Restructuring and the Changing Locations of Jobs." In *State of the Union: America in the 1990s*, edited by Reynolds Farley. New York: Russell Sage Foundation.

Klein, Bruce W., and Philip L. Rones. 1989. "A Profile of the Working Poor." *Monthly Labor Review* 112 (no. 10): 3–13.

Kosters, Marvin H. 1990. "The Outlook for Jobs and Living Standards." In *Jobs, Earnings, and Employment Growth Policies in the United States*, edited by John D. Kasarda. Boston: Kluwer Academic Publishers.

Levitan, Sar A., Frank Gallo, and Isaac Shapiro. 1993. *Working but Poor: America's Contradiction.* Rev. ed. Baltimore: Johns Hopkins University Press.

Levy, Frank. 1995. "Incomes and Income Inequality since 1970." In *State of the Union: America in the 1990s*, edited by Reynolds Farley. New York: Russell Sage Foundation.

United States Bureau of the Census. 1993. *Census of Population and Housing, 1990: Public Use Microdata Sample U.S. Technical Documentation.* Washington, D.C.: Government Printing Office.

United States Department of Labor, Bureau of Labor Statistics. 1993. *A Profile of the Working Poor, 1991.* Report 847. Washington, D.C.: Government Printing Office, June.

Wetzel, James R. 1995. "Labor Force, Unemployment, and Earnings." In *State of the Union: America in the 1990s,* edited by Reynolds Farley. New York: Russell Sage Foundation.

Wilson, William J. 1987. *The Truly Disadvantaged: The Inner City, the Underclass, and Public Policy.* Chicago: University of Chicago Press.

Appendix A

Poverty Thresholds in 1989 by Size of Family and Number of Related Children under 18 Years

Size of Family Unit	Weighted average thresholds	Related children under 18 years								
		None	One	Two	Three	Four	Five	Six	Seven	Eight or more
One person										
(unrelated individual)	$6,310									
under 65 years	6,451	$6,541								
65 years and over	5,947	5,947								
Two persons	8,076									
householder under 65 years	8,343	8,303	$8,547							
householder 65 years and over	7,501	7,495	8,515							
Three persons	9,885	9,699	9,981	$9,990						
Four persons	12,674	12,790	12,999	12,575	$12,619					
Five persons	14,990	15,424	15,648	15,169	14,798	$14,572				
Six persons	16,921	17,740	17,811	17,444	17,092	16,569	$16,259			
Seven persons	19,162	20,412	20,540	20,101	19,794	19,224	18,558	$17,828		
Eight persons	21,328	22,830	23,031	22,617	21,738	21,738	21,084	20,403	$20,230	
Nine persons or more	25,480	27,463	27,595	27,229	26,921	26,415	25,719	25,089	24,933	$23,973

Source: Bureau of Census, *1990 Census of Population and Housing,* "Public Use Microdata Sample: Technical Documentation," July 1993.

4

Hardly Making It: The Increase in Low Earnings and What to Do about It

SHELDON DANZIGER AND PETER GOTTSCHALK

Since the early 1970s, Americans have experienced "hard economic times," characterized by slow economic growth and increasing inequalities in living standards. The gaps between the living standards of the rich and the poor and between those of the rich and the middle class have widened. These gaps have also grown among families within racial and ethnic groups. That is, a few white families have fared very well, while many more have lost ground. The same is true for persons of color—the most advantaged have moved ahead, while the least advantaged have fallen behind.

The economic hardship that affects so many Americans represents a sharp break with our recent economic history. Family incomes, adjusted for inflation, doubled in the two decades following World War II, while they have grown very little since the early 1970s. Many workers now earn lower real wages than they did two decades ago. Our focus in this essay is on the increased percentage of workers who are "hardly making it," that is, those who fail to earn enough during a year to support a family of four persons at the poverty line.

During the 1950s and 1960s, most men were employed at jobs that paid "good wages." The percentage of these jobs that provided health insurance and pensions also increased over these decades. Inflation-adjusted wages rose steadily from year to year and most men earned enough to support a family on their own. This was an era during which the American dream was fulfilled for most families. It was characterized by a steady improvement in living standards that was shared by most families and interrupted only occasionally by mild recessions. This rapid economic growth, coupled with the fact that income inequality also diminished somewhat over these two decades, reinforced the conventional wisdom that a "rising tide lifts all boats," and that a healthy economy would generate continuously falling poverty rates.

The economic experiences of families and workers since the early 1970s differs dramatically from the post-World War II era. Many jobs pay relatively low wages and often do not provide health insurance or private pensions. Workers, whether white collar or blue collar, have experienced higher unemployment rates and tend to spend fewer years working for any single firm. In many families, both the husband and wife must work to earn enough to support the family. A rising tide no longer lifts all boats. The recent period can be better characterized as one of "uneven tides" (Danziger and Gottschalk 1993). In the current era, the large yachts are anchored in safe harbors where they ride out the uneven tides, while small boats are left unprotected and run aground. No matter how measured, income and earnings inequality have increased over the past twenty years.

The Magnitude of the Problem

The extent of economic hardship is more widespread than many Americans realize. There is a tendency in popular portrayals of economic hardship to focus on inner-city poverty, single-mother families, and displaced factory workers and to associate poverty with their lack of work effort or lack of skills. But in recent years, inequalities increased within most broader groups across the population as well. That is, while white-collar workers fared better on average than blue-collar workers, and married couples fared better on average than mother-only families, many white-collar workers and many workers in married-couple families were also permanently laid off or experienced reductions in their real earnings.

Not even the most-advantaged groups were immune from the changing labor market conditions. For example, college graduates earn much more than less-educated workers, and the earnings of college graduates have grown much faster than the earnings of other workers since the late 1970s. In today's turbulent labor market, however, a college degree no longer guarantees high wages, as an increasing number of college graduates can attest.

Table 4.1 uses published data from the Current Population Survey (CPS) to document how hard it is for young workers to "make it." The data report, for 1992, the percentage of workers between the ages of 25 and 34 who earned less than $15,000, which was quite similar to the official poverty line for a family of four persons, $14,335. Many low earners are not income poor because the official poverty measure is based on total family income from all sources and from all family members. A low earner may not be poor if he or

Table 4.1
Percentage of Workers, Ages 25–34,
Who Earned Less than $15,000 in 1992[a]

	High School Graduates[b]	College Graduates[c]
All Males, 25–34	32.5	16.6
White Male	29.1	15.8
Black Male	51.3	14.5
Hispanic Origin Male	40.6	22.7
All Females, 25–34	58.2	25.1
White Female	57.3	24.8
Black Female	63.4	37.7
Hispanic Origin Female	62.3	24.3

[a] In 1992, the official poverty line for a family of four persons was $14,335.
[b] Includes persons with an equivalency degree and those who have completed 12 years of high school.
[c] Excludes college graduates who have achieved higher degrees.

Source: U.S. Bureau of the Census (1993). *Money Income of Households, Families, and Persons in the United States: 1992.* Series P–60, No. 184, Table 29.

she lives in a smaller family (for example, in 1992, the poverty line for a family of two persons was $9443) or if he or she has property income or government assistance or if there are other earners in the family. Nonetheless, the table provides a good measure of the extent of labor market hardship among *workers.* Any young person who did not work at all during 1992 is excluded from the table.[1]

Among college graduates who did not have post-graduate degrees, about one-sixth of men and one quarter of women worked during 1992 but earned less than $15,000. The corresponding percentages were about twice as large for high school graduates who had not completed any post-high school education—32.5 percent for men and 58.2 percent for women.

The number of workers whose own annual earnings are below the poverty line has increased dramatically over the past two decades for most age, education, and race/ethnic groups (see U.S. Bureau of the Census, 1992, and Acs and Danziger, 1993). The child of the blue-collar worker who graduates from high school can no longer expect to earn the wages and benefits her or his father earned when he left high school and went to work in a unionized factory in the early 1970s. And, the child of the corporate manager who graduates from college can no longer expect the secure employment and promotion opportunities that his or her father had two decades ago.

As we have documented (Danziger and Gottschalk 1995), changes in labor markets were primarily responsible for generating the pervasive economic hardships of poverty and inequality. Contrary to the assertions of conservative social critics (Murray 1984; Mead 1992; Magnet 1993), these problems were not caused by well-intentioned government social policies that distorted the work ethic and family structure of program recipients. The poor have not turned away from the economy; rather, the economy has pulled away from the poor. If the average living standard of American families had doubled since the early 1970s and if that rising living standard was widely shared by the poor, the middle class, and the rich, as was the economic experience of the quarter-century following World War II, then America would now have a very small poverty problem. Poverty remains high and inequalities have increased, not because of a failure of social policy or a failure of personal responsibility, but because of a failure of the economy to perform as expected.

In this essay, we focus on how prime-age male workers fared in the labor market in the nation's largest metropolitan areas during the 1980s. It is well known that, for the nation as a whole, the economy grew modestly and poverty and inequality increased. However, is it still possible that in metropolitan areas where economic growth was strong a rising tide still lifted all boats? That is, were there metropolitan areas where earnings growth was rapid and as widely shared as was the case in the quarter-century following World War II? We know that some metropolitan areas grew rapidly during the 1980s (Boston boomed during the Massachusetts miracle) while others suffered (Houston was dragged down by the collapse of the domestic oil industry). If poverty and inequality fell in booming places and rose in places suffering from economic dislocations, then one still might conclude that economic growth was a very effective antipoverty policy.

To foreshadow our results, the data analyzed below are consistent with and reinforce the conclusions drawn from the national data. We find that the incidence of low earnings and earnings inequality increased in most metropolitan areas during the 1980s. Areas with the most rapid increase in mean earnings did experience the smallest increases in poverty and inequality. However, no metropolitan area escaped the "uneven tides" that swept across the national labor market and diminished the economic prospects of millions of workers. In the next section, we review unpublished data from the computer tapes of the 1980 and 1990 Decennial Censuses. In the final section of this essay, we propose some policy reforms that would raise the earnings of those who have been left behind.

Trends in the Level and Distribution of Earnings

It is now widely acknowledged that earnings growth slowed and inequality increased over the past two decades (see Levy and Murnane 1992, for a comprehensive review). Our reading of the literature leads us to conclude that there is no single cause for this increased earnings inequality. Many factors moved the economy in the same direction. The decline in the percentage of the work force that was unionized, reductions in the percentage of workers who were employed in manufacturing, increased employment in the service sector, increased global competition and the consequent expansion of the import and export sectors, all contributed to rising inequality of earnings. As a result of the automation associated with the introduction and widespread use of computers and other innovations, employers increased their demand for skilled personnel who could run the more sophisticated equipment. Simultaneously, they reduced their demand for less-skilled workers, who were either displaced by the automated system or had to compete with new imports. The wages of the most-skilled workers increased, while those of less-skilled workers actually declined in real terms.

We begin by reviewing trends in mean earnings, low earnings and inequality for our sample, drawn from the computer tapes containing the 1 in 100 Public Use Samples of the 1980 and 1990 Decennial Censuses. In order to focus on those who are most attached to the labor force, we include only men between the ages of 25 and 54 who historically have the highest labor force participation rate as measured by the Bureau of Labor Statistics (1979 for the 1980 Census, 1989 for the 1990 Census). We exclude the self-employed, those in the military, and those reporting that they were not in the labor force (that is, they were not working and had not looked for work in the four weeks prior to the Census).

Women are much more likely to have annual earnings below the poverty line than are men. An analysis of trends in the low earnings rate of women is more complex, however, because their labor force attachment is affected more by marital status and child-care responsibilities than is the attachment of men. One way to avoid these complexities is to compare labor market outcomes *only* for those men and women who worked full-time for the entire year. From national data, we know that the incidence of low earnings increased for both men and women over the 1980s. For example, among year-round, full-time workers, 16 years and older, whose highest degree was a high school diploma, the low earnings rate increased between 1979 and 1989 by 7.2 percentage points, from 7.8 to 15.0 percent for men, and by 6.8 points, from

21.1 to 27.9 percent for women (U.S. Bureau of the Census, 1994). Our analysis is based only on men's experience, but our conclusions would not be affected if we had also examined women's earnings in these metropolitan areas.[2]

Our sample includes about 314,000 men in 1980 and 377,000 men in 1990; of these observations, 168,000 and 195,000 resided in one of the nation's fifty largest metropolitan areas in each of the two sample years. Only the Census provides large enough samples to measure labor market outcomes for specific metropolitan areas. Our sample sizes for the smallest areas among the top fifty metropolises are around 1000 workers; they are around 20,000 for the largest metropolitan areas.

Coincidentally, 1979 and 1989 were both business cycle peaks, with an average unemployment rate of 5.8 percent in the earlier year and 5.3 percent in the later year. We express all monetary values in 1989 dollars using the CPI-U-X-1. We define a one earner as a male worker whose annual earnings are less than the poverty line for a family of four, defined by the CPI-U-X-1, $11,570 in 1989 (see U.S. Bureau of the Census, P-60, No. 178, p. 2).[3] A man who works full-time year-round and is a low earner had a wage rate of $5.75 or less. Low earners represent those who fare badly in the labor market, whether or not they happen to live in a poor family.

Table 4.2 presents the summary statistics for prime-aged working men classified by race and ethnicity and by their completed education. All men are classified into one of four mutually exclusive race/ethnic groups: white non-Hispanics, black non-Hispanics, Hispanics, and non-Hispanics of other races. This latter group includes Native Americans, Asian-Americans, Pacific Islanders, and others. They comprise such a small, but heterogeneous, part of the total population that we include them in the totals, but we do not show their group-specific outcomes.[4]

Familiar differences are apparent in Table 4.2. Holding education constant, earnings are higher and the incidence of low earnings is smaller for white non-Hispanics than it is for black non-Hispanics or Hispanics. Within each group, earnings are much higher for college graduates than they are for high school graduates. The ratio of the annual earnings of college graduates to those of high school graduates was quite similar for the three groups—1.63 for whites, 1.64 for blacks, and 1.71 for Hispanics. High school graduates are more than twice as likely as college graduates to have low earnings.

Our sample includes only the most-advantaged workers—men of prime age. They earned on average over $30,000. Yet, because inequality was quite high, about 13 percent earned less than $11,570.

Table 4.2
The Level and Distribution of Annual Earnings,
Males 25–54 Years of Age, 1989

Race/Ethnicity and Educational Attainment	Mean Earnings	Percent Low Earners	Coefficient of Variation (X 100)
White, non-Hispanic			
Without H.S. Diploma	$19,659	25.2	75.60
High School Graduate	25,781	12.1	61.49
Some College or Associate's	31,300	8.5	65.53
Bachelor's	42,004	5.2	72.30
Graduate Work	54,062	3.9	75.03
Black, non-Hispanic			
Without H.S. Diploma	14,347	39.6	91.62
High School Graduate	18,445	27.0	74.38
Some College or Associate's	22,594	18.0	67.96
Bachelor's	30,286	8.9	63.86
Graduate Work	39,258	8.3	67.57
Hispanic			
Without H.S. Diploma	15,018	36.1	79.78
High School Graduate	20,270	22.1	69.70
Some College or Associate's	25,635	15.4	71.14
Bachelor's	34,562	8.4	79.66
Graduate Work	44,280	10.9	90.67
Largest 50 CMSAs	33,221	11.8	83.11
United States	30,250	13.2	81.87

Table 4.3 shows that there was very little real earnings growth on average over the decade. Despite an unusually long economic recovery (it lasted from November 1982 to July 1990), real earnings grew by only 1.32 percent in the U.S. and 3.85 percent in the largest fifty metropolitan areas. The percentage of men who had low annual earnings rose by more than 2.5 percentage points and the coefficient of variation increased by about 30 percent.[5]

The view that anyone who works hard can get ahead is so widely held that there is a tendency to attribute the lower earnings of minorities to race-specific factors. Table 4.3, however, demonstrates that the slow growth and rising inequality of the 1980s had very similar effects on whites and minorities. The causes of this disappointing performance are *not* primarily due to behavioral differences among the races; they are due to changes in the econ-

Table 4.3
Changes in the Level and Distribution of Earnings
1979–1989

Race/Ethnicity and Educational Attainment	% Change[a] Mean Earnings	% Point[b] Change Low Earners	% Change[a] Coefficient of Variation
White, non-Hispanic			
Without H.S. Diploma	-18.87	9.84	24.32
High School Graduate	-11.70	4.16	19.53
Some College or Associate's	-1.98	1.31	17.19
Bachelor's	8.18	-0.23	20.79
Graduate Work	28.58	-1.43	26.14
Black, non-Hispanic			
Without H.S. Diploma	-15.04	10.31	19.23
High School Graduate	-11.49	7.87	17.91
Some College or Associate's	-3.41	1.31	14.00
Bachelor's	12.25	-1.75	18.76
Graduate Work	19.54	0.71	18.72
Hispanic			
Without H.S. Diploma	-14.35	9.60	15.92
High School Graduate	-12.66	6.93	17.63
Some College or Associate's	-2.73	2.54	20.31
Bachelor's	12.23	-2.74	15.49
Graduate Work	24.97	1.26	31.28
Largest 50 CMSAs	3.85	2.13	30.73
United States	1.32	2.65	29.57

[a] Defined as 100 × (1989 value −1979 value) / 1979 value.
[b] Defined as 1989 low earnings rate less 1979 low earnings rate.

omy. Large racial differences remain in any year, but the trends over time for the race/ethnic groups were quite similar. For example, the earnings of high school graduates declined by about 12 percent for whites, blacks, and Hispanics during the 1980s. White college graduates earned 8 percent more, while minority graduates gained about 12 percent. Inequality increased in double-digits for all fifteen race-ethnic-education groups shown, and the incidence of low earnings increased for eleven of the fifteen groups.

Table 4.4 focuses on changes in the level and distribution of earnings between 1979 and 1989 in the fifty largest metropolitan areas. It shows that the seven areas with the largest increases in mean earnings all grew by more than

Table 4.4
Changes in the Level and Distribution of Male Earnings in the Largest Metropolitan Areas, 1979–1989

Metropolitan Area	% Change[a] Mean Earnings	% Point[b] Change Low Earners	% Change[a] Coefficient of Variation
Largest Increase in Mean			
New York, NY–NJ–CT	19.59	-0.18	26.90
Boston, MA	18.12	-1.17	26.30
Hartford, CT	13.52	-0.18	20.51
Greensboro, Winston Salem, NC	13.02	-2.82	20.09
Philadelphia, PA—NJ–DE–MD	11.18	-0.46	28.88
San Francisco, CA	9.22	0.84	25.68
Albany, NY	8.72	-0.02	14.29
Largest Decrease in Mean			
Houston, TX	-9.52	7.69	34.29
New Orleans, LA	-9.10	6.80	32.30
Salt Lake City–Ogden, UT	-6.70	4.17	39.63
Louisville, KY-IN	-6.59	5.51	27.75
Pittsburgh, PA	-6.37	6.82	53.14
Oklahoma City, OK	-5.79	5.80	31.20
Largest 50 MSAs	3.85	2.13	30.74
United States	1.32	2.65	29.57

[a] Defined as 100 × (1989 value − 1979 value/ 1979 value.
[b] Defined as 1989 low earnings rate less 1979 low earnings rate.

8.72 percent. The incidence of low earnings declined slightly in six of these areas. Inequality, however, increased substantially in all seven. At the other extreme, the six metropolitan areas that fared the worst during the 1980s had real earnings declines of more than 5.79 percent. These declining areas had very large increases in the incidence of low earnings and the coefficient of variation of earnings.

Figure 4.1 plots the percentage change in mean earnings (on the *x*-axis) against the percentage point increase in the low earnings rate (on the *y*-axis). Figure 4.2 plots the change in mean earnings against the percentage change in the coefficient of variation. In both figures, each diamond represents the experience of one of the metropolitan areas.

If a rising tide had lifted all boats, those metropolitan areas which experienced earnings growth would have had reductions in their low earnings rates.

Figure 4.1

Earnings Growth vs. Change in Low Earners

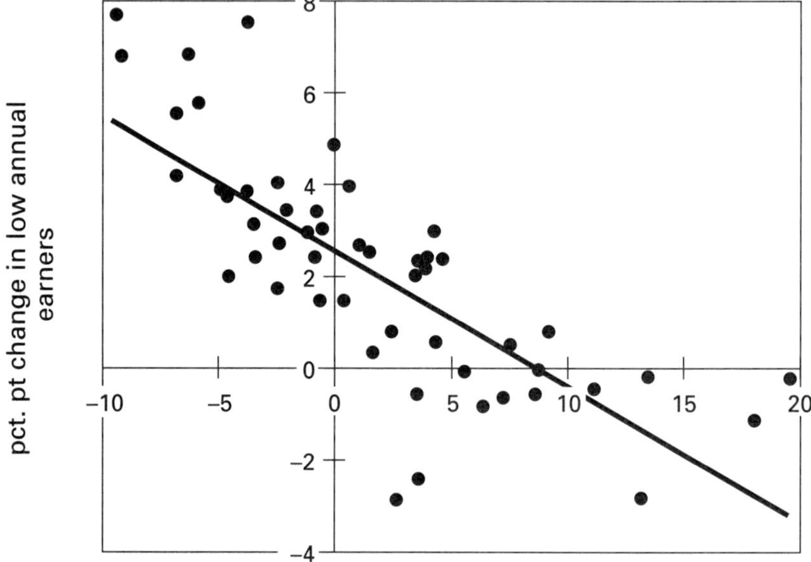

If the earnings growth was equally shared, a downward-sloping line in Figure 4.1 would pass through the origin. The origin would represent a metropolitan area in which the real wage of every worker remained constant—that is, no change in mean earnings and no change in either the low earnings rate or the coefficient of variation. The data points for the other metropolitan areas would be clustered in the northwest quadrant—areas with declining average wages would have rising rates of low earnings—and in the southeast quadrant—areas with rising wages would have declining low earnings rates.

This clearly was not the situation during the 1980s. The data trace out a downward-sloping line, but the line is shifted out toward the northeast quadrant and crosses the *y*-axis well above the origin. Mean male earnings grew in twenty-seven of the fifty largest metropolitan areas. However, the low earnings rate fell in only thirteen of them.[6] And, in most of the areas where the low earnings rate fell, it fell by less than one percentage point. The intercept indicates that, because of rising inequality, areas with no real wage growth had, on average, more than a 2 percentage point increase in the incidence of low earnings.

Figure 4.2

Earnings Growth vs. Change in Inequality

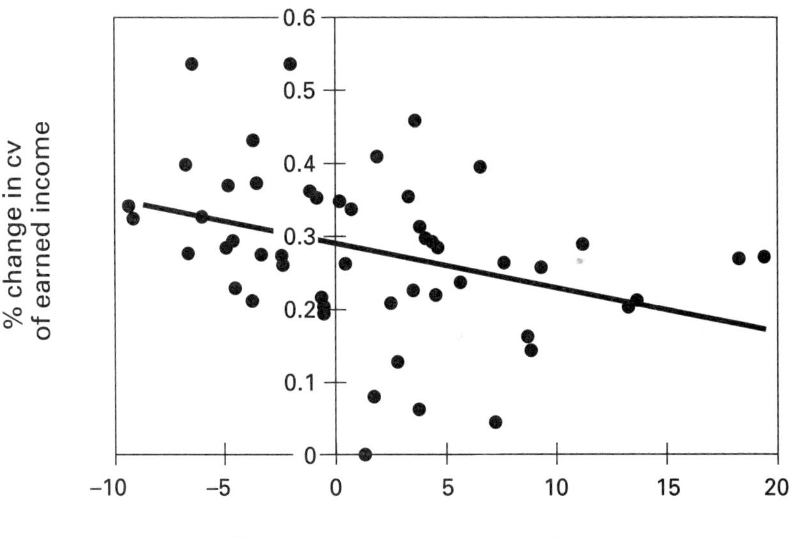

Figure 4.2 is even more dramatic—the coefficient of variation (CV) increased in every one of the fifty largest metropolitan areas. The rather flat slope of the line indicates that there is only a modest relationship between earnings growth and the change in inequality. The CV increased in fast-growing as well as slow-growing areas. A metropolitan area with no real earnings growth (where the line intersects the *y*-axis) had an increase in the coefficient of variation of about 28 percent.

These data clearly document that the 1980s was a decade of uneven tides across metropolitan areas. There was slow growth in the mean and rising inequalities, with increased variation both between and within metropolitan areas.[7] While most of the largest areas contain inner-city neighborhoods of concentrated poverty in which living conditions are bleak, regardless of the overall economic conditions in the metropolitan area, the trends documented here apply well beyond the inner-city.

Policies to Aid Low Earners

The economic forces that have increased inequality, such as technological change and increased globalization of markets, have direct efficiency benefits as well as the negative distributional effects that we have documented. They provide the potential for increases in our overall standard of living by introducing new goods and services and reducing prices on existing products. Increased returns to skill, no matter what their cause, widen the earnings gap between those who have marketable skills and those who do not. They also provide incentives for workers to upgrade their skills. Thus, these changes in the economy are not unambiguously bad.

One of government's primary roles is to undertake policies to deal with the equity costs arising out of these changes without introducing unnecessary inefficiencies. We now turn to some of those policy options. First, we note an economic truism—that rapid economic growth is the best antipoverty strategy. It goes without saying that if the engine of the American economy *could be* retooled so that the rate and distributional patterns of economic growth during the immediate post–World War II decade were restored, it would be much easier to reduce poverty.

Based on the labor market experiences of the last two decades, however, we doubt that the American economy will return to the patterns of the "golden age" in the foreseeable future. The problem is *not* that economic growth is necessarily ineffective in reducing poverty. Rather it is the fact that since 1973 economic growth has been both uneven and relatively slow and, as a consequence, much less effective in reducing poverty than was the case during the 1950s and 1960s. The gaps between the wages of low-skilled and high-skilled workers have grown so large that earnings and family income inequality will remain high for many years, even if the uneven growth pattern of the 1980s can be reversed. As a result, we are not likely to grow our way out of the problems caused by increasing inequality in the labor market. We still need macroeconomic policies that promote economic growth, but we also need enhanced labor market and antipoverty policies to augment the incomes of those workers and families who have not been benefiting from economic growth.[8]

Market forces, on their own, will lead to some adjustments that, in the long run, should reduce these labor market inequalities. For example, the rising returns to education since the late 1970s should induce individuals to take greater advantage of human capital–enhancing opportunities and invest more of their own resources to increase their education and improve their skills.[9] While such a market adjustment is likely to occur in the long run, the wages of the less-skilled are likely to remain low for a long period. In addition, the most responsive workers are likely to be those young people who have the ability to afford higher education, not today's less-skilled, prime-age workers who have already borne the brunt of the recent labor market changes.

Because such supply-side responses are likely to take so long, and because so many workers have fared so badly in the labor market over the past two decades, there is an urgent need to implement policies that can offset the economic hardships generated by the market without unduly interfering with the market itself. The policies we propose are directed toward the workers who have been most affected by the decline in employers' demand for their skills. They would supplement the earnings of low-wage workers and offset some of the detrimental impacts of the slow growth and rising inequality of the past two decades.

Our first policy proposal would build on a successful antipoverty initiative—the Earned Income Tax Credit (EITC)—by significantly increasing the assistance it provides to childless workers. The EITC was enacted in 1975, and expanded in 1986, 1990, and 1993. It has retained bipartisan support because of a number of its features—it assists only those who work; it helps two-parent as well as single-parent families; it raises the employee's take-home pay without increasing the employer's labor costs.

By 1996, for every dollar earned, the EITC will provide an additional 40 cents (for families with two or more children) up to a maximum of $3,560 for workers earning between $8,900 and $11,620. This will make the minimum wage, supplemented by the EITC, equal to $5.95 for these families. The amount of the credit will then be reduced at a rate of 21 cents for each dollar earned above $11,620, so that it will phase out at $28,524.[10] For families with one child, the EITC will be 34 cents for every dollar earned, up to maximum of $2,095 for workers earning between $6,160 and $11,290. Above $11,290, the amount of the EITC will be reduced at a rate of 16 cents for every dollar earned, so that it will phase out at $24,395.

The 1993 Act also provided, for the first time, a small EITC to childless workers between the ages of 24 and 65. Their EITC, beginning in 1994, is 7.65 cents for every dollar earned up to $4,000. The maximum benefit, $306, just offsets the employee's share of the Social Security payroll tax, which is 7.65 percent, over this income range. From $5,000 to $9,000, the EITC for single workers is phased out, so the EITC is less than their Social Security taxes.

When fully implemented, the EITC will have substantially offset the decline in real wages over the past two decades for workers at the bottom of the distribution who work full-year, and reside in families with children. Single earners and childless couples, however, need greater earnings supplementation than the 1993 law provides.

An EITC expansion to all persons regardless of age or family status is, however, expensive and potentially inefficient if it provides tax credits to persons, such as students or grown children living with their parents, who have low annual earnings but are otherwise not needy. The 1993 law attempts to address this problem by restricting the EITC to childless persons between the ages of 25 and 64. An expanded EITC for childless workers in this age range offers an excellent opportunity for assisting those who have been left behind by the slow growth and rising inequality of the last two decades.

For childless couples, we would raise the subsidy from 7.65 to 20 cents per dollar of earnings, with a maximum payment of $1,000 for workers earning between $5,000 and $9,000. The credit would be reduced at a 15 percent rate so that it would be phased out at close to $17,000. For single workers, the subsidy rate would raise to 15 cents per dollar, reaching $750 for workers earning $5,000. It would remain at that level for earnings up to $9,000, after which it would be phased out at 15 cents per dollar of earnings, aiding workers with earnings below $14,000. This would be a substantial expansion of assistance for about 9.5 million single workers and childless couples, and we estimate that it would cost the Treasury about $5 billion per year.

We also advocate an expansion of child-care subsidies to help low-income working parents.[11] We would expand the existing Dependent Care Credit (DCC) and make it refundable. The DCC is a nonrefundable credit against federal income tax liability. A taxpayer may claim the credit for expenses, incurred for a child less than 13 years of age, that are required for the taxpayer to work. All working single parents with qualifying dependents are eligible to claim the DCC. Two-parent families can claim the credit only when both parents work. The amount of expenses claimed cannot exceed $2,400 if there is one dependent or $4,800 if there are two dependents. Families with incomes below $10,000 can claim a nonrefundable tax credit of 30 percent of child care expenses up to a maximum credit of $720 for one child and $1,440 for two or more children. The credit is then reduced for families with higher incomes until it reaches $480 for one child ($960 for two children) for parents whose family earnings exceed $20,000 per year. The intent of the credit is to reduce the costs of working for all families with children. However, the working poor gain very little from the nonrefundable DCC because they typically have no federal income tax liabilities. For example, because a single-parent family does not pay federal income tax until its income exceeds $10,500 and a two-parent family pays no federal tax until its income is above $14,000, the value of the credit is zero for most of the working poor. Steffick and Giannarelli (1993) estimate that, if the existing DCC were changed from nonrefundable to refundable, an additional 1.1 million low-income families would be aided at a cost of about $700 million in 1994.

Even if the DCC were made refundable, however, the 30 percent maximum subsidy–rate does not cover enough of the actual costs of day care for workers at the bottom of the wage distribution. We would follow Robins (1990) and raise the maximum subsidy to 80 percent of child-care costs for families earning less than $10,000, and then lower the rate by 4 percent for every $1,000 earned, so the rate would be 40 percent for families earning $20,000 and 20 percent for families earning $25,000 or more. Given the high cost of child care, we would also raise the maximum amount of allowable expenses to $3,000 per year for one child and $6,000 for two or more children.

Under this scenario, a single mother earning $10,000 and spending $4,000 on child care for her two children would receive a refundable credit of $3,200. A family with two children earning $25,000 would be eligible for a maximum credit of $1,200 as compared to a maximum of $960 today. Thus, most of the added subsidies for child care resulting from this proposal would be targeted on poor and near-poor working families. We estimate that such a DCC expansion would cost an additional $5 billion per year.[12] Taken together, the recently expanded EITC and a refundable DCC would go a long way toward reducing poverty in families with children in which the parents work at low-wage rates for most of the year.[13]

The popular view that anyone who works hard can get ahead in America is still so widely held that it fosters the view that anyone who remains poor must be personally responsible for his or her situation. Behavioral issues, such as increases in out-of-wedlock childbearing, divorce, and participation in illegal rather than legal activities, do contribute to the continuing high poverty rate. But poverty remains high because of the major economic trends of the past two decades—slow improvement in living standards and rising inequality that made it increasingly difficult for many families to escape poverty. In addition, public policy responses were not put in place to counter those trends. We have experienced a continuum of economic hardship which has kept millions of families from achieving the living standard that they expected and millions of others from achieving even a poverty-line standard.

Supplementing wages and reducing child-care costs would help make work pay and would strengthen our safety net. Such a safety net might not have been essential during the 1950s and 1960s when the private economy rapidly generated job opportunities and higher real wages across the board. If those times do return, our economic safety net would be relevant for a smaller number of people. However, if the patterns of the last two decades continue through the 1990s, then the expansions to the safety net that we have proposed could significantly reduce economic hardships for tens of millions of Americans. It is imperative that we, as a society, address the adverse consequences of slow growth and rising inequality.

Notes

1. In his essay in this volume, Kasarda uses a family-income definition to define the "working poor." We focus instead on *individuals* who are "low earners."

2. For a more detailed analysis of trends in labor market outcomes for women, and a comparison of trends in poverty and family incomes between male-headed and female-headed households, see Danziger and Gottschalk (1995), chapters 4 and 6.

3. Problems arose with the official consumer price index (CPI-U) in the 1970s because of the way it reflected changes in the costs of home ownership. This was a period of rising home prices and interest rates and too large a weight was given to home ownership costs, particularly mortgage interest rates. This produced an overstatement of inflation. As a result, a new price index, the CPI-U-X1, was adopted in 1983. It is less affected by current housing prices and mortgage interest rates because it estimates the cost of renting and not purchasing a home. This better reflects the experience of low earners who are more likely to rent than to purchase a home. The Census Bureau adopted the CPI-U-X1 in 1983. The CPI-U-X1 poverty line is about 10 percent lower than the official poverty line. We use it here for both 1979 and 1989.

4. Our classification differs from the one used by the Bureau of the Census in its publications. The census categories are not mutually exclusive—whites, blacks, and Hispanics, with Hispanics double-counted in the former categories.

5. Our low earnings measure can be affected by changes in both wage rates and hours worked by the workers in our sample. If we focus only on wage rates, however, we find similar results. The percentage of men whose hourly wage rate was so low that they would have been a low earner even if they had worked full-time, year-round increased by 3.29 percentage points in the U.S. and by 2.60 percentage points in the fifty largest metropolitan areas.

6. When we measure the incidence of low earnings based on wage rates evaluated at full-time, year-round work, we find that the rate fell in only eight of the metropolitan areas. This indicates that the rising low earnings rate is not due to declining work effort as Mead (1992) has suggested.

7. The coefficient of variation of the mean annual earnings of the fifty areas increased by about 15 percent over the decades, indicating that earnings growth was faster in areas that had higher earnings in 1979.

8. Blank and London, in this volume, discuss government policies that impact on work among poor households; we focus on policies to supplement low wages.

9. We are assuming that increased education raises productivity, and, hence wages, and that employers do not use degrees solely as a screening device.

10. One unavoidable disadvantage of the tax credit approach is that phasing out the credits yields high cumulative marginal tax rates for families with incomes between about $15,000 and $30,000. Their cumulative marginal tax rate is the sum of the social security payroll tax (7.65%), the personal income tax (15% or 28% depending on family

size and income in this range), and the phase-down rate for the earned income tax credit (21%).

11. See Hofferth, in this volume, for an analysis of the supply and demand for child care.

12. The $5B costs of this DCC expansion could be reduced by restricting the credit to high-income families. This would, however, raise their cumulative tax rate.

13. There is no empirical evidence that expanded tax credits for the working poor will lead employers to lower wages. In this period of rapid technological advancement, employers in all industries have substituted college-educated for less-educated workers even though their relative wage has increased. Market forces are not leading employers to raise the wages they pay less-skilled workers. Tax credits are the best way to raise the incomes of low earners.

References

Acs, Gregory, and Sheldon H. Danziger. 1993. "Educational Attainment, Industrial Structure, and Male Earnings through the 1980s." *Journal of Human Resources* 28 (Summer): 618–648.

Danziger, Sheldon H., and Peter Gottschalk. Eds. 1993. *Uneven Tides: Rising Inequality in America.* New York: Russell Sage Foundation.

Danziger, Sheldon H., and Peter Gottschalk. 1995. *America Unequal: How Slow Growth and Increasing Inequality Have Diminished the Prospects of the Poor and the Middle Class.* Cambridge, Mass.: Harvard University Press.

Levy, Frank, and Richard J. Murnane. 1992. "U.S. Earnings Levels and Earnings Inequality: A Review of Recent Trends and Proposed Explanations." *Journal of Economic Literature* 30 (September): 1333–1381.

Magnet, Myron. 1993. *The Dream and the Nightmare: The Sixties' Legacy to the Underclass.* New York: W. Morrow.

Mead, Lawrence. 1992. *The New Politics of Poverty: The Working Poor in America.* New York: Basic Books.

Murray, Charles. 1984. *Losing Ground: American Social Policy, 1950–1980.* New York: Basic Books.

Robins, Philip. 1990. "Federal Financing of Child Care: Alternative Approaches and Economic Implications." *Population Research and Policy Review* 9 (no. 1): 65–90.

Steffick, Diane, and Linda Giannarelli. 1993. "Results of TRIM2 Simulations of a Refundable Child Care Tax Credit." Washington, D.C.: Urban Institute. Unpublished memo, November 11.

U.S. Bureau of the Census. 1993. *Money Income of Households, Families, and Persons: 1992.* Current Population Reports, Series P-60, no. 184, September. Washington, D.C.: Government Printing Office.

U.S. Bureau of the Census. 1992. *Workers with Low Earnings: 1964 to 1990.* Current Population Reports, Series P-60, No. 178, March. Washington, D.C.: Government Printing Office.

U.S. Bureau of the Census. 1994. Workers with Low Earnings: Note to Data Users. Unpublished tables prepared by Jack McNeil.

5

Trends in the Working Poor: The Impact of Economy, Family, and Public Policy

REBECCA M. BLANK AND REBECCA A. LONDON

The public discussion of poverty continually emphasizes the importance of work as a route out of poverty. Recent national reforms of the welfare system are aimed at encouraging welfare recipients to work. Educational reforms aimed at the non–college-bound population emphasize getting youth into jobs and facilitating the school-to-work transition. The presence of a substantial number of workers among the poor, however, raises questions about this strategy. It suggests that work may not be sufficient to escape poverty; if many of the jobs available to less-skilled workers are too poorly paid to provide a route out of poverty, then policy must be as concerned with wage and income supplementation as with employment. Evidence indicates that fundamental changes in the labor market have led to falling wages among less-skilled workers. As a result, one might expect that the number of working poor may be increasing and the opportunities to escape poverty through employment may be shrinking.

This essay focuses on changes in the working-poor population and relates these changes to changes in the economic, family, and policy environment over the past fifteen years. The first section explores the extent of employment among the poor and recent trends in the working poor. The second section relates these trends to changes in the U.S. economy. The third, fourth, and fifth sections look at policy issues and relate changes in the number of working poor to economic policy, family composition, and the effect of government programs on work behavior of the poor. The last section summarizes the results and suggests several long-term policy implications.

This essay does not focus specifically on the issue of *urban* poverty alone, but provides a description of nationwide shifts that are affecting all poor families and persons. By the early 1990s, however, poverty is predominantly an urban phenomenon and any general discussion of poverty is primarily a discussion of the urban poor. Only 26 percent of the poor lived outside major metropolitan areas in 1992. It is also important to note that over one third of the poor in metropolitan areas live in the suburbs, not in the central cities.[1] The shrinking share of rural poverty has been matched by a growing share of poverty in both central cities and in their suburbs.

Describing the Working Poor

The term "working poor" has been used in a wide variety of ways in the research literature.[2] In some articles, it is used to describe work behavior among women who receive Aid to Families with Dependent Children (AFDC), the primary program that provides low-income cash assistance and is typically referred to as welfare.[3] Others have taken care to include only poor persons who are involved in the labor market (either through employment or active job search) for a substantial part of the year.[4] In this essay, we typically distinguish between those poor persons who report some employment over the previous year and those who do not. This is a relatively broad definition of the working poor and is the easiest one to implement in a consistent way across available data sources. While we will refer to those who worked at all during the past year as "working poor," the more accurate (but much more unwieldy) reference might be "persons who have had some experience with jobs and employment over the year." When possible, we will separate out those with full-time year-round work experience from the more partially employed.

It is also important to note that *poverty* status is based on the total income of all related persons who live together, while *work* is typically an individual-level concept. Poverty is calculated by comparing the total cash income among all related individuals in a household against a federally defined poverty line that varies by family size.[5] Thus, family composition is a key element in determining the link between work and poverty. Two adult workers who are married to each other are much less likely to face poverty than are two workers who are the single heads of two separate households. For this reason, we present work behavior among adults by family configuration in many of the tables.

Finally, a definitional note on family configuration is in order. When the U.S. Bureau of the Census calculates poverty status, it assumes that all related people who live together share expenses, and poverty is defined relative to their total income. Anyone who lives with one or more relatives (spouse, child, parents, siblings, etc.) is considered part of a *family*. Those who do not live with any relatives are considered *unrelated individuals*, and their poverty status is based only on their own income. These people may be living alone or living with people to whom they are not related. For instance, poverty status for two unrelated roommates is calculated for each person, based only on his or her income. In contrast, if these roommates are sisters, they are considered a family and their poverty status is based on their combined incomes. The language of this essay is consistent with the Census terminology. Thus, when we refer to a family, this will always mean a group of related people and will never include unrelated individuals. Unfortunately, the Census has no terminology to refer broadly to both families and unrelated individuals. This essay uses the term "family unit" to refer to an economically independent living unit, which may be either a family or an unrelated individual. For instance, when we calculate the percent of family units with at least one worker, this is the share of all families and all unrelated individuals that contain at least one person who worked over the past year.

Who Are the Working Poor in 1992?

There are various ways to look at the nature and extent of work behavior among the poor. "How many workers are poor?" is a different question than "How many of the adult poor are working?" One may also be interested in the question "What share of poor individuals are in a family unit where at least one adult is working?"

Table 5.1 looks at the question of how many workers are poor, distinguishing between adult men and women. Less than 3 percent of full-time year-round workers[6] are poor (live in a family unit with income below the poverty line), while over 30 percent of non-workers are poor. Interestingly, given similar work behavior, men and women are equally likely to be poor; women have an overall higher poverty rate because they are more likely to be non-workers or part-time workers.

Part I of Table 5.2 asks the question the other way around, looking at how many persons in poor family units are working. For comparison, the table also shows work behavior among persons in non-poor family units. For every family type in Table 5.2, individuals in poor family units are much less likely to be working than equivalent individuals in non-poor family units. Among all adults in poor family units, 48 percent worked at some point during 1992, while 88 percent of adults in non-poor family units worked. In poor married-couple families, 69 percent of the husbands and 36 percent of the wives work, compared to 94 percent and 75 percent among husbands and wives in non-poor married-couple families. Among single women who had families, 44 percent work in poor families while 89 percent work in non-poor families.

Table 5.1
Incidence of Poverty, Tabulated by Work Behavior, 1992
All persons, 16–64

Individual Work Behavior	Percent of Poor among		
	All persons	Men	Women
Full-time year-round workers	2.6	2.6	2.6
Workers, not full-time year-round	14.5	14.8	14.3
Non-workers	30.3	30.4	30.4
All persons (Workers and non-workers)	11.9	9.7	14.1

Source: U.S. Department of Commerce, 1993, tabulated from data in table 14.

Table 5.2
Work Behavior among Non-elderly Poor and Non-Poor Adults, by Family Type, 1992

Family Type	Adults in Poor Family Units			Adults in Non-Poor Family Units		
	All Adults[a]	Men	Women	All Adults[a]	Men	Women
Part I. Percent Working						
Unrelated individuals	52.1	57.4	47.2	93.8	94.2	93.3
Married couples	50.2	68.6	36.3	82.0	93.5	75.0
Single heads of families	na	na	44.4	na	na	89.0
All family units	47.7	57.6	41.0	88.4	92.2	84.2
Part II. Percent Working Full-time, Year-round						
Unrelated individuals	8.5	10.4	6.7	67.9	67.5	68.4
Married couples	16.0	29.0	7.7	52.6	77.0	42.7
Single heads of families	na	na	9.5	na	na	67.2
All family types	10.9	16.1	7.4	54.4	65.8	48.7

[a]Counts include all adults in family units where the head is not over age 65.

Source: U.S. Department of Commerce, 1993, tabulated from data in table 14.

Table 5.3
Share of All Poor in Non-elderly Family Units with Some Labor Market Involvement, 1992

	Share of poor persons in the indicated type of family unit containing	
Type of family unit	**At least one worker**	**At least one full-time year-round worker**
Unrelated individuals[a]	52.1	8.5
Male-headed	57.3	10.4
Female-headed	47.2	6.7
Families[b]	64.7	22.2
Male-headed	79.5	33.4
Female-headed	50.2	11.4
Married couple families	76.0	32.9
Single adult families	54.5	12.6
All family units	62.6	19.9
Male-headed	75.8	29.6
Female-headed	49.7	10.6

[a]Ages 16 to 64.
[b]Calculated from all persons in families, assuming persons in elderly-headed families do not work.

Source: U.S. Department of Commerce, 1993, tabulated from tables 5, 14 & 19.

Part II of Table 5.2 investigates full-time year-round work behavior. Although a substantial minority of married-couple poor families have a full-time worker in them, among other groups of the poor, full-time work is relatively rare. While close to a third of the men in poor married-couple familes work full-time year-round, 77 percent of men in similar non-poor families work as much. Similarly, only 10 percent of poor women who head families work full-time, while among the non-poor 67 percent of such women work full-time.

Finally, Table 5.3 looks at how many persons (children and adults) live in poor family units where someone is employed at least part-time over the year, excluding those persons who live in poor family units headed by an elderly person. Fifty-two percent of all non-elderly unrelated individuals and 65 percent of all persons in non-elderly families are in family units where at least one person works. This means that almost two thirds (63 percent) of all poor persons are in living situations where there is at least one worker, as the bottom rows of Table 5.3 indicate. Twenty percent of all persons are in family units where there is at least one full-time year-round worker. This suggests that many of the poor have connections to the labor market and rely at least in part upon earnings. Not surprisingly, these numbers are lowest among single-adult families, although over half of all persons in this type of family have some reliance on earnings: 54 percent of all persons in single-adult families are in a family with at least one worker, while 13 percent are in a family with a full-time year-round worker.

In summary, in 1992 quite a large number of poor adults had some contact with the labor market, and around two-thirds of all poor persons were in family units where there was at least one worker. This suggests that many poor adults do find jobs with some regularity. Yet, few of these workers are full-time year-round workers. In comparison to the non-poor, full-time work is quite a rare phenomenon among most groups of poor, although one-third of poor married couples have at least one full-time worker. This of course raises the question of causality: Is it intractable constraints in their lives and in the labor market that prevent the poor from working more, or is this a reversible behavioral choice?

Trends in work among the poor over time are one place to start answering this question. If work behavior is highly cyclical, this suggests that labor market constraints are important. If work behavior shows relatively stable upward or downward trends, this suggests more long-term behavioral or economic shifts.

What Has Happened to the Working Poor over Time?

Figure 5.1 plots the percent of all workers and of full-time year-round workers who live in poor family units. The percent of workers who are poor rose sharply with the back-to-back recessions of the early 1980s, declined during the long expansion between 1983 and 1990, and rose again with the stagnant economic environment of 1990–1992. Overall, there is no indication of any substantial trend in poverty among workers over the past fifteen years. If the economy expands for a period of years in the mid-1990s, the share of poverty among workers will again decline. Similar conclusions are evident if one focuses only on poverty among full-time year-round workers. While the percent of poor workers has increased by 0.8 percentage points over the past fifteen years, this is not a substantial change.

The work experiences of the poor also show few trends over time. Figure 5.2 plots the percent of various types of poor family units who have at least one or more workers. Over the past fifteen years, about 70 percent of married-couple poor families contained a worker, with no discernable trend. There has been a slight upward trend in work among single women who head

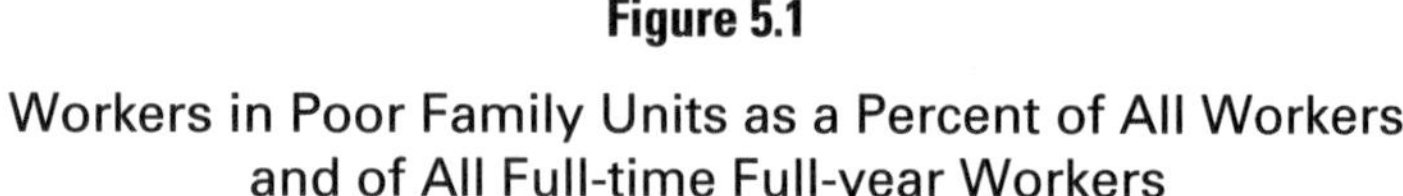

Figure 5.1

Workers in Poor Family Units as a Percent of All Workers and of All Full-time Full-year Workers

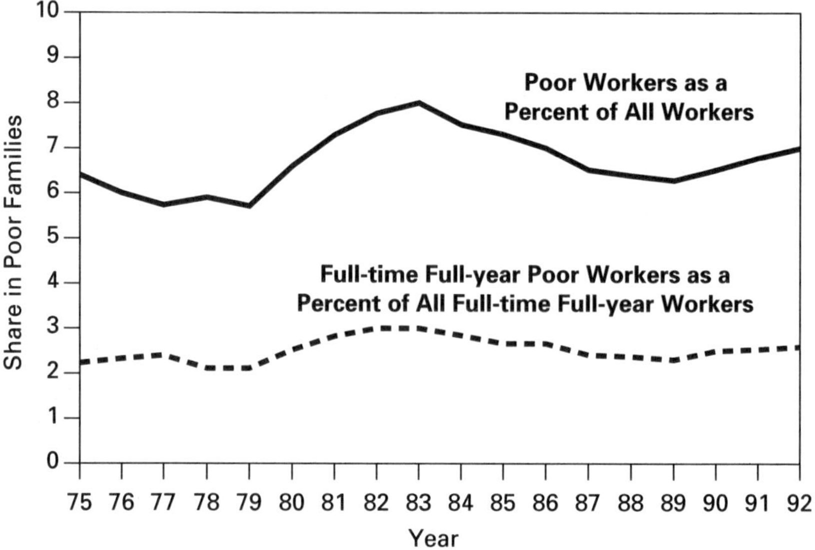

Source: U.S. Department of Commerce, P-60 series, various issues.

families, from 47 percent to 50 percent. Data on unrelated individuals is only recently available.

Figure 5.3 shows the equivalent graph for full-time year-round workers. As expected, the number of poor family units with a year-round full-time worker is much lower in all years. While there has been a slight decline in full-time year-round work in married-couple families, there has been an upward trend in full-time year-round work among single female family heads. Note that the data used in Figures 5.2 and 5.3 include elderly-headed families. When we look only at non-elderly low-income families (using data described below), there is a more notable trend toward decreasing work effort among married couples and increasing work effort among single-female family heads.

The above data have come from reports on the poverty population published annually by the U.S. Bureau of the Census. One problem with these data is that they are based on family units whose income falls below an arbitrarily defined poverty line. Over time, the poverty line has fallen in the in-

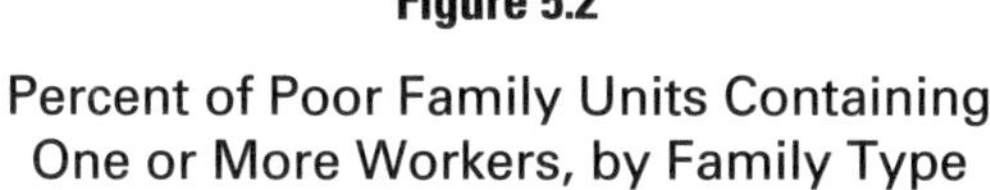

Figure 5.2

Percent of Poor Family Units Containing One or More Workers, by Family Type

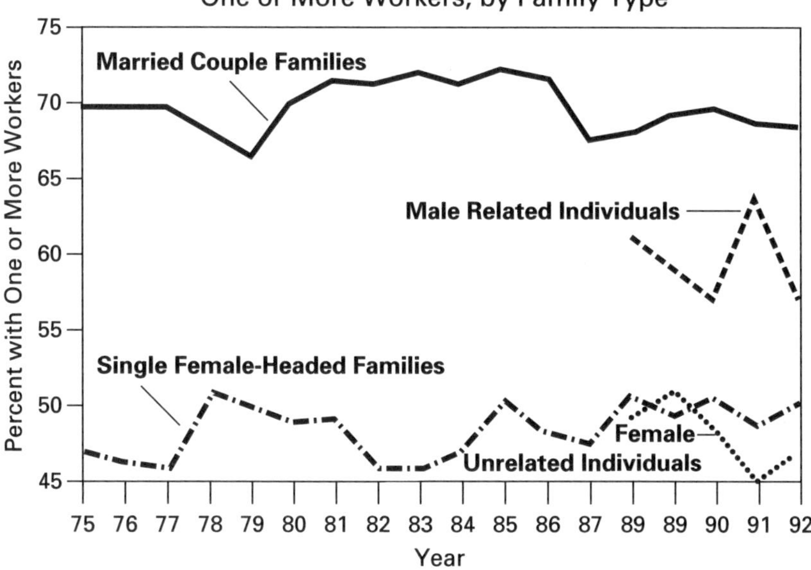

Source: See Figure 1.
Note that this figure includes elderly-headed family units, which were not separately tabulated in earlier years.

come distribution, meaning that there has been an increase over time in how far below median income a family's income has to fall in order to be counted as poor. To provide a somewhat more consistent measure of work behavior among those at the bottom of the income distribution, we switch from looking at individuals and families whose income is below the U.S. poverty line to looking at those whose income is in the bottom quintile (bottom 20 percent) of the income distribution among all family units.

The data used to define who is and is not in the bottom quintile of the income distribution comes from the *Current Population Survey* (March) from 1968 through 1992, a random national sample of families and individuals that asks family units about their work experience and income sources over the past year, providing information on the years 1967–1991, a twenty-five–year period.[7] The income distribution is obtained by ordering all family units by their reported annual cash income. The bottom quintile contains the bottom 20 percent of family units in the United States, based on this ordering.

Figure 5.3

Percent of Poor Family Units Whose Head Works Full-time Full-year, by Family Type

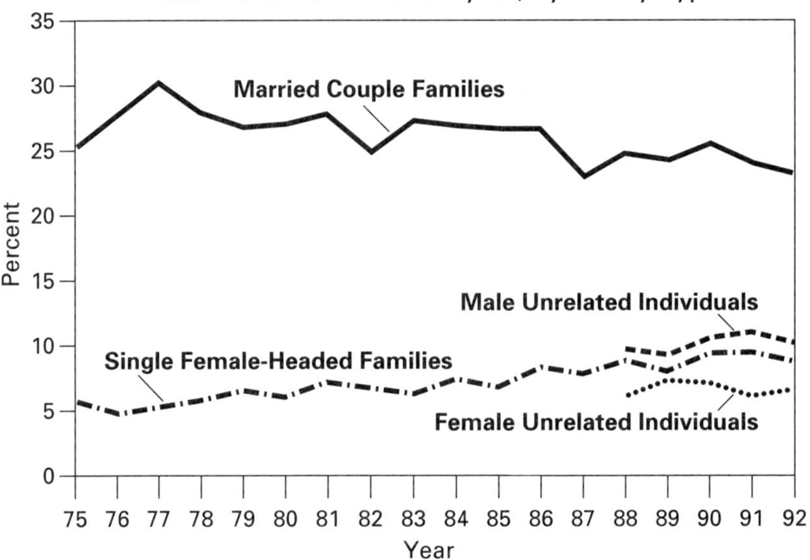

Source: See Figure 1.
Note that this figure includes elderly-headed family units, which were not separately tabulated in earlier years.

Within the bottom quintile, we are particularly interested in work behavior among the heads and other adults within low-income family units headed by non-elderly adults. Figure 5.4 plots the percent of non-elderly family units in the bottom quintile with a working person at their head. The overall trend (solid line) moves downward from 1967–1982, from around 67 percent to 60 percent, but has been quite flat since then.

Also graphed on Figure 5.4 is the probability of head's employment in two selected family types within the bottom quintile of the income distribution. Among married couples with children in the bottom quintile of the income distribution, there is a marked decline in the probability that the family head is a worker. This is offset, however, by an increase over the past fifteen years in the probability of work among single family heads.

The amount of work that household heads perform may be of as much interest as whether or not they work. Figure 5.5 graphs annual weeks of work among non-elderly working heads of family units in the bottom quintile of

Figure 5.4

Percent of Heads Working among All Family Units in the Bottom Quintile and for Two Selected Groups

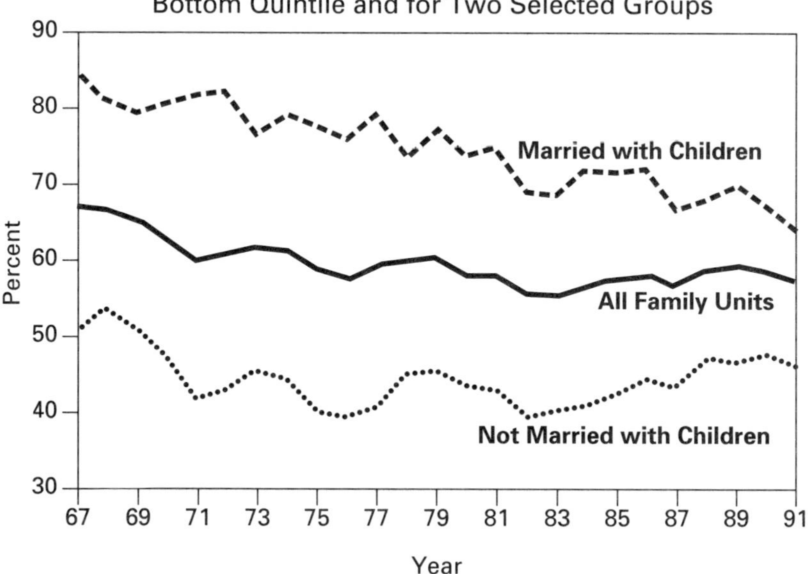

Source: Authors' tabulations, March Current Populations Survey data.

the income distribution. Overall, weeks of work decline from 1967 through about 1983, and rise since then. Again, this is the result of offsetting trends among different groups of family units, of which two are shown in Figure 5.5. The recent increase in weeks of work among poor heads of family units is primarily due to increases in weeks of work among single family heads.

The conclusion from Figures 5.4 and 5.5 is that work behavior has changed in very different ways among different groups of low-income families. Among married couples, both the probability of working and the weeks of work have declined substantially over the past twenty-five years, evidence of a deterioration in work behavior. Among single family heads, particularly among women with children, the probability of working and the average weeks of work have increased. These trends are entirely consistent with other evidence on labor market changes by gender. Less-skilled adult men (who are the primary heads of low-income married-couple families) have steadily decreased their labor market involvement over the past twenty years.[8] Adult women have steadily increased their labor market involvement for several

Figure 5.5

Heads' Average Weeks of Work if Working among All Family Units in the Bottom Quintile and for Two Selected Groups

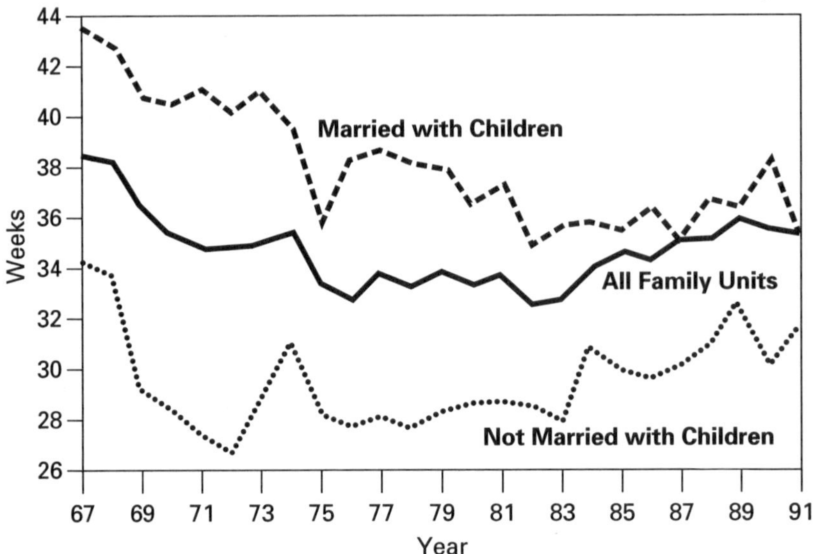

Source: See Figure 4.

decades. While these increases have been smallest among least-skilled women, among women with high school or college degrees there has been a large and continuing increase in work effort.[9] This is driving the increased labor market behavior of single-adult family units. While our focus in this essay is on work behavior, it should be noted that even with these trends in employment and hours, single-headed family units are still poorer than married-couple family units.

Finally, it is worth noting that labor market involvement does not only mean employment. If there were an increase in the number of people actively (but unsuccessfully) seeking work this would be registered as an increase in work effort among low-income family units. Figure 5.6 graphs the average weeks of unemployment experienced by family heads in the bottom quintile of the income distribution. Consistent with aggregate unemployment trends, the solid line shows a steady rise in the extent of unemployment among low-income family units throughout the 1970s. After 1983, however, aggregate unemployment rates start trending downward, and unemployment among low-income family unit heads trends downward as well. These patterns occur

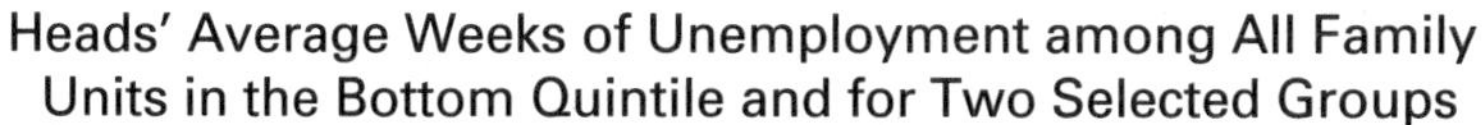

Figure 5.6

Heads' Average Weeks of Unemployment among All Family Units in the Bottom Quintile and for Two Selected Groups

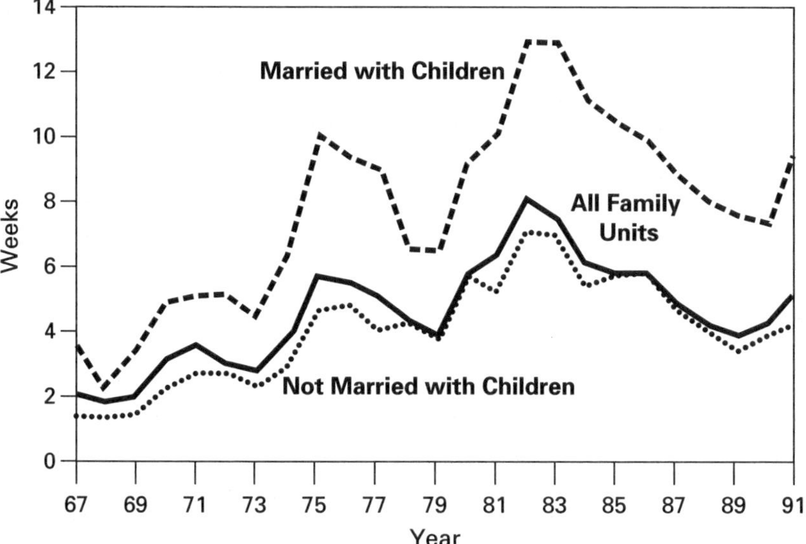

Source: See Figure 4.

among all low-income family types. Thus, there is no evidence that unemployment has gotten worse among low-income family units over the past decade.

To summarize the evidence on trends in work among low-income family units, there has been an increase in the weeks of work and the probability of working among heads of low-income family units over the past ten years, consistent with the idea that the number of working poor has increased. Not all low-income family units have shown this same trend, however. Single mothers who head their own families are working more than they were a decade ago, while the men who head married-couple families are working less.

The Working Poor and the Changing Economy

In recent years there has been an explosion of interest in changes in the labor market for more- and less-skilled workers driven by the fact that wage inequality is widening. Wages among less-skilled workers have fallen steadily, while wages among more-skilled workers have risen steadily since about 1979.

This suggests that earnings opportunities among poor adults have become more limited.

These results differ by gender and it is worth a brief discussion of the trends in weekly earnings among low-income men versus women.[10] Since 1979, real wages for male high school drop-outs and high school graduates have fallen in all sectors of the economy. Less-skilled men in both manufacturing and non-manufacturing industries have experienced wage declines, which means that the long-term sectoral shift away from manufacturing into services is not the primary cause of these changes; they would have occurred even in the absence of that shift. In addition, both younger and older men are experiencing these changes, so it is not just a deterioration in the work skills of younger workers that is driving these changes.

Among women, real wages of high school drop-outs have been stagnant, while wages among their more-educated sisters have increased steadily, with the largest increases among the college educated. It is notable, however, that wages among less-educated women remain far below those of equivalent men. The decline in the male-female wage differential at the bottom end of the labor market is not occurring because women are doing better, but because men are doing worse. Thus, the problems facing low-skilled women are less those of a deteriorating labor market than they are the problems of a stagnant labor market that still provides the same low-paying jobs as it always has.[11]

Table 5.4 presents evidence on these trends among men and women by education level. Over the 1980s, average weekly earnings among men with less than twelve years of education have fallen by 13 percent, while they have risen 11 percent among men with more than twelve years of education. In contrast, women without a high school degree have faced virtually stagnant weekly earnings since 1969 (still well below the earnings of their equivalent male colleagues), while women with more than twelve years of education have seen their earnings grow by 25 percent.

The causes of these labor market changes are much discussed. In general, most of the research indicates that it is changes in the demand for more- versus less-skilled labor that is driving these trends, rather than changes in worker productivity and labor supply.[12] Two particular economywide changes in the U.S. have been strongly linked to these wage changes: the growing importance of international competition to U.S. firms, and the presence of non-neutral technological shifts that have increased demand for more-skilled workers and decreased demand for less-skilled workers. In addi-

Table 5.4
Average Weekly Earnings by Years of School and Sex among Non-elderly Adults Who Work
($1992)

	Men			Women		
	1969	1979	1989	1969	1979	1989
All workers	$593	$580	$613	$282	$299	$364
Percent change		−2.2	+5.7		+6.0	+21.7
Less than 12 years of education	$470	$440	$384	$221	$224	$223
Percent change		−6.4	−12.7		+1.4	−0.4
12 years of education	$580	$548	$526	$278	$280	$308
Percent change		−5.5	−4.0		+0.7	+10.0
More than 12 years of education	$763	$693	$768	$366	$362	$453
Percent change		−9.2	+10.8		−1.1	+25.1

Source: Tabulations from the Current Population Surveys, March 1970, 1980, and 1990, based on the civilian population ages 18-65. Inflation adjustments are based on the GDP deflator.

tion, declines in unionization (which are closely related to these other changes) have contributed to these problems.

In recent work investigating the reasons for persistently high poverty rates during the extended economic expansion of the 1980s, Blank (1993) indicates that the primary cause was the decline in real wages among less-skilled workers, which worked against expansions in employment and jobs to produce only small declines in overall poverty.

These wage changes have also been linked to work behavior among those whom they effect. Juhn (1992) indicates that the majority of the decline in work among less-skilled men since 1979 can be directly attributed to their declining wage levels. We present estimates below that suggest these wage changes are responsible for about a 2 percent decline in the probability of work among family heads in the bottom quintile since 1979.

Interestingly, these wage changes have not been correlated with rising unemployment. As Figure 5.6 indicated, weeks of unemployment among family units at the bottom of the income distribution have actually fallen somewhat over the 1980s. Thus, the problem appears not to be the availability of jobs, but the nature of the jobs available to less-skilled workers. But the returns to work have clearly fallen, particularly among men. It is perhaps not surprising that the result has been decreasing work effort among less-skilled men.

Much of our anti-poverty policy is aimed at encouraging work effort among poor adults. In the next three sections we review many of the major issues relating to work effort among poor persons, and relate them to policy. Given the discussion in this section about recent economic changes in the labor market for poor adults, we start by talking about job availability and economic policy. We then turn to the impact of changes in family composition, a key concern with regard to work behavior, although this may be less readily affected by public policy. Finally, we end with a discussion of some of the major anti-poverty programs that have an impact on work behavior among the poor.

Economic Policy and Work Behavior among the Poor

Work among the poor is closely related to the health of the U.S. economy. Any policy that aims at increasing work opportunities for the poor must be concerned with two issues: first, whether there are jobs available, and second, whether these jobs provide an opportunity to escape poverty.

With regard to the first question, job availability, there is substantial evidence that low unemployment is necessary to ensure work opportunities for low-income adults. Unemployment is very unequally distributed. Blank and Card (1993) indicate that a one-point rise in the unemployment rate increases weeks of unemployment among persons in family units at the bottom quintile of the income distribution about twice as much as among family units at the top quintile of the income distribution.

Table 5.5 looks at the effects of unemployment on family units in the bottom quintile of the income distribution. The coefficients reported in Table 5.5 can be directly interpreted as the effect of a one-point rise in the unemployment rate on the indicated variable.[13] For instance, the first row indicates that a one-point rise in unemployment leads to a 1.7 point rise in the probability of unemployment among family unit heads in the bottom of the income distribution. Row 4 indicates that a one-point rise in unemployment leads to a 1.2 point fall in the probability of work among family unit heads. Total weeks of unemployment among heads goes up by 0.7 weeks, while weeks of employment among heads goes down by 0.8, indicating some (but not many) heads leave the labor market rather than seek further work. Wages among

Table 5.5
Effect of a One-point Rise in the Unemployment Rate on Selected Variables among Family Units in the Bottom Quintile of the Income Distribution

Dependent Variable	Coefficient on the Unemployment Rate	
Percent of heads who are unemployed	1.707**	(.147)
Average weeks of unemployment:		
Among heads	.696**	(.040)
Among all adults	.864**	(.049)
Percent of heads who are working	−1.221**	(.192)
Average weeks of work:		
Among heads	−.844**	(.082)
Among all adults	−.982**	(.108)
Average weekly wages among heads (in dollars)	−2.711**	(.704)
Average annual earnings (in dollars):		
Among heads	−149.5**	(23.9)
Among all adults	−162.7**	(25.5)

Standard errors in parentheses.
Earnings and wages in 1992 dollars.

** Significant at 1 percent level.

Source: Tabulations by authors. See note 14.

heads are procyclical and also show declines as unemployment rises. The net effect of these wage and hour changes is a decline of $163 in average annual earnings among all adults in bottom quintile family units when unemployment rises by one point.[14]

Table 5.5 emphasizes the negative effects of high unemployment rates on families at the bottom of the income distribution; the previous section discussed the economywide trend toward a widening wage inequality that has presumably depressed wages among less-skilled workers. Evidence of the effect of changes in unemployment and in wage inequality on low-income family units' work behavior is shown in Table 5.6. The results in Table 5.6 are based on a series of regressions not shown here.[15] The first column of Table 5.6 shows the actual 1991 value of five measures of work behavior among family units in the bottom quintile of the income distribution. The second column simulates the 1991 values, based on regression coefficients.[16] It should be clear that the regressions are fitting the data very well.

The third column indicates what work behavior among family units at the bottom quintile of the income distribution would have looked like if unemployment had been at 5.5 percent in 1991 rather than at 6.7 percent. (Over the 1980s, 5.5 percent unemployment was the lowest annual rate of unemployment achieved, and by some accounts is quite close to the so-called "natural rate" of full employment consistent with non-accelerating inflation.) Heads' unemployment would have been lower, and close to one percent more of these families would have had a working head, with about 0.8 more weeks of employment in general. This would have increased average weekly wages moderately (by $2.36), and increased average earnings by $122.

The fourth column of Table 5.6 shows the impact of widening wage inequality on work behavior in the bottom quintile of the income distribution. If wage inequality had remained at the same level in 1991 as it was in 1979,[17] it would have increased the percent of working heads by one percent and increased average weekly wages by $4.04, leading to $142 more earnings over the year (a 4.4 percent increase). If wage inequality had remained unchanged since 1979 and unemployment had been at its low of the last decade, column 5 indicates that earnings among low-income families would have been $264 or 8.2 percent higher in 1991.

The policy lessons to be drawn from the results in Tables 5.5 and 5.6 are not necessarily straightforward. Strategies that maintain strong employment and foster job growth will clearly increase work and earnings among low-income families. Yet, anyone involved in macro-economic policy will immediately remind us that there are multiple goals for macro-policy. Maintaining low inflation, encouraging investment, and maintaining long-term balance in international trade accounts are also important and sometimes policy moves that decrease unemployment might worsen some of these other objectives. If the primary concern of policy is to relieve poverty and encourage employment among low-income families, however, low unemployment rates are almost surely a more important policy goal than these others.

With regard to the widening wage inequality, there is little reason to believe that we could (or should) reverse these trends in the U.S. economy. To the extent that these wage changes reflect shifts in the U.S. competitive position in the international labor market, they are long-term economic trends over

Table 5.6
Simulated Effect of Various Economic Alternatives upon Selected Variables among Family Units in the Bottom Quintile of the Income Distribution

			Simulated Values in 1991 if		
Dependent Variable	**Actual 1991 Value**	**Simulated 1991 Value[a]**	**Unemployment rate = 5.5%**	**Wage Inequality at 1979 value**	**Unemployment rate = 5.5% and wage inequality at 1979 value**
Percent of heads employed	25.4	25.4	23.6	25.4	23.6
Average weeks of unemployment among adults within family unit	6.6	6.6	5.6	6.6	5.6
Percent of heads working	58.0	57.9	58.9	59.0	60.0
Average weeks of work among adults within family unit	23.0	23.0	23.8	23.2	23.9
Head's average weekly wage	94.26	94.19	96.55	98.23	100.56
Average earnings within family unit	3,219	3,221	3,343	3,363	3,485

Earnings and wages in 1992 dollars.

[a]Simulation based on regression coefficients using actual 1991 values of all independent variables.

Source: Authors' tabulations. See note 15.

which policymakers have little control. The question instead is how much the U.S. will choose to protect the incomes of poor workers in the face of declining wages, either by providing wage supplements or by providing other forms of income support. In the past decade, the vast expansion in wage supplementation through the income tax system via the Earned Income Tax Credit (EITC) demonstrates an interest on the part of policymakers to "make work pay" for low-wage workers. This policy is discussed in more detail below.

Demographic Change and Work Behavior among the Poor

Another causal issue that is closely related to changes in work behavior and poverty is changes in family composition. There have been dramatic compositional changes in American family structure over the past several decades. Figure 5.7 shows how the population in the bottom quintile of the income distribution has been divided among family types over the past two decades. The area between each set of lines shows the relative share of the indicated family type. In particular, the share of low-income family units headed by elderly individuals has plummeted, and the share of childless married-couple families has also decreased. With the rise of divorce and childbearing outside of marriage, the share of low-income single adults who head a family with children has increased from 10 percent to 19 percent since 1969. In addition, the share of single adults living without children has also soared, from 29 percent to 41 percent of low-income family units between 1967 and 1991. Many of these single adult family units are female-headed, so that a growing proportion of low-income family units are headed by women.

These changes in the composition of family units are necessarily linked to changing work behavior for low-income family units. For instance, because women tend to work fewer weeks than men, a shift from male-headed to female-headed family units would decrease work hours among the poor family units. At the same time, however, work hours among women have gone up while work hours among men have gone down, as noted above. These changes should offset the effect of shifts in family composition.

Table 5.7 provides a simple decomposition of changes in a few key variables that measure work effort among bottom-quintile family units. Part I focuses on the 1967–1991 period. Using the first variable, percent of heads working, as an example, columns 1 and 2 show the percent of heads who work among family units in the bottom quintile in 1967 and 1991, while column 3 shows the change between these years. Column 3 indicates that all four measures of work effort in Table 5.7 have declined between 1967 and 1991. The per-

Figure 5.7

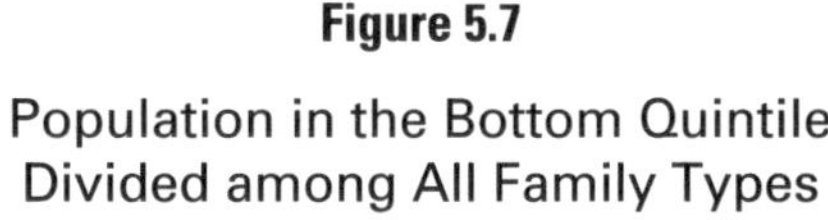

Population in the Bottom Quintile
Divided among All Family Types

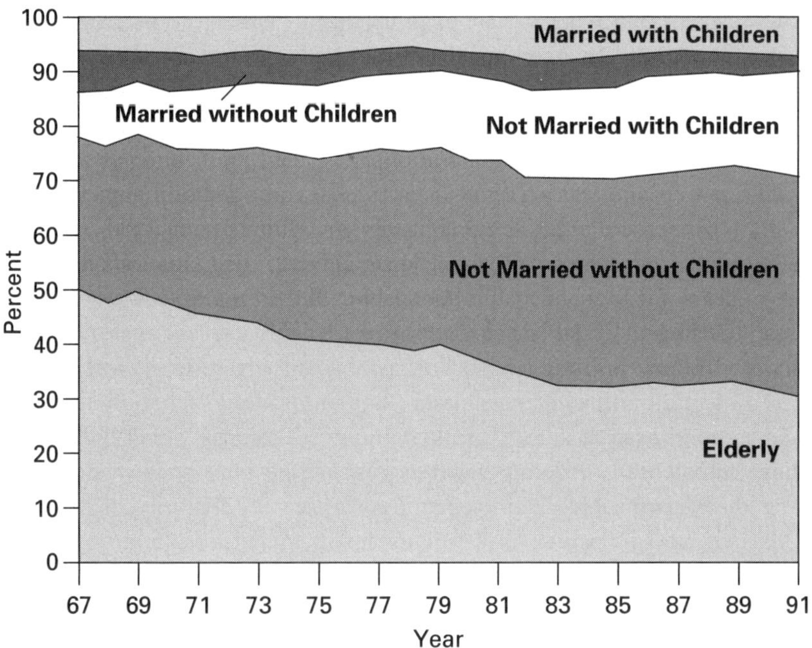

Source: See Figure 4.

cent of working heads has declined 9 points, and the average weeks of work within families has declined nine weeks. Real wages have also declined, leading to a $1209 decline in annual family earnings. Part II, which provides similar analysis for the more recent 1979–1991 time period, indicates that most of these changes (except for the decline in real wages) occurred over the 1970s and not during the 1980s.

Column 4 (row 1) shows the percent of heads who would work if family configuration had been held constant at its 1967 levels. We hold family configuration constant across four types of family units in Table 5.7: Not married, with and without children, and married, with and without children. Any changes in column 4 that occur are due to changes in work behavior within the different family types. Column 5 shows the percent of heads who would work if the changes in family configuration had occurred, but no changes in

Table 5.7
Effect on Selected Variables of Changes in Family Configuration Versus Behavioral Changes within Family Types[a] among Family Units in the Bottom Quintile

Part I. 1967–91

	Actual 1967 Value	Actual 1991 Value	Actual Change 1967–91	Family configuration constant; work behavior within family type changes	Work behavior within family type constant; family configuration changes
Percent of heads working	67.3	58.0	–9.3	–8.7	–0.6
Average weeks of work among adults within family unit	32.4	23.0	–9.4	–7.3	–2.1
Average weekly wages among heads within family unit	120.02	94.25	–25.77	–26.34	0.57
Average earnings within family unit	4,428	3,219	–1,209	–1,067	–141

Part II. 1979–91

	Actual 1979 Value	Actual 1991 Value	Actual Change 1979–91	Family configuration constant; work behavior within family type changes	Work behavior within family type constant; family configuration changes
Percent of heads working	60.2	58.0	–2.1	–1.7	–0.4
Average weeks of work among adults within family unit	23.6	23.0	–0.6	0.0	–0.6
Average weekly wages among heads within family unit	107.03	94.25	–12.78	–12.32	–0.46
Average earnings within family unit	3,485	3,219	–266	–216	–50

Earnings and wages in 1992 dollars.

[a] "Family type" in this table refers to four types of family units: not married with children, not married without children, married with children, and married without children

Source: Authors' tabulations. See text.

work behavior within family categories had occurred. Thus, column 5 shows the effect of family configuration, holding work behavior constant. Columns 4 and 5 sum to the total change in column 3.

In part I, showing the 1967–1991 time period, it is clear that the primary cause of changes in work behavior among bottom-quintile family units was changes in work behavior within the four family types. Only a small share of the change in any of these four variables can be explained by changes in family configuration alone. For instance, while the percent of working heads declined by 9.3 percentage points, 94 percent (8.7 percentage points) of this was due to changes in work behavior within family types, and only 6 percent was due to changes in configuration across family types. This is true in the 1979–1991 time period as well, when family configuration changes were also relatively unimportant.

It is clear from Table 5.7 that both shifts in the configuration of families and changes in work behavior within particular types of families have affected low-income households, but the overwhelming changes have occurred in behavior within family types. Even in the absence of any significant demographic shifts, within-group behavioral changes would have produced substantial aggregate declines in work behavior.

In many ways, the fact that family composition changes have not been a primary cause of changes in work behavior among low-income families is good news from a policy perspective. Although our ability to stimulate economic growth and decrease unemployment may be limited, economic policy levers are still far more effective than any policy levers which address family configuration and marriage/fertility behavior. If changes in family configuration had been the primary cause of aggregate changes in work among low-income families, the appropriate policy response would be uncertain. In fact, if the concern is to increase work effort among the poor, the trends in work behavior among different family types lead to a conclusion that many would find unpalatable: the increase in work among single women who head households, in contrast to the decrease in work among low-income men who head households, implies that we should encourage the move to single-female families. This emphasizes the problem of viewing work behavior as a single policy objective. Concern about parental time available to raise and nurture children might lead to an alternative conclusion. At best, the discussion of family configuration change suggests that these changes are second-order effects in their impact on work behavior over the past few decades.

Government Policies That Directly Impact Work among Poor Households

These policies fall into three types: first, those that involve direct employment, job placement, and training efforts designed to move individuals toward greater work hours and more lucrative employment; second, those that are designed to help redistribute income and offset poverty, which have incentive effects for work behavior built into them; and third, those designed to increase or supplement earnings.

Direct Employment and Training Programs

U.S. policies aimed at increasing employment through job placement, job creation, or job training can be dealt with quickly because these have historically been relatively small programs. Since 1982, the primary job training program has been the Job Training Partnership Act (JTPA), which offers job training and search assistance to disadvantaged workers. JTPA is run by local private sector cooperatives, known as private industry councils (PICs). PICs determine what type of training and job placement would be most beneficial to clients and local employers, leading to substantial variance in how the program is run among different cities.

JTPA is a small program, serving only about 550,000 persons in 1991, of which slightly under half were teenagers.[18] A major recent evaluation of the effectiveness of JTPA found that the program had a positive effect on the earnings and employment of adult men and women, increasing earnings by about $500 per year and increasing employment by 2 to 3 percentage points.[19] The results for youth are more disappointing, with no evidence that this population gained from its participation in JTPA programs.

At present, the U.S. has no public job creation programs designed to make jobs in the public sector available to workers who have difficulty finding employment in the private sector. In the 1970s, a relatively limited public sector job creation program was run, known as the Comprehensive Employment and Training Act (CETA). In part because of mixed results and in part because of budget difficulties, CETA was replaced by JTPA in 1982.

The largest recent effort aimed at directly increasing employment among low-income families has occurred as part of welfare reform. In the 1980s, a number of states received permission to experiment with welfare-to-work programs that provided job search and employment assistance to AFDC recipients. While some of these programs were voluntary, most were mandatory, meaning that women who were assigned to the program had to participate in order to keep their full welfare eligibility. A series of evaluations on these state programs indicated that they were successful at significantly increasing employment and earnings among women on AFDC. For instance, in Arkansas, by the end of the third year of their state program, the employment rate among work-welfare participants was 6.2 percentage points higher than the 18.3 percent employment rate among non-participants; participant's earnings were 31 percent ($337) higher.[20]

In part because of the success of these evaluations, Congress passed the Family Support Act in 1988, directing all states to run mandatory welfare-to-work programs. These programs were to provide job search assistance, but also required states to provide training and education for some groups of women, particularly teenage mothers. The results of this new legislative mandate are still unclear. An early evaluation of California's program, known as GAIN, indicates that it has produced significant employment and earnings benefits for its participants.[21]

While this sounds promising as a way of increasing work behavior among AFDC recipients, there are two important caveats. First, it is not clear that these programs will reduce the number of working poor; in fact, the evidence indicates that few women who participate in these programs escape poverty. While they work more and their earnings increase, their welfare income decreases at the same time. Given very low wage rates, few of them experience large income gains. Thus, such programs may only be successful at moving women out of poverty if they are combined with earnings supplement programs like the EITC. Second, these programs are relatively limited. Few states are providing these services to more than 5 to 7 percent of their total AFDC caseload. While the law requires that this increase over time, it is not clear how successful states will be at expanding these programs.

The most recent discussion of welfare reform within the Clinton Administration proposes to push these welfare-to-work programs even further. The current proposal would require long-term AFDC recipients to work, either on created (public sector) jobs or in private sector job placements. There is little reason to believe that a high percentage of this population will be successful at escaping poverty through work alone, particularly since long-term recipients tend to be the most disadvantaged in terms of labor market skills. Thus, while additional reforms may increase future work among AFDC recipients, they may also increase the share of the working poor.

It is worth emphasizing that all of these direct employment programs affect a very small number of the poor. No more than 3 to 5 percent of all poor adults participated in JTPA or welfare-to-work programs in 1992. Thus, the effects on work behavior among the poor of direct employment and work placement programs are necessarily quite small.

Government Programs Whose Structure Impacts Work Behavior among the Poor

A wide variety of government programs redistribute income in ways that create incentives or disincentives for work. A full review of all these programs is far beyond the scope of this essay.[22] We will focus instead on one major program that is typically considered highly important for low-income families: AFDC or welfare. The issues relating to this program, however, are quite similar to those involved in virtually all income supplementation programs, whether in the form of cash or in-kind assistance.

Exclusive of welfare-to-work programs, welfare assistance is designed to provide support to low-income (predominantly single-adult) families. It does this by paying a basic guaranteed benefit to families with no alternative sources of income and then reducing this benefit as other income (including earnings) becomes available.

This embeds two work disincentives.[23] First, paying support to persons who do not work at all makes non-work more attractive. The higher the guaranteed benefit at zero hours of work, the greater the work disincentive. Second, reducing the benefit level as earnings increase essentially imposes a tax on earnings. For every dollar the family earns, they lose some of their benefits, so their total income gain is less than one dollar. The higher the benefit reduction rate, the greater the work disincentive.

Over the past fifteen years, these two work disincentives have changed in offsetting ways. On the one hand, AFDC benefit levels have steadily declined. Note that these benefits are not determined by the federal government, but are set within each state, resulting in a wide variance in benefit payments. Figure 5.8 graphs the median value of state AFDC benefits, as well as the additional value of (nationally set) food stamp benefits, which are received by most AFDC recipients. While the value of food stamps has been relatively constant since 1979, the value of AFDC has declined, leading to a decline in the maximum benefits available to a welfare recipient who does not work. This should have led to increased work effort.

At the same time, the benefit reduction rate on earnings increased in the early 1980s. Since 1981, for every dollar of earnings, AFDC benefits are reduced by $.67 for the first four months of work, and by $1 afterwards. Theoretically, this means that a woman who earns a dollar may lose a dollar of benefits, making her financially no better off after working than before. In reality, because of various income exemptions for such things as child care and

Figure 5.8

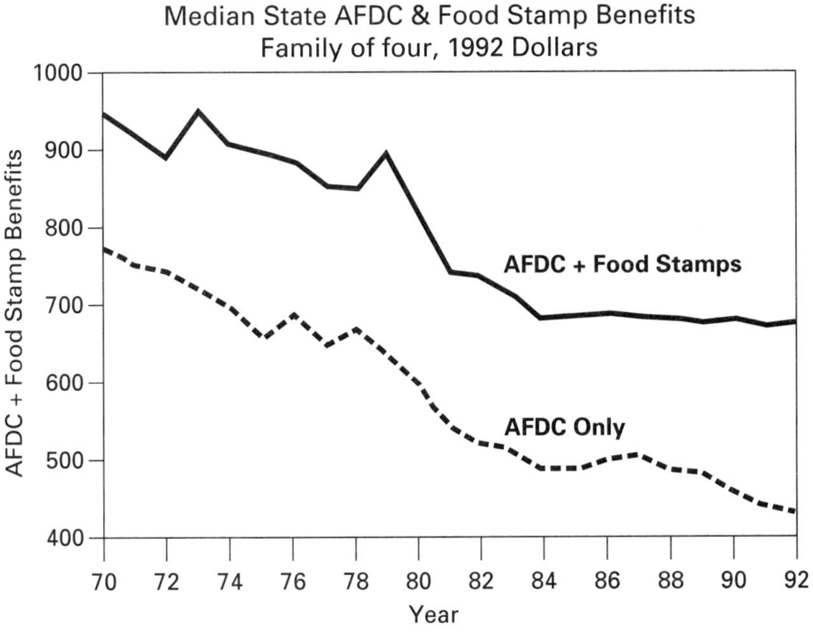
Median State AFDC & Food Stamp Benefits
Family of four, 1992 Dollars
AFDC + Food Stamp Benefits
1000
900
800
700
600
500
400
AFDC + Food Stamps
AFDC Only
70
72
74
76
78
80
82
84
86
88
90
92
Year

work expenses, the actual benefit reduction rate is typically less than dollar-for-dollar, but it is still quite high. This should have decreased work effort.

In part, it was frustration with trying to calibrate benefit levels and benefit reduction rates that stimulated an interest in direct welfare-to-work programs. Rather than relying on program incentives and trying to encourage women to work in the face of high benefit reduction rates, welfare-to-work programs mandate that eligible welfare recipients must participate in job training and placement programs.

There is little agreement on the net effects of AFDC program structure on work behavior and on the number of working poor. Moffitt (1992) has summarized the literature on the effect of welfare support on the labor supply of recipients by stressing the "considerable uncertainty regarding the magnitude of the effects" even after twenty years of research. In general, those who tend to believe that the poor work too little see very large work disincentives within AFDC (and within other income transfer programs.) Those who are less concerned about this problem tend to read the research results as showing relatively small and second-order effects. Thus, there is an ongoing argument about the extent to which changes in work behavior and economic self-sufficiency can be induced by changes in the structure of income transfer programs.

Policies to Increase and/or Supplement Wages

Our discussion of the changing economy emphasized the decline in earnings opportunities among less-skilled workers over the past few years. The primary policy response to this decline has been increased attention to wage supplementation programs. Wage supplements encourage work by increasing the returns to work. Because of this, they avoid the potential work disincentives of income transfer programs that may encourage persons to remain out of the labor market and collect maximum transfer benefits. In order to receive a wage supplement, a person must be working. We discuss two policies aimed at increasing or supplementing wages: the minimum wage and wage supplements available through the tax system.

The minimum wage and work behavior. The minimum wage is not a wage supplement program, but a mandate on employers concerning the wage levels they must pay. While initially only a minority of jobs were covered by minimum wage mandates, currently almost all jobs are subject to minimum wage provisions. The level of the minimum wage is determined by Congress, which has raised it in some years, and let it remain unchanged in others. Figure 5.9 graphs the real value of the minimum wage from 1946 to 1992 in 1992 dollars. At $4.25 per hour in 1992, the minimum wage had a much higher value throughout the 1960s and 1970s. It declined in the 1980s as its constant dollar level was eroded by inflation.

Surprisingly, the minimum wage is less important for the working poor than many might believe. The majority of workers in minimum wage jobs are not poor. In particular, the majority of minimum wage recipients are second and third earners (particularly teens) from middle or upper income families. (Of course, because of low wages, some adolescents may have no choice but to continue to live with their parents.) For instance, Mincy (1990) estimates that only 18 percent of minimum wage earners are in poor families in 1986. Horrigan and Mincy (1993) estimate that if the minimum wage in the 1980s had kept up with inflation, this would have had only a very small effect on the widening wage inequality of that decade. In this sense, the minimum wage is a very inefficient anti-poverty tool. It affects many jobs filled by persons who do not live in poor families.

Yet, while many minimum wage workers are not poor, many of the poor are minimum wage workers. Increases in the minimum wage might be a way to offset some of the wage declines that have occurred. There are reasons to

Figure 5.9

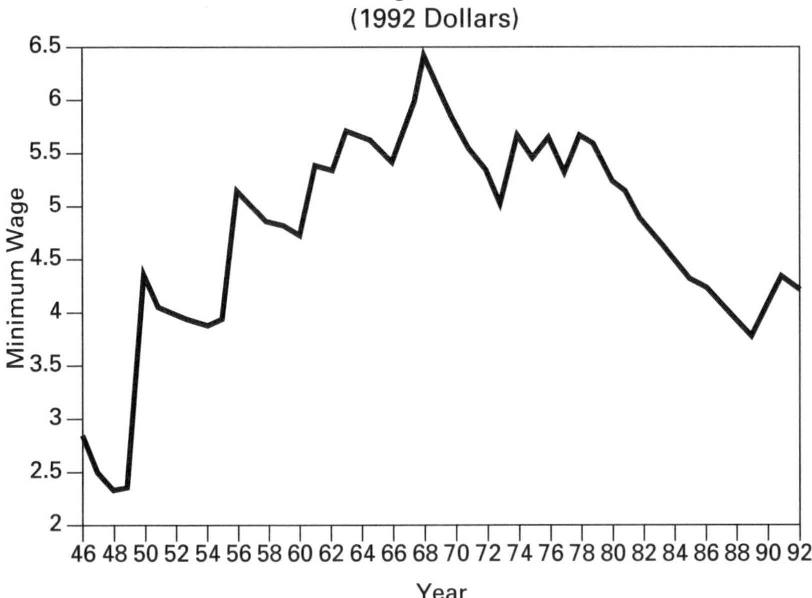

believe that a moderate rise in the minimum wage, say to $5/hour (still well below its highest values in the late 1960s) might help working poor adults. It is also true, however, that if demand for less-skilled work is falling (as indicated by the decline in wages for less-skilled work), mandated increases in wages for less-skilled workers might result in the loss of these jobs. Without addressing some of the underlying skill- and demand-related reasons why wages are so low, merely mandating higher wages may raise unemployment as much as it raises earnings.

A substantial research literature has studied the disemployment effects of higher minimum wages. The increase in 1989 and 1990 appeared to have small disemployment effects.[24]In part, this was surely due to the very low level to which the minimum wage had fallen, so that very few workers were affected by it. But larger increases that begin to affect more and more workers may well have increasing disemployment affects. This suggests that there is a limit to how much increases in the minimum wage can be used to increase work incentives among the poor.

Tax policy to supplement earnings. Tax policies are also integrally related to work behavior. If tax rates rise, workers get to keep less of their income; this

Figure 5.10

Combined Taxes as a Percent of Income at Poverty Level by Size of Family Unit

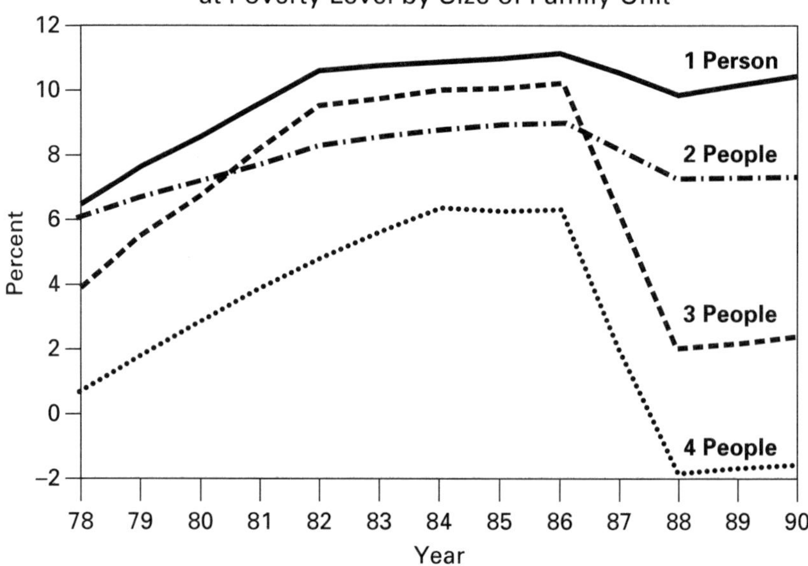

Source: U.S. House of Representatives, 1993, table 9.

should result in an increase in the number of working poor as well as a decline in the incentive for low-income families to work. The 1980s saw major changes in the tax rates facing working low-income adults. Figure 5.10 graphs the tax rates faced by poor families over the 1980s. As the graph shows, tax burdens rose steadily through the early 1980s, and dropped sharply after the tax reforms of 1986.

Underlying these tax changes are three primary components: first, the tax rates and exemption levels embedded in the federal income tax system changed. During many years of high inflation in the 1970s, exemptions levels were not indexed, which meant that tax burdens on poor families increased. These exemption levels were raised in 1986 and are now inflation indexed, which means that few poor families will be subject to federal income taxes. Second, the payroll tax that supports social security has steadily increased. This is currently a flat-rate tax of 7.65 percent on all earnings up to an income level in excess of $50,000. Thus all poor workers pay this tax, and its rate has almost doubled since 1980. So, as federal income tax burdens were falling, the payroll tax burden on poor families was rising.

Third and most importantly, in recent years Congress has greatly expanded the Earned Income Tax Credit (EITC), mentioned above. The EITC supplements earnings for workers in low-income families. It is paid through the federal income tax system, typically as a lump sum refund at the end of the tax year. The exact structure of the EITC is well described elsewhere and will not be repeated here.[25] Essentially, the EITC supplements earnings up to a given point, and then slowly tapers off as earnings go above this level. For instance, in 1980, the EITC provided an additional $.10 per $1 of earnings on the first $5000 of earnings. By 1994, this had increased to a supplement of $.26 per $1 of earnings on the first $7750 of earnings. Over the next few years, the EITC is scheduled to increase even further. The intention is that low-wage workers will receive a supplement large enough to ensure that full-time work, together with the EITC and food stamps, will bring them out of poverty.[26]

Because the recent large expansions in the EITC are just now occurring, and because we lack good data on who uses the EITC and when they receive it, we know little about the effect of the EITC on poor families. On the one hand, a substantial number of eligible families (around 80 percent) seem to be receiving the supplement.[27] This clearly increases their family income and offsets any wage declines they may have experienced. On the other hand, few recipients appear to understand exactly how the EITC operates, thus it is unclear that it provides them with any additional work incentives. One of the strongest arguments for the EITC is that it should promote greater work effort by providing a larger reward for work, but this will only happen if recipients understand the extent to which the EITC increases their earnings.

The EITC is potentially the most important policy change for the working poor of the last decade. It offsets the deterioration in earnings opportunities for less-skilled workers, and produces higher rewards from work. Table 5.8 indicates how the EITC changes the income levels of a selected group of low-income families in 1994. Part I looks at a married couple with two children and one full-time year-round worker, part II looks at a single adult family with two children and a full-time year-round worker, while part III looks at a single adult family with two children and a part-time year-round worker. In column 1 we assume the head works full-time year-round at the minimum wage of $4.25. In column 2 we assume the wage is $6 per hour, and in column 3 it is $10 per hour. In both columns 1 and 2, changes in the federal tax schedule mean that these households owe only payroll taxes, which are more than offset by the EITC, resulting in substantial refunds. The full-time earner at $10 per hour pays taxes in both families, but the EITC reduces the tax burden.

The net effect of the EITC is to move all of these families closer toward or

Table 5.8
Selected Tax Burdens in 1994 by Family Type

	Wage rate of:		
	$4.25	**$6.00**	**$10.00**
Part I. Married couple with two children One earner working 40 hours/week, year-round			
Earnings	8,500	12,000	20,000
– Standard deduction	6,350	6,350	6,350
– Exemptions	9,800	9,800	9,800
= Taxable Income (0 if negative)	0	0	3,850
FICA tax	650	918	1,530
+ Income tax	0	0	578
– EITC	2,528	2,351	937
+ Tax payment (refund)	(1,878)	(1,433)	1,171
After tax income	10,378	13,433	18,829
Percent of poverty line	70.8	91.7	128.5
Part II. Single adult with two children One earner working 40 hours/week, year-round			
Earnings	8,500	12,000	20,000
– Standard deduction	5,650	5,600	5,600
– Exemptions	7,350	7,350	7,350
= Taxable Income (0 if negative)	0	0	7,050
FICA tax	650	918	1,530
+ Income tax	0	0	1,058
– EITC	2,528	2,351	937
+ Tax payment (refund)	(1,878)	(1,433)	1,651
After tax income	10,378	13,433	18,829
Percent of poverty line	89.1	115.4	186.0
Part III. Single adult with two children One earner working 25 hours/week, year-round			
Earnings	8,500	7,500	12,500
– Standard deduction	5,600	5,600	5,600
– Exemptions	7,350	7,350	7,350
= Taxable Income (0 if negative)	0	0	0
FICA tax	406	574	956
+ Income tax	0	0	0
– EITC	1,594	2,251	2,263
+ Tax payment (refund)	(1,188)	(1,677)	1,307
After tax income	6,501	9,177	13,807
Percent of poverty line	55.8	78.8	118.6

Source: Authors' tabulations.

further above the poverty line. In fact, by 1996 when the expansions in the EITC are fully phased in, the single-mother full-time worker in part II will be out of poverty at every wage level, and the married-couple full-time worker will be out of poverty at $6 and $10/hour, and closer to the poverty line at the minimum wage.

As the EITC expands in the years ahead, there are at least two questions of importance about which we know little. First, we need to better understand how recipients view the EITC, and whether it is creating the work incentives that its supporters claim. Second, we need to see how effective this policy will be (particularly with the current expansions) in assuring working-poor adults that their families will be able to escape poverty.

This quick review of a few of the policies that affect the working poor can be summarized in four main points. First, the U.S. has remarkably few programs that directly attempt to increase employment among low-income adults through job placement and training. Recent and upcoming welfare reform efforts have increased these efforts among that population, but this still remains small relative to the total number of poor adults. Second, a vast array of other U.S. programs affect work behavior. The structure and design of most anti-poverty programs embed certain incentives for or against work. For instance, recent changes in AFDC benefits and benefit reduction rates seem to be rather perversely designed to increase work incentives in some ways and decrease them in others.

Third, the most important policy change affecting the working poor in recent years has been the expansion in the EITC. This has essentially reduced the federal taxes paid by low-income families to zero, and raised most families with full-time year-round workers close to the poverty line. If these expansions are successful in making work pay, this could mean that virtually no full-time, year-round workers in moderate-sized families will still be below the poverty line in the U.S.

Fourth, it is worth remembering that efforts to increase work effort are not the same as efforts to reduce the number of working poor. Given the low wages and limited labor market opportunities facing many less-skilled workers, reforms designed primarily to increase work among low-income adults may also increase the number of working poor. Only in combination with wage supplement programs will increases in work effort guarantee a decrease in poverty.

This essay has focused on changes in the working poor and related these to economic, demographic, and policy changes. A substantial number of poor adults work, and almost two-thirds of all poor persons are in family units where someone has worked in the past year. Only a small share of these workers are employed full-time year-round, however. While the actual share of the poor who have some connection with the labor market has increased slightly in recent years, this hides two quite divergent trends: an increase in work among single women who head families, offset by a decline in work among men heading married-couple families.

These trends in work behavior among low-income men and women since 1979 mirror trends in wages. Less-skilled men have experienced substantial real wage declines. Less-skilled women have seen either stagnant wages (for high school drop-outs) or real wage increases (for high school graduates). The economic trends that have led to a widening distribution of wages and declining earning opportunities among less-skilled workers make it harder than in past decades for less-skilled workers to escape poverty through work.

Anti-poverty efforts have long emphasized the importance of work as a route out of poverty. Given this, policies designed to encourage work among low-income families are important. One of the most important policy issues is the level of unemployment in the overall economy, which disproportionately affects less-skilled workers. Employment and earnings opportunities within poor families are significantly harmed by rising unemployment; strategies that focus on employment growth and low unemployment will encourage work and increase earnings among poor families.

Family configuration changes have been relatively unimportant in affecting work behavior since the late 1960s. Most changes in work behavior would have occurred even if family configuration had not changed. Changes in the population share of married-couple and single-headed family units have had only secondary effects on work behavior among the poor. This is reassuring from a policy perspective, since we have fewer policy instruments through which we can effectively influence family configuration and formation.

Anti-poverty efforts by government also influence work behavior. Programs aimed at directly assisting workers to increase their training and work effort are a relatively small part of U.S. anti-poverty efforts, although efforts are being made to expand such programs for welfare recipients. The main effect of anti-poverty programs on work effort are through program structure. All income supplementation programs, such as AFDC, are designed in ways that discourage work. While there is broad agreement that these programs affect work behavior, there is much less agreement on whether these effects have been particularly large.

Direct efforts to supplement and increase wages should also increase work incentives and decrease the number of working poor. Increases in the EITC are increasingly seen as the best policy instrument to supplement earnings, offset declines in real wages, and encourage greater work effort. With the current EITC expansions, full-time year-round workers will find it much easier to escape poverty through work. The long-term effect of this on the number of working poor is still unknown, but the expanded EITC promises to do more to reduce the extent of the working poor than any other intervention currently under discussion.

Finally, we note that our results indicate that it is full-time work that is most effective in reducing the number of working poor. Very few full-time workers are poor; the EITC expansions will only reinforce this. The fact that most of the working poor are not full-time year-round workers, however, suggests that for at least some substantial group of poor adults, full-time work may not be a viable option. Particularly for single parents with younger children, full-time employment and full-time parenting may be especially difficult. For this reason, other non–employment-related anti-poverty strategies, such as increased child support enforcement, will continue to be necessary.

Notes

1. In 1992, 74.2 percent of all poor persons lived in metropolitan areas, and 42.4 percent lived within central city jurisdictions (U.S. Department of Commerce 1993, Table 8.) See Blank (1993, Table 2.7) for trends over time in these numbers.

2. The most thorough recent discussion of the working poor is in Levitan and Shapiro (1987).

3. For instance, see Moscovice, Craig, and Pitt (1987).

4. For instance, see Klein and Rones (1989), Gardner and Herz (1992), or Kasarda (this volume).

5. There are many potential problems involved in the current definition of poverty that will not be discussed in this essay. See Ruggles (1990).

6. Full-time year-round workers are those working at least 35 hours per week and 50 or more weeks per year.

7. These data are described in more detail in Blank and Card (1993).

8. Coleman and Pencavel (1993a).

9. Coleman and Pencavel (1993b). See also Blank (1995) for a summary of work behavior trends by gender and skill level.

10. The evidence summarized in this section is presented in Danziger and Gottschalk (1993), Juhn et al. (1993), Blackburn et al. (1990), and Levy and Murnane (1992).

11. For a more extended discussion of changes in the low-wage labor market, especially for women, see Blank (1995).

12. In addition to the literature cited in note 9, other research that investigates causes includes Katz and Murphy (1992), Bound and Johnson (1992), and Davis and Haltiwanger (1991).

13. The regressions that underlie the results in Table 5.5 are based on the same data used in Blank and Card (1993). In particular, the regressions use 225 year-by-region observations, based on nine U.S. Census regions across fifteen years (1967–1991). The data are tabulated from the March CPS tapes for each year. The bottom quintile of the income distribution is calculated each year, based on family unit income. The dependent variable (defined for each region and year) in Table 5.5 is regressed against the region-specific unemployment rate, as well region and year fixed effects.

14. If the regressions in Table 5.5 are done separately for different family types in the bottom of the income distribution, the results indicate that rises in unemployment significantly reduce work and earnings among all family heads, regardless of age or marital status. Not surprisingly, the effects are largest on those family units who are most involved in the labor market and who lose substantial weeks of work and earnings when they become unemployed.

15. The regressions in Table 5.6 use the same region-by-year data set as in Table 5.5, but are based only on the 1973–1991 period (9 regions by 19 years = 171 observations). Included in each regression are region and year effects, as well as unemployment rates, median log wages, and the standard deviation of log wages within each region and year. Also included are region-specific control variables for the percent of family units in central city and rural areas, for the percent of family units headed by single adults and by blacks, and average education levels. Regressions identical to these for the bottom quintile of the income distribution are reported in Table 7 of Blank and Card (1993), where the sources of these data are described.

16. Column 2 uses the estimated coefficients from the regressions described in the previous note, based on region-by-year data, multiplied by the 1991 value of the independent variables for the entire United States.

17. Between 1979 and 1991, the standard deviation of log wages increased by about 5 percent.

18. U.S. House of Representatives (1993).

19. Bloom et al. (1993). These results are based on earnings and employment comparisons between a group of JTPA participants and a randomized group of "controls," eighteen months after the start of JTPA training.

20. Gueron and Pauly (1991) provide a summary of the results from these programs.

21. Friedlander et al. (1993).

22. For instance, a list of such programs would include unemployment insurance, social security, housing assistance, Supplement Security Income, etc.

23. For a complete summary of the research on work incentive effects on welfare programs, see Moffitt (1992). For a discussion of the recent institutional changes in AFDC and their effects on work incentives see Blank (1994).

24. See Card (1992). Neumark and Wascher (1992) find some disemployment effects, but they are still relatively small.

25. See Hoffman and Seidman (1990). For a discussion of recent expansions and changes in the EITC, see Scholz (1994b).

26. Of course, it is worth noting that for single parents with small children, the cost of child care may still make work—even at incomes slightly above the poverty line—relatively unattractive.

27. Scholz (1994b)

References

Blackburn, McKinley L., David E. Bloom, and Richard B. Freeman. 1990. "The Declining Economic Position of Less-Skilled American Men." In *A Future of Lousy Jobs?* edited by Gary Burtless. Washington, D.C.: Brookings Institution.

Blank, Rebecca M. 1995. "Outlook for the U.S. Labor Market and Prospects for Low-Wage Entry-Level Jobs." In *The Work Alternative: Welfare Reform and the Realities of the Job Market*, edited by Demetra Nightingale and Robert Haveman. Washington, D.C.: Urban Institute Press.

Blank, Rebecca M. 1994. "The Employment Strategy: Public Policies to Increase Work and Earnings." In *Confronting Poverty: Prescriptions for Change*, edited by Sheldon Danziger, Gary Sandefur, and Daniel Weinberg. Boston: Harvard University Press.

Blank, Rebecca M. 1993. "Why Were Poverty Rates So High in the 1980s?" In *Poverty and Prosperity in the USA in the Late Twentieth Century*, edited by Dimitri B. Papadimitriou and Edward N. Wolff. London: Macmillan.

Blank, Rebecca M., and David Card. 1993. "Poverty, Income Distribution, and Growth: Are They Still Connected?" *Brookings Papers on Economic Activity* Number 2.

Bloom, Howard S., Larry L. Orr, George Cave, Stephen H. Bell, and Fred Doolittle. 1993. *The National JTPA Study*. A report to the U.S. Department of Labor. Bethesda, Md.: Abt Associates.

Bound, John, and George Johnson. 1992. "Changes in the Structure of Wages in the 1980s: An Evaluation of Alternative Explanations." *American Economic Review* 82 (no. 3, June): 371–392.

Card, David. 1992. "Using Regional Variation in Wages to Measure the Effects of the Federal Minimum Wage." *Industrial and Labor Relations Review* 46 (no. 1, October): 2237.

Coleman, Mary T., and John Pencavel. 1993a. "Changes in Work Hours of Male Employees, 1940–1987." *Industrial and Labor Relations Review* 46 (no. 2, January): 262–283.

Coleman, Mary T., and John Pencavel. 1993b. "Trends in Market Work Behavior of Women since 1940." *Industrial and Labor Relations Review* 46 (no. 4, July): 653–676.

Danziger, Sheldon, and Peter Gottschalk. 1993. *Uneven Tides: Rising Inequality in America*. New York: Russell Sage Foundation.

Davis, Steve J., and John Haltiwanger. 1991. "Wage Dispersion between and within U.S. Manufacturing Plants: 1963–86." In *Brookings Papers on Economic Activity: Microeconomics*, edited by Martin Neil Baily and Clifford Winston. Washington, D.C.: Brookings Institution.

Friedlander, Daniel, James Riccio, and Stephen Freedman. 1993. *GAIN: Two-Year Impacts in Six Counties*. New York: Manpower Development Research Corporation.

Gardner, Jennifer M., and Diane E. Herz. 1992. "Working and Poor in 1990." *Monthly Labor Review* 115 (no. 12, December): 20–28.

Gueron, Judith M., and Edward Pauly. 1991. *From Welfare to Work*. New York: Russell Sage Foundation.

Hoffman, Saul D., and Laurence S. Seidman. 1990. *The Earned Income Tax Credit*. Kalamazoo, Mich.: W. E. Upjohn Institute.

Horrigan, Michael W., and Ronald B. Mincy. 1993. "The Minimum Wage and Earnings and Income Inequality." In *Uneven Tides: Rising Inequality in America*, edited by Sheldon Danziger and Peter Gottschalk. New York: Russell Sage Foundation.

Juhn, Chinhui. 1992. "Decline of Male Labor Market Participation: The Role of Declining Market Opportunities." *Quarterly Journal of Economics* 107 (no. 1, February): 79–122.

Juhn, Chinhui, Kevin M. Murphy, and Brooks Pierce. 1993. "Wage Inequality and the Rise in Returns to Skill." *Journal of Political Economy* 101 (no. 3, June): 410–442.

Katz, Lawrence F., and Kevin M. Murphy. 1992. "Changes in Relative Wages, 1963–87: Supply and Demand Factors." *Quarterly Journal of Economics* 107 (no. 1, February): 35–78.

Klein, Bruce W., and Philip L. Rones. 1989. "A Profile of the Working Poor." *Monthly Labor Review* 112 (no. 10, October): 3–13.

Levitan, Sar A., and Isaac Shapiro. 1987. *Working But Poor.* Baltimore: Johns Hopkins University Press.

Levy, Frank, and Richard J. Murnane. 1992. "U.S. Earnings Levels and Earnings Inequality: A Review of Recent Trends and Proposed Explanations." *Journal of Economic Literature* 30 (no.3, September): 1333–81.

Mincy, Ronald B. 1990. "Raising the Minimum Wage: Effects on Family Poverty." *Monthly Labor Review* 113 (no. 7, July): 18–25.

Moffitt, Robert. 1992. "Incentive Effects of the U.S. Welfare System: A Review." *Journal of Economic Literature* 30: 1–61.

Moscovice, Ira, William Craig, and Laura Pitt. 1987. "Meeting the Basic Needs of the Working Poor." *Social Service Review* 61 (no. 3, September): 420–431.

Neumark, David, and William Wascher. 1992. "Evidence on Employment Effects of Minimum Wages and Subminimum Wage Provisions from Panel Data on State Minimum Wage Laws." *Industrial and Labor Relations Review* 46 (no. 1, October): 55–61.

Ruggles, Patricia. 1990. *Drawing the Line.* Washington, D.C.: Urban Institute Press.

Scholz, John Karl. 1994a. "The Earned Income Tax Credit: Participation, Compliance, and Antipoverty Effectiveness." *National Tax Journal* 47 (no. 1, March): 59–81.

Scholz, John Karl. 1994b. "Tax Policy and the Working Poor: The Earned Income Tax Credit." *Focus.* Madison, Wisc.: Institute for Research on Poverty. Winter.

U.S. Department of Commerce, Bureau of the Census. 1993. *Poverty in the United States: 1992.* Current Population Reports, Series P60–185. Washington, D.C.: U.S. Government Printing Office, September.

U.S. House of Representatives, Committee on Ways and Means. 1993. *1993 Green Book.* Washington, D.C.: Government Printing Office, July 7.

6

Out-of-School Time: Risk and Opportunity

SANDRA L. HOFFERTH

"Out-of-school hours constitute the single biggest block of time in the life of a young adolescent" (Task Force on Youth Development and Community Programs 1992). About 40 percent of the waking hours of school-age children ages 9–14 are not committed to any particular activity and much of this time is spent alone or with peers. This time presents both a risk and an opportunity for school-aged children and the preschoolers they sometimes care for. It presents a risk in that, not productively used, out-of-school time can lead to undesirable behavior; an opportunity in that it presents the potential for positive involvement. Whether or not youths use out-of-school time to get into trouble or to get involved in productive activities depends greatly on the income level of the family and on the characteristics of the community in which they reside.

The large amount of time children and young adolescents spend alone or with peers is partially a function of two factors: increased female labor force participation and the increased proportion of children being raised in single-parent families due to divorce or out-of-wedlock childbearing. Between 1970 and 1990, the proportion of married mothers of school-age children in the labor force rose from 49 to 74 percent (U.S. Bureau of the Census 1994). At the same time, the proportion of families headed by a female doubled from 10 to 20 percent. While the large increases have been primarily among married mothers, the proportion of unmarried mothers in the work force is expected to continue to increase with welfare reform efforts. The goal of welfare reform is to "end welfare as we know it." This means moving nonemployed mothers into meaningful jobs leading to self-sufficiency.

In doing this, however, more thought needs to be given to where these families are headed and how to get them there. Many families will remain poor because the entry-level jobs for which they qualify do not pay well. It may take years to improve their incomes to the point where they will truly become self-sufficient. Thus, families will need more, not fewer, services. If services are not expanded, children may be left in inadequate care or to care for themselves and mothers may wind up back on welfare.

Of the services that such families will need, child care is critical. Children need care and supervision when they are not in school and their parents are not available. Considerable research has focused on the child-care needs of preschool-age children; less attention has focused on school-age children. While the need for child-care arrangements declines as children age and parents monitor them less closely, this does not mean that families need fewer services. The needs of school-age children for supervision in spending their free time productively are only recently beginning to be acknowledged (Task Force on Youth Development and Community Programs 1992). This is especially important for poor children in communities where opportunities for involvement in risky activities may exceed those for involvement in positive, skill-producing activities.

If efforts to maintain parental self-sufficiency are to succeed, the needs of children above the poverty line should be viewed as equally important as the needs of those below the line. This essay examines the need for and use of services and programs for school-age children by working-poor and working-class families compared with middle-income families. It then examines the constraints working-poor and working-class households face pertaining to availability/access to services, the cost of services, and the quality of services. It concludes by outlining policy options that would improve the ability of poor and working-class families to work and would, at the same time, promote the health and development of children.

The Need for Supervision of School-Age Children during Nonschool Hours

Below I discuss estimates of the numbers of school-age children in self-care before and after school, the consequences of lack of adequate supervision, and the history of U.S. investment in child care for school-age children. Following this section I describe the data sets used for this essay.

Number in Self-Care

Why is the supervision of school-age children important? In 1990 there were an estimated 29 million school-age children between the ages of 5 and 12. Estimates of the number of children caring for themselves have ranged from a high of 15 million (as measured by Zigler and Long 1983) to a low of 1.8 million (as measured by the Census Bureau in 1984 [U.S. Bureau of the Census 1987]). The latter implies a self-care rate of about 6 percent while the former implies that half of all school-age children had no adult supervision for at least part of the day. Part of the explanation for differences in rates of self-care are due to the way the estimates are calculated. The low estimates have been based on questions asked directly of parents about unsupervised time that occurs on a regularly scheduled basis each week. These estimates are likely to underestimate the number of children caring for themselves if parents view self-care as socially undesirable and therefore underreport its occurrence. This view is supported by the results of two statewide surveys which found that about one-quarter of school-age children (but nowhere near one-half) regularly cared for themselves when parents were employed (Kuchak 1983).

The high estimates, in contrast, are not generally based upon questions asked of mothers, but upon the proportion of mothers working full-time whose children are not reported to be enrolled in child care. It is assumed that such mothers need child care after school. However, these high estimates do not take into account the fact that, in a two-parent dual-earner family, parents may arrange their schedules so that one parent can care for the children before or after school while the other parent works (or studies). Finally, these high estimates include all self-care, whether on an occasional or a regular basis. Since many children occasionally care for themselves, even if this is not regularly scheduled, such estimates will substantially exceed those which only include regularly arranged self-care.

Although it is often assumed that the number of children in self-care, popularly called latch-key children, has been increasing as the number of mothers working outside the home has grown, little empirical evidence has been available to examine changes in self-care over time. Recent national estimates of the proportion of school-age children *regularly* caring for themselves before or after school yield a national estimate of 3.4 million children or 12 percent (Hofferth et al. 1991). This is almost double the 1984 national estimate of 1.8 million (U.S. Bureau of the Census 1987). Although these 1990 estimates are also subject to underreporting, they seem plausible because they are derived from a survey entirely about child care rather than from a short set of questions added to a larger unrelated survey as was done in 1984. Whether the difference between the two estimates represents a real change or simply differences in the ways the questions were asked cannot be determined.

Consequences of Lack of Supervision

What are the consequences of the lack of supervision and the lack of opportunity to participate in after-school programs and activities? A number of studies have examined the consequences for children of caring for themselves.

Early research examining the effects of self-care on children found high levels of fear among latch-key children compared to adult-supervised children (Long and Long 1982). However, recent research suggests a more complex story. The more recent studies have found no difference between self-care and adult-supervised children on measures such as independence, self-esteem, locus of control, social adjustment, and interpersonal relationship (Rodman, Pratto and Nelson 1985; Vandell and Corasaniti 1988; Posner and Vandell 1994). Steinberg (1986) found that self-care is not an all-or-nothing concept. The degree of supervision varies even when the parent is not physically present. In some cases children were supervised via telephone and were expected to check in with parents or neighbors upon their return home. Other children went to friends' homes or to shopping malls. Steinberg concluded that the less the adult supervision, the more susceptible were children to peer pressure to engage in anti-social behavior. Posner and Vandell found, however, that there were only small differences in the actual amount of adult supervision between self-care and informal adult care.

Only a few research studies have examined the effects of participation in organized after-school programs. One of these studies found participants in an after-school program for kindergarten students to have more advanced social skills than children not enrolled in the program (Howes, Olenick, and Der-Kiureghian 1987). Another study found after-school program participants to have more advanced math and reading skills (Mayesky 1979). An early study of middle-income children found that those who went to a for-profit day care center after school had lower academic achievement and social adjustment than either mother-care or self-care children. In contrast, a study of four different types of after-school care for low-income children found that children in a formal after-school program spent more time in academic activities and enrichment lessons and less time watching television and playing outdoors unsupervised (Posner and Vandell 1994). Children in formal after-school programs also spent more time engaging in activities with peers and adults and less time with siblings than did other children. In brief, those studies that control for maternal education, race, and family income find that the time spent in after-school programs was correlated with better academic achievement and social adjustment. Although the lack of opportunities to participate in enrichment activities may exact a price later on, the long-term effects are unknown (Seligson and Fink 1989). Little research has focused on the effects of participation in other types of after-school activities, such as sports and lessons, on the development of young children.

Finally, the consequences may very likely depend on the characteristics of the children in self-care:

> Although researchers have addressed the consequences of self-care for the children involved, they have not focused as much on choice of self-care, perhaps because it has not been seen as a choice, or because the number of cases is small. However, the consequences may very well depend as much on the children as on the arrangement. If children care for themselves because their parents are poor and unable to find or afford adequate care, the consequences are likely to be severe. If, in contrast, middle class parents choose this option for more mature responsible children, then the consequences may be slight or nonexistent. So it is important to identify the parental and child characteristics associated with use of self-care. (Cain and Hofferth 1989)

History of Investments in School-Age Child Care

In recent years, we have heard increasingly lively debate over the part that schools should play in the lives of children beyond the formal school day, and policymakers have increased the incentives for schools to provide before- and after-school programs for children (Kagan and Zigler 1987). How recent is this concern and what is the level of investment in child care for school-age children in 1994? In order to obtain a better picture of present policy, a review of previous policies is helpful.

In farming societies children learned from their parents, relatives, and neighbors by working beside them in the day-to-day activities of planting, harvesting, and food preparation. Opportunities for formal learning were limited. The movement off the farm occurred at about the same time that schooling became increasingly located outside the home (Hernandez 1993). According to one report, the average proportion of days in the year during which children ages 5 to 17 attended school nearly quadrupled between 1870 and 1988, from about 12 to 43 percent (Hernandez 1993). Most of the increase occurred between 1870 and 1930, when compulsory school laws for children ages 6 to 14 were instituted (Seligson et al. 1983).

As the amount of time needed to care for school-age children declined, the education and potential wages of mothers rose, and with declining marriage stability, mothers entered the work force in large numbers. In 1950, one-quarter of all married mothers of school-age children were in the labor force, while three-quarters were at home (U.S. Bureau of the Census 1994). By 1990 this ratio was reversed: three-quarters of married mothers with school-age children were in the work force and only one-quarter of mothers with school-age children remained at home full-time.

School-age child care first became a national issue during World War II when many mothers went to work. Under the Lanham Act of 1940, the federal government greatly expanded support for child care. At the height of the war effort, approximately 3,000 extended school programs served over 100,000 children (Seligson et al. 1983). A 1941 amendment to the Lanham Act authorized the provision of community facilities for extended care programs (Ribar 1991). Many of the facilities for school-age children were under the auspices of the Department of Education and were located in school buildings (Seligson et al. 1983).

After World War II, employment ended for many young women. This also spelled the end of most child-care centers (Cahan 1989). Only the California and New York school systems retained school-age child-care programs (Seligson et al. 1983). It was not until 1978, when the Elementary and Secondary Education Act was amended, that public schools were officially permitted to house community activities.

In the 1970s there was considerable argument about whether schools were or were not the logical agency to operate services for school-age children. In 1972, an Interagency School-Age Day Care Task Force—consisting of staff from the Department of Health, Education, and Welfare and the Department of Labor—recommended supporting school-age programs in centers, family day care homes, and schools through agency-school collaborations, but it stopped short of supporting school-run programs (Seligson et al. 1983). Albert Shanker, president of the American Federation of Teachers, was in favor of school-provided services. Fearing that the support of teacher unions for school-provided services was centered more on the needs of teachers than the needs of children, child-care advocates were generally opposed to programs operated by the schools (Seligson et al. 1983). Given recent changes in the child population, and the difficulties schools currently face in meeting their educational mandate, advocates today are even more skeptical of the ability of schools to take on yet another obligation (Kagan and Zigler, 1987). However, the need for school-age care continues to increase. Because of the pressing need to care for these school-aged children, other child advocates have begun to shift their position. A number of these experts now agree that schools are certainly the appropriate location for child-care services, whether the services are operated by the schools or by private agencies (see, for example, the Child Care Action Campaign 1993).

During the late 1970s operating funding was provided through Title XX and, after 1980, through Social Services Block Grants. Although funds for services were generally cut and/or consolidated in the early 1980s, new funds for school-age children were authorized through the Dependent Care Block Grant of 1984. Annual expenditures as high as $20 million were authorized, though appropriations have not exceeded $13 million per year since 1989 (Hofferth 1993). These authorizations supported program start-up and expansion, but did not support ongoing activities. Sixty percent of these funds were for school-age child care and 40 percent were for resource and referral services for children, the elderly, and the disabled. In 1990, the total amount of funding available for child care amounted to about $6.3 billion annually. While school-age care could be subsidized under all programs, only one small program—the Dependent Care Block Grant—was specifically targeted at school-age children.

The Child Care and Development Block Grant was established in 1990. Three-quarters of these funds were authorized to subsidize child care for eligible children under age 13. The remaining one-quarter of the funds were to be used for quality improvements, start up or expansion of preschool and school-age child-care programs, and some service provision. More than $900 million was spent in FY94 and spending is projected to be $1.1 billion in FY95. Of this, about $180 million is specifically targeted toward school-age children (and other activities). Thus the amount of funding for school-age children has increased from about $13 million annually to about $193 million at the federal level. Meanwhile the total federal budget for child care and early education in 1994 has increased to almost $12 billion dollars (Hofferth, 1993).[1]

Welfare reform has also increased the funding of programs for low-income households, including those with school-age children. As part of the Family Support Act of 1988, a one-year transition period was instituted which allowed mothers to retain their Medicaid coverage and to continue to receive subsidized child care on a sliding fee scale basis. Called "Transition Child Care," this program was funded at about $545 million in FY94 (Hofferth, 1993). In 1990, an additional program of child-care assistance was authorized to provide child-care assistance for low-income, non-AFDC (Aid to Families with Dependent Children) families that need child care in order to work and who would otherwise be at risk of becoming dependent upon AFDC. This program has been funded at about $300 million annually (Hofferth, 1993).

Finally, numerous states have established their own grant programs (Seppanen et al. 1993). In 1991, for example, "the Indiana legislature mandated that all public school corporations provide after-school programs for school-age children by the 1992–93 academic year" (Seppanen et al. 1993, A–48). In addition to the federal funding sources mentioned above, the State of Indiana has made available close to one million dollars for start-up costs for after-school programs. In order to underwrite the costs of the program, since 1985, a percentage of revenues from cigarette sales has been targeted for school-age child care. Community groups such as the YMCA/YWCA and other private nonprofit agencies have been instrumental in developing new school-based programs.

Data

The availability of new data from surveys of parents and providers in the same community makes it possible to explore some of these issues in an integrated manner. The remainder of this essay relies on two unique data sets: the National Child Care Survey 1990 (Hofferth et al. 1991) and the 1991 National Study of Before- and After-School Programs (Seppanen et al. 1993). Both urban and rural families are included in these data sets. While differences between urban and rural residents may be of interest to the reader, once controls for family structure, family income, and area cost-of-living were included, urban-rural differences never reached significance. Consequently the essay uses results for both urban and rural residents.

The National Child Care Survey 1990

The National Child Care Survey (NCCS) 1990 was a nationally representative survey of families with children under age 13—some 27 million families with 47.7 million children—fielded from November 1989 through May 1990. Through random digit dial techniques and computer-assisted telephone interviewing methods, approximately 4,400 households in 144 counties representative of the United States were interviewed by phone (Hofferth et al. 1991). The overall response rate to the survey was 57 percent. A variety of data quality checks indicate close agreement between the results of this survey and other national surveys conducted in person and by phone with respect to child-care arrangements (Hofferth et al. 1991). The objectives of the NCCS were to obtain a comprehensive picture of how families care for their children and to examine how families make their child-care choices. The unique aspects of the study are the data on the employment patterns of the mothers (and husbands, if present) and child-care arrangements for as many as five of the family's children during the previous week.

Definition of Working Poor. Since decisions about the care of children are family decisions, the total income of the family was used to define poverty, and the employment of both parents were taken into account to define "working." Because child-care arrangements were identified at the time of the survey, the employment of family members during the survey week was used to define the employment status of the family.[2] A working-poor family is one whose total household income was below the poverty line and whose head, spouse, or both worked for pay during the survey week. Few of these families have older children who are also participating in the work force.

Definition of Poverty. The official poverty index was originally established in 1964. This index was based on the cost to a family (of different sizes) of a minimally adequate diet. It was assumed that food represented about one third of all family expenditures; therefore, by multiplying food expenditures by three, minimal living costs were estimated (U.S. Bureau of the Census 1994). The estimate is adjusted each year for inflation. Given this index, in 1989 the poverty threshold was $10,000 for a family of three and about $12,500 for a family of four. A family of seven with an income of $19,000 per year would be considered poor. In 1989, 15 percent of American families with children were poor. Since poor families tend to have more children, a larger proportion (about 20 percent) of children under age 18 were poor.

Adequacy of Definition. There is much debate over the adequacy of the official definition of poverty. Some argue that the definition is too narrow because income does not include the value of in-kind transfers through means-tested programs (medical care, housing, food stamps) in the estimate of family income. Such transfers, if counted, would reduce the proportion of individuals in families with related children considered poor by the traditional definition by 14 percent (Committee on Ways and Means 1991). Others argue that the definition of poverty is outdated because it has not kept up with changing standards of living (Ruggles 1990). Updating the definition would double the proportion of the population living in poverty to about one out of four and would raise the estimates of child poverty from 20 to 30 percent.

Because there is considerable ambiguity about the definition of poverty, I have included a second group in this analysis: those whose family incomes lie between the poverty line and $25,000—which is about 75 percent of the median family income in 1989 of $32,000. Most of these families would be eligi-

Figure 6.1

Percentage of Families with Youngest Child Age 5–12 in Six Subgroups

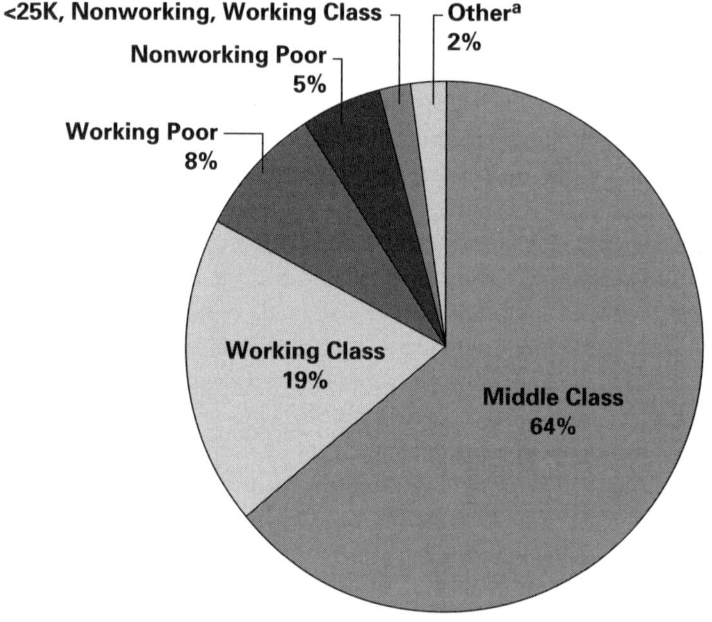

Source: Original tabulations from the National Child Care Survey 1990
[a]"Other" refers to families with children who are living with relatives, not parents.

ble for assistance if the new Child and Dependent Care Block Grant were completely funded.[3]

Finally, because of the large differences in employment status among poor, working-class, and middle-income groups, I divided the study population into six groups, as shown in Figure 6.1: *nonworking poor*, household income below the poverty line, no employed member; *working poor*, household income below the poverty line but at least one employed member; *working class*, household income above the poverty line but under $25,000, at least one employed member; *nonworking working class*, household income above the poverty line but under $25,000, no employed member; *middle-class* families, households with incomes of $25,000 or more; and a small "*other*" category which consists of children and nonparental relatives. In this essay we focus only on working-poor, working-class, and middle-class families.[4] The "working poor" comprise 8 percent of families with children ages 5 to 12; the "working class" constitute almost 20 percent of all families with a school-age child; and the "middle class" constitute 64 percent of families with a youngest child of school age in the 1990 study group (Figure 6.1).

The National Study of Before- and After-School Programs

In 1991, the National Study of Before- and After-School Programs interviewed a sample of 1300 before- and after-school programs selected in the same 144 counties in which the National Child Care Survey 1990 was conducted (Seppanen et al. 1993). The sample includes formal public school–based programs and other formal before- and after-school programs such as licensed center-based programs, public school–based programs, church-operated programs, programs operated by private schools, and programs operated by youth organizations. The universe includes formal institutional programs that provide before- and/or after-school care for children ages 5–13 for at least two hours per day four days a week. Individually arranged activities such as music lessons or scouts are excluded. In addition, home-based family day care was excluded from the sample. The purpose of the study was to obtain information about the number and capacity of existing school-age care programs, the organizational characteristics of providers, the nature of programs, and features that characterize programs serving children from low-income families such as higher- vs. lower-quality programs.

Parents' Use of Before- and After-School Services and Programs

Table 6.1 shows the distribution of children ages 5 to 12 by their primary child-care arrangement, that is, the regularly scheduled arrangement used for most nonschool hours. Center-based programs are nonresidential settings where children are cared for in a group for all or part of the day (Willer et al. 1991). Care by a relative includes care by related persons other than the parents, such as siblings, aunts, and grandparents. Children may be cared for in their own home or that of the relative. In-home care is care by a sitter in the child's home. Family day care is care provided for a small group of children in the home of the provider. Lessons include educational, sport, and other activities that occur on a regularly scheduled basis.

Consistent with findings for preschool children (Hofferth et al. 1991), we see that, compared to children of middle-class families, children from working-poor families are less likely to be enrolled in a center-based program and are more likely to be in the care of a relative. Children from working-class families fall in between. They are more likely than middle-class families to be in

Table 6.1

Percentage Distribution of School-Age Children in Primary Child-Care Arrangement, by Age and Income Group

	Parent	Center	Relatives	In-house	Family Day Care	Self Care	Lessons	Other	Total	N
All Children 5–12										
Working Poor	50	3	24	5	3	3	10	2	100	318
Working Class	43	8	19	2	8	3	15	2	100	743
Middle Class	43	10	11	3	4	2	26	1	100	3,053
Total	44	8	14	3	4	2	21	3	100	4,463
Children 5–7										
Working Poor	54	5	26	5	5	0	5	0	100	123
Working Class	42	16	17	3	12	0	9	1	100	299
Middle Class	46	16	11	4	5	0	17	1	100	1,231
Total	46	14	14	4	6	0	14	2	100	1,816
Children 8–10										
Working Poor	47	3	27	4	2	5	10	2	100	124
Working Class	45	5	19	2	7	2	17	3	100	300
Middle Class	43	7	11	3	5	2	30	1	100	1,177
Total	44	6	15	3	5	2	24	3	100	1,728
Children 11–12										
Working Poor	46	0	17	5	3	3	19	7	100	71
Working Class	43	1	20	2	2	10	23	0	100	144
Middle Class	37	3	13	2	2	7	35	2	100	645
Total	39	3	14	2	2	7	31	3	100	919

Source: National Child-Care Survey,1990

Figure 6.2

Proportion of Youngest School-Age Children in Any Self-Care

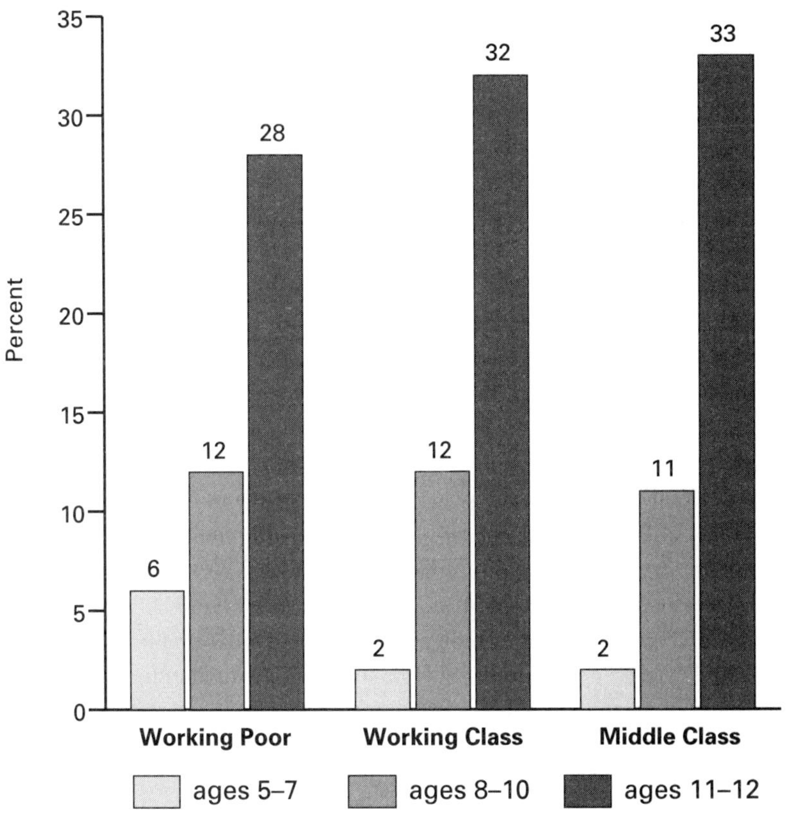

Source: Original tabulations from the National Child Care Survey 1990.

relative care, and more likely than either middle-class or poor families to be in family day care. The use of centers by working-class families is similar to that of middle-class families. There is little use of self-care as a primary arrangement until the child becomes age 11. Working-poor parents are least likely to use self-care as the primary arrangement for their school-age children. Finally, the use of lessons is higher for the middle-class than for other groups. As children age, the use of center-based programs declines while the use of lessons and other activities rises.

Figure 6.2 shows the proportion of children, by age and family income group, who care for themselves in part, not necessarily as the primary care arrangement. By comparing Table 6.1 and Figure 6.2, we see that the proportion of children in some self-care arrangement is considerably higher than it is for those in self-care as the primary arrangement. For example, in Table 6.1 we see that 3 percent of working-poor children ages 11–12 use self-care as the primary arrangement, while in Figure 6.2 we see that 28 percent of working-poor children ages 11–12 use some self-care. This pattern holds true for children of all ages and all income groups.

Figure 6.2 shows differences by income and age. Age differences in self-care are highly significant, with more older than younger children caring for themselves. Income differences are not significant. Neither differences by age nor income are statistically significant for sibling care (not shown). Thus, working-poor families are not significantly more likely to leave their children either in self-care or in sibling care when these children are not in school and their parents are not home to care for them.

In contrast, there are major differences among income groups in the enrollment of children in activities such as lessons, sports, and other activities that supplement their schooling. Figure 6.3 reveals substantial differences by income group in the enrollment of school-age children in extracurricular activities. The difference between the enrollment of children ages 5–7 in working-poor and working-class families is not statistically significant; however, all other differences are statistically significant. Thus enrollment in enrichment activities rises, as expected, with income. It is interesting that the enrollments of working-class and middle-class children in these activities increase with age, while there is only a very small enrollment increase with age among working-poor children. This also illustrates the importance of family income in providing important enrichment opportunities to children.

The difference in the use of programs that enable children to further develop their skills and to be exposed to a variety of other opportunities is important. Are these differences due to differences in preferences or to differences in constraints? Below we examine the constraints to the use of before- and after-school programs.

How Family Structure and Employment Affect the Need for After-School Supervision

How many children need care and supervision is an important question that is not simple to answer. Need is not necessarily synonymous with maternal employment. Some dual-earner couples are able to adjust their schedules so that one partner can stay home while the other works. Of course, single parents do not have this option. Thus, the number of parents and number of

Figure 6.3

Proportion of Youngest School-Age Children in Lessons, Sports, and Similar Activities

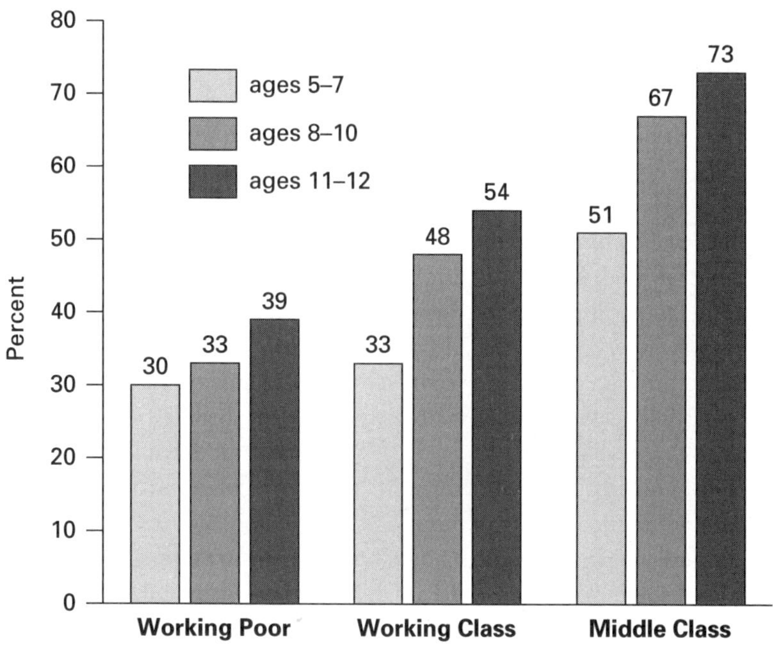

Source: Original tabulations from the National Child Care Survey 1990.

earners within a household and the nature of their work schedules are important factors affecting whether or not children need supervision before and after school.

Families with two earners are at an advantage. One of the ways families have managed to improve their standard of living even as the wages of males have stagnated is by increasing the number of family earners (Levy and Michel 1991). Consequently, we see in Figure 6.4 that almost two out of three middle-class families have two earners, compared with fewer than one out of four working-poor families and three out of ten working-class families.

The major reason working-poor families have one earner is that they are less likely to have two parents. Forty-nine percent of working-poor families and 55 percent of working-class families are two-parent families, compared with 90 percent of middle-class families (Figure 6.4). Even among families

Figure 6.4

Percentage of Families with Youngest Child Age 5–12 by Family Structure, Number of Earners, and Income Group

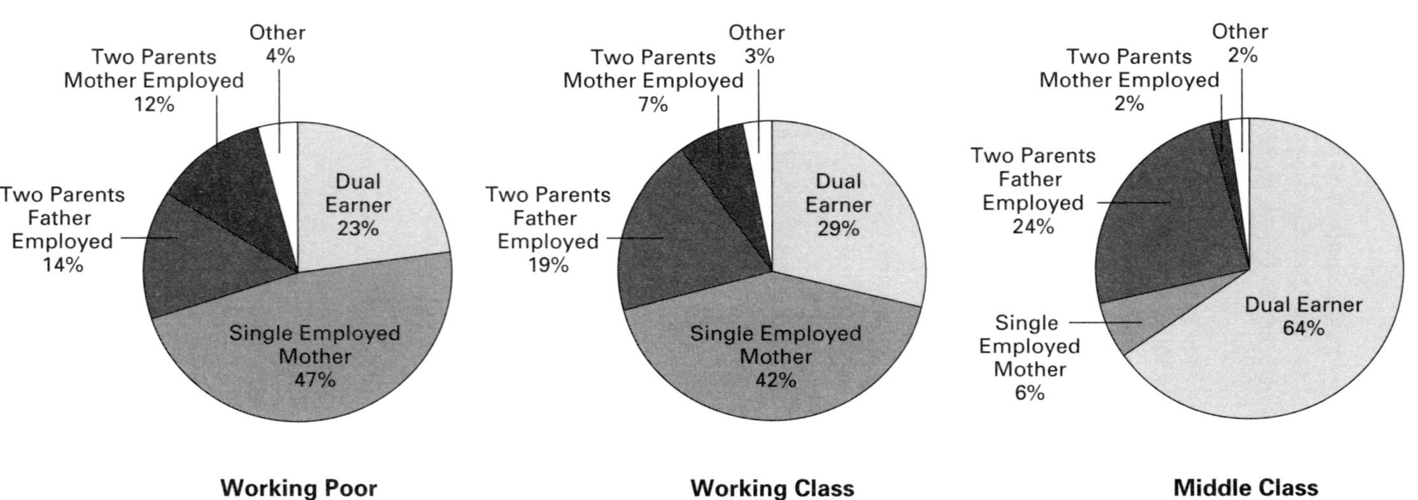

Source: Original tabulations from the National Child Care Survey 1990.

with two parents, however, working-poor and working-class families are less likely (about 50 percent) than middle-class families (71 percent) to have two earners (not shown). This may be due to different lifestyle choices or to factors limiting the father's ability to work.

Constraints on Families' Use of Programs

Based on the types of arrangements parents use, we might speculate that low-income parents are more likely to have access to relatives than high-income families, but equal access to centers. The National Child Care Survey probed this issue. It asked parents who were not using a given type of arrangement whether it was available to them and, if so, how far away it was located. Parents were least likely to report that a relative was available and most likely to report that a center was available. There were no significant income differences in the availability of relatives, in-home, and family day care (not shown).[5] However, there were substantial differences in perception of the availability of center care, with low-income families much less likely to report it available (49 percent) than high-income families (70 percent). Thus, except for center-based care, perceived differences in availability cannot explain differences in usage. However, perceptions of availability may depend not just upon physical closeness but on availability of slots, convenience, cost, and quality of programs.

Availability and Access to Programs

Although programs are located nearby, they may not meet parental needs in other ways: they may have no spaces open, they may provide care only for young children, and their schedules may not fit those of parents.

Spaces Available. Overall, there appear to be spaces in before- and after-school programs. In 1991, 41 percent of licensed spaces were available and unfilled (Figure 6.5). One-third of before- and after-school programs had vacancy rates of 25 percent or less but 25 percent have vacancy rates of 75 percent of capacity (not shown). These rates suggest that programs are under-enrolled in many areas. Whether programs actually want and are able to take children up to their licensed capacity is unclear.

Ages of Children Accepted by Programs. The older the child, the fewer the number of programs and slots available. Enrollment in before- and after-school programs peaks at kindergarten, dropping by grade, with only 18 percent of all children in after-school programs enrolled in fourth grade or higher (not shown). Program availability declines as well. While 90 percent serve first graders, 53 percent of programs serve fourth graders (Figure 6.5),

Figure 6.5

Percentage of Programs

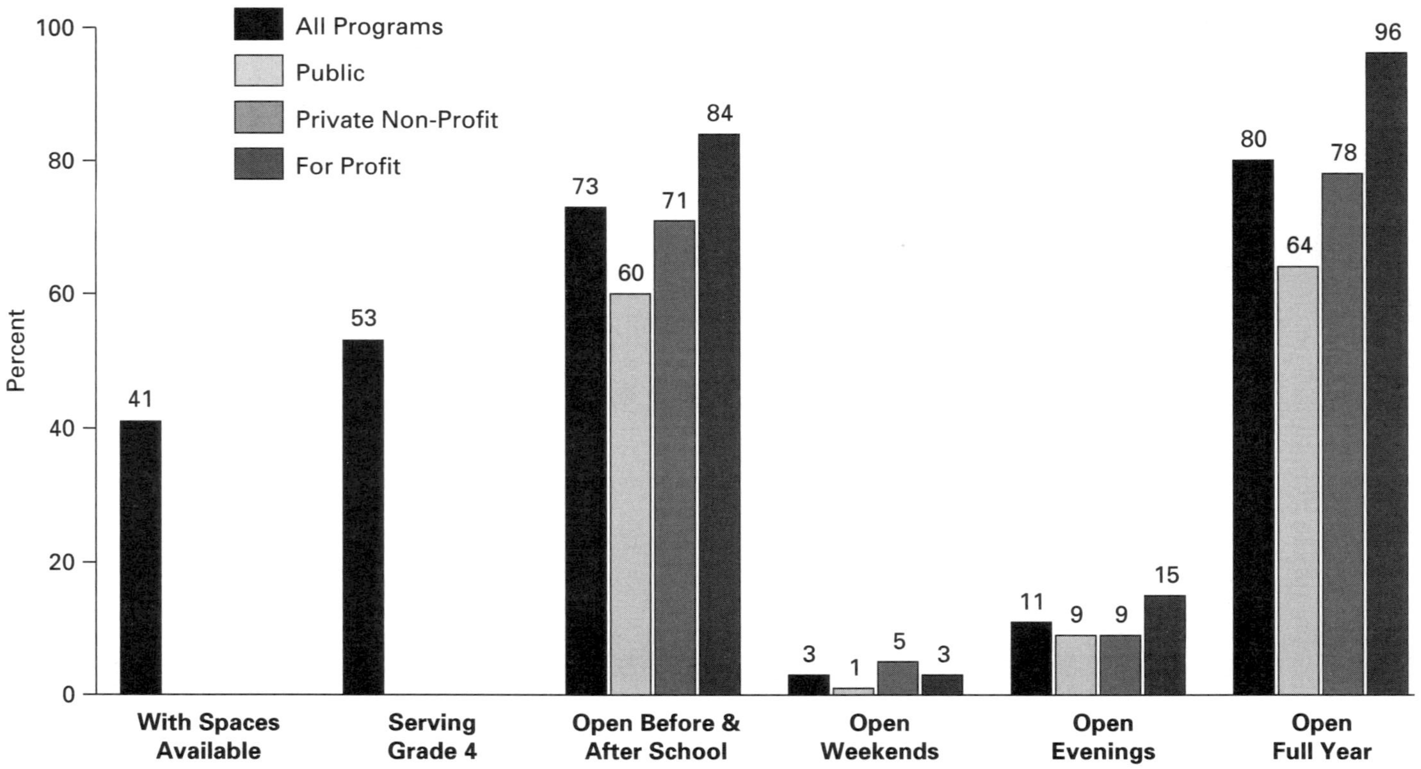

Source: Seppanen et al., 1993.

39 percent serve fifth graders, and only 27 percent serve children in sixth grade and higher. This is consistent with evidence from parents that children begin caring for themselves about ages 8 to 10, in the third to fifth grades. It also suggests that lack of appropriate and available care might be a barrier to the use of before- and after-school care for older children.

Sponsorship of Programs (not shown). The sponsorship may affect the characteristics of programs. In 1991, 66 percent of school-age programs were run by not-for-profit organizations such as public schools (18 percent); private schools (10 percent); state, county, and local governments (5 percent); church groups (6 percent); private organizations (19 percent); private youth groups (7 percent); and other organizations (1 percent). Thirty-four percent were run by for-profit organizations such as private schools (3 percent), private corporations (29 percent), and similar organizations (2 percent).

Parent Work Schedules and Program Hours. An important consideration is whether programs meet parental needs for care. Are parents working full-time or part-time? Do they work full-year or part-year? Do they work weekends and evenings or daytime only? Slots may be available but not convenient for parents.

Of those mothers employed at the time of the 1990 NCCS survey, only 45 percent of those in working-poor families worked full-time, compared with three-quarters of mothers in other families (Table 6.2). Differences among fathers' employment were small. Fathers in poor families were less likely than other fathers to be working full-time (84 percent versus 96 percent).

The majority of programs operate either after school only or before and after school. Seventy-three percent of all programs are open both before and after school (Figure 6.5). Twenty-six percent are open only after school and only about one percent of the programs are open only before school (not shown). A higher proportion of for-profit (84 percent) than nonprofit (71 percent) or public (60 percent) programs are open both before and after school (Figure 6.5). Ninety-nine percent of all programs are open five days a week (not shown).

As illustrated in Table 6.2, only 18 percent of working-poor mothers who worked at all during the previous year were employed full-time, full-year, compared with 42 percent of mothers in families with higher incomes. Fifty-six percent of working-poor fathers who worked in the last year worked full-time, full-year, compared with 71 percent of working-class fathers and 81 percent of middle-class fathers. As seen in Figure 6.5, while 80 percent of all programs operated the full-year (summer and on school holidays and vaca-

Table 6.2

Work Schedule, Occupation, and Wages of Employed Parents with Children under 13 years of Age (in percentage)

	Working Poor		Working Class		Middle Class		Total	
	Mothers	**Fathers**	**Mothers**	**Fathers**	**Mothers**	**Fathers**	**Mothers**	**Fathers**
Work full-time	45	84	76	96	71	97	70	96
Work full-time, full-year	18	56	42	71	42	81	39	78
Work weekends	33	29	27	28	16	23	20	24
Work nights	8	15	10	9	8	9	9	9
Employed in service work	39	8	27	9	13	5	18	6
Employed as operators/laborers	14	27	12	26	5	13	7	16
Employed in professional occupations	9	9	10	10	32	27	25	23
Earns <$5 per hour	62	64	48	27	17	3	29	10

Source: Original tabulations from the National Child Care Survey 1990.

tions), for-profits were the most likely to be open these times (96 percent), while public programs were least likely to be open (64 percent).

Even if programs operate all year, they may still not fit the work schedule of parents. One-third of working-poor and more than one-quarter of working-class mothers worked weekends, along with more than one-quarter of working-poor and working-class fathers (Table 6.2). These parents do not have access to most centers and family day care homes. In terms of working evenings, differences among mothers in different income groups were small (a range of 8 to 9 percent). Working-poor fathers were most likely to work at night (15 percent), compared with other fathers (9 percent). Although the proportion of parents who work nights is relatively small, those who do so are unlikely to be able to use center-based care. Even centers that operate full-day have limited hours. In particular, few are open after 6 PM (11 percent), and almost none (3 percent) are open on weekends. For evening and weekend hours there is little variation across program sponsor.

The Issue of Cost

Besides whether a program is located nearby and the convenience or inconvenience of the schedule, the income of parents and the cost of care constrain parents' child-care choices.

Ability to Pay for Care

The types of occupations in which parents work will affect their wages and schedules. Table 6.2 indicates that about 40 percent of working-poor and 27 percent of working-class mothers are employed in service occupations, compared with only 13 percent of middle-class mothers. Few working-poor (9 percent) and working-class (10 percent) mothers are in professional occupations. Working-poor and working-class fathers are more likely to be employed as operators or laborers than middle-class fathers and are less likely to be employed in managerial, professional, technical, sales, or administrative positions.

Many of the jobs going to working-poor and working-class parents pay poorly. For example, 62 percent of all employed mothers in working-poor families earned less than $5 per hour at their main job in 1989, compared with 48 percent of mothers in working-class families and 17 percent of mothers in middle-income families (Table 6.2). Sixty-four percent of working-poor fathers earned under $5 per hour at their main job in 1989, compared to 27 per-

Table 6.3
Who Paid and Who Received Financial Assistance in Paying for Any Type of Before- or After-School Care or Lessons for School-Aged Children, 1990 (percentage)

Percentage	Working Poor	Working Class	Middle Class
Using care who paid for it	63	63	57
Who received direct assistance in paying for it	9	8	2
Using center-based care who received direct assistance in paying for it	51	11	4
Who claimed the Child and Dependent Care Tax Credit in 1990	16	38	32

Source: Original tabulations from the National Child Care Survey 1990

cent of working-class fathers and 3 percent of middle-income fathers. Even for parents who worked full-time and full-year (2,000 hours per year), hourly earnings of $5 will still earn only $10,000, which is the poverty threshold for a family of three. The ability to pay for child care is further limited by the fact that many low-paying jobs provide few benefits such as health insurance and sick leave, further reducing the disposable income of these families.

Who Pays for Care?

About 58 percent of NCCS parents with a school-age child in care reported paying for child care in 1990. Of those families with a school-aged child, about 63 percent of working-poor and working-class households, and 57 percent of middle-class families whose youngest child is school-age personally paid for the care of their children (Table 6.3). Paying for care is more likely if the mother is employed and if the child is in a formal center-based program. Almost nine out of ten parents paid for care if their child was enrolled in a center (Hofferth et al. 1991).

Figure 6.6 shows families with a single employed mother were the most likely to pay for care—70 percent of working-poor families, 73 percent of working-class families, and 80 percent of middle-class families. Dual-earner families were the next most likely to pay—57 percent of working-poor families, 53 percent of working-class families, and 57 percent of middle-class families.

Figure 6.6

Percentage of Families Who Pay for Child Care by Income, Structure, & Employment Status of Family

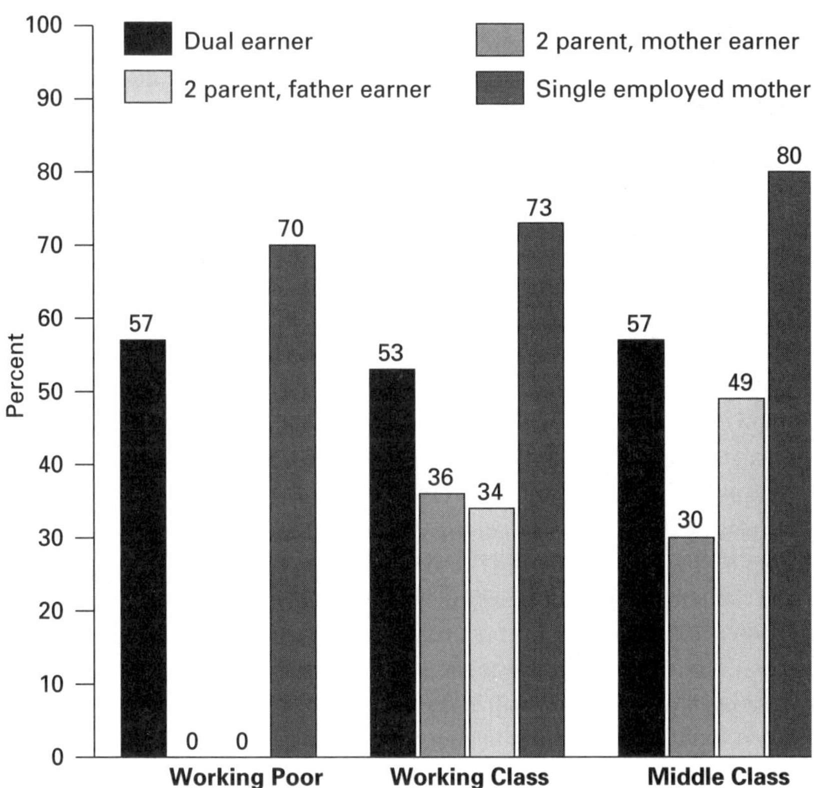

Source: Original tabulations from the National Child Care Survey 1990.

Financial Assistance in Paying for Care

Only a small proportion of families with a school-age child receive direct assistance in paying for child care. Of families relying on before- and after-school care, in 1990, 9 percent of working-poor families, 8 percent of working-class families, and 2 percent of middle-class families received assistance in paying for child care (Table 6.3).

However, it should be noted that the assistance that is available is directed toward working-poor children in center-based care. Half of working-poor families with a school-age child in center care received assistance in paying for care (Table 6.3). Only 11 percent of working-class families and 4 percent of middle-class families with a child in center care received direct financial assistance.

Data from before- and after-school programs corroborate this report from parents. According to data from the National Study of Before- and After-School Programs, in one-third of these center-based programs a government agency pays for the care of some children, one-quarter of the programs adjust fees based on family income, and one-quarter offer tuition grants and scholarships. Still, 86 percent of parents are estimated to pay the full fee for care of their children (Seppanen et al. 1993).

Finally, parents may pay for care and receive a credit on their income taxes for a portion of those expenditures. About one-third of NCCS families with school-age children reported that they claimed a tax credit for child care expenses in 1988, about the same proportion as families with a preschool child. This percentage varies by income, with 16 percent of working-poor, 38 percent of working-class, and 32 percent of middle-class families claiming the credit (Table 6.3). Parents do not consider the tax credit to be direct financial assistance because only 2 percent of middle-income families said they received direct assistance, despite the fact that 32 percent claimed the tax credit.

Budget Shares

NCCS families were also asked their income and how much in total they paid for care for all their children. Although families pay more per hour of care for school-age children than for preschool children ($2.78 compared with $1.56), because families with school-age children use fewer hours (13 instead of 37), the amount spent on child care per week is smaller for families with only school-age children compared to those families with preschool children. On average center-based after-school programs charged about $1.96 per hour and center-based before-school programs charged $2.89 per hour in 1991 (Seppanen et al. 1993). According to the NCCS, the average price parents paid for both before- and after-school center-based care was $2.52 per hour in 1990 (Hofferth et al., 1991).

In 1990, the average weekly expenditure on child care for all children was $30 for a family with an employed mother and the youngest child of school age. Although the absolute amount families pay is of interest, of more importance is the size of that payment relative to income, that is, the "budget share." On average, families with school-age children paid about 6 percent of their family budget on before- and after-school care.

As seen in Figure 6.7, there are substantial differences in budget share

Figure 6.7

Weekly Expenditures and Percentage of Income Spent on Child Care by Income Group

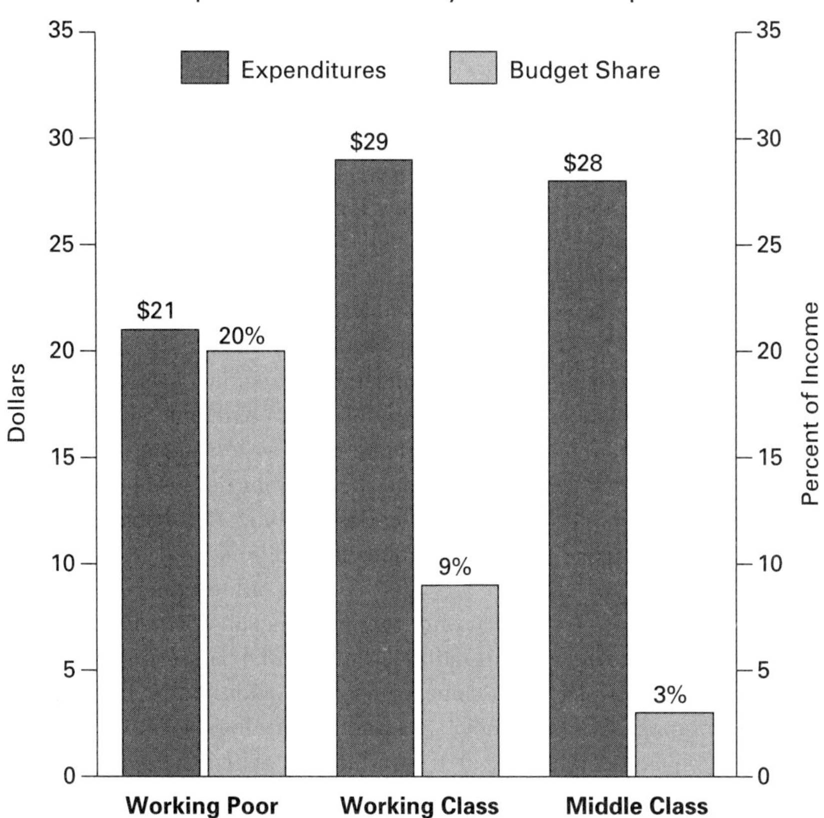

Source: Original tabulations from the National Child Care Survey 1990.

spent for child care by income group. For example, among those who paid for care in 1990, working-poor families paid, on average, $21 per week for the care of all their school-age children, which represented 20 percent of their family income. Working-class families, on average, spent $29 per week, which represented 9 percent of family income, and middle-class families paid, on average, $28 per week, which represented a mere 3 percent of their total family income. It is somewhat surprising that the average amount paid per week by working-class and middle-class families is about the same. This is consistent, however, with the finding discussed earlier that most parents pay the full fee for care.

Quality of Programs

The most important program characteristics related to quality are basic health and safety; structural features such as child/caregiver ratios, group sizes, and teacher training; and the nature of the interaction between provider and parent. The National Study of Before- and After-School Programs found that 84 percent of programs surveyed were either licensed by the state or were under state departments of education. There were no differences in program licensing or accreditation by income of the children served. Consequently, minimal standards for health, safety, and development were assured.

Child/caregiver ratios, which averaged eight to nine children per adult, according to programs surveyed, are excellent and are clearly within regulatory requirements of states. There were no differences in ratios in programs by the income levels of the children served. A high proportion of programs, though not all, report a wide range of enrichment activities offered. Programs for low-income children were more likely to offer tutoring and homework help than programs for higher-income children.

Compared with either regular classroom or preschool teachers, however, levels of compensation and benefits for before- and after-school program staff are low. Because of this and, in part because of the part-time work hours, turnover rates are high. Overall, turnover averages 35 percent per year, with 58 percent of programs reporting an average staff turnover rate of 60 percent per year. This is likely to detract from quality programming. Again, there were no differences in turnover among programs serving low-income compared with those serving higher-income children.

Policies for School-Age Children

Availability of Programs

Are spaces for school-age children in short supply? Evidence in this study suggests that, while there are spaces for younger school-age children that are not utilized, spaces and appropriate programs for older school-age children are scarce. Parents tend to leave their children to care for themselves as they enter middle childhood and young adolescence (ages 8 to 10). Do those facts reflect parents' preferences, lack of program access, the failure of programs to satisfactorily serve the needs and appeal to the interests of young adolescents, or the cost of these programs? This study indicates that the use of private lessons, sports, and similar activities becomes more widespread as middle-class and working-class children mature, but children in working-poor families do *not* participate more in such activities as they mature. While we cannot be sure whether such activities are not affordable or simply not available for them, the data suggest that cost may be the important issue. Eighty-six percent of parents pay the full fee for their children's programs. Given the widespread importance of such programs to young adolescents, more attention needs to be paid both to expanding organized programs, providing more scholarships and financial assistance, and to educating parents about the importance of individual skill-developing activities such as lessons. Community agencies could expand both group and individual activities in low-income communities to fill this rather large gap between different income groups.

The availability of programs on weekends and during the evening is another issue that needs consideration. According to the data presented here, more than one out of four working-poor and working-class families have a parent who works on the weekend. About one out of ten working-poor mothers and one out of seven working-poor fathers was likely to work a night shift. Few programs are open during the evenings and even fewer on weekends. This limits care options for parents with school-age children.

Finally, consideration needs to be given to developing a different type of program for older school-age children. Older children do not feel comfortable in child-care programs, yet these children are often not mature enough to be left to care for themselves. The National Study of Before- and After-School Programs found few examples of high quality programming for older children.

Schools versus Private Enterprise

Should schools or private enterprise be responsible for the care of children? According to the study described here, in 1991, 28 percent of programs were run by public and private nonprofit schools, with about 18 percent in the public schools. It was surprising that so few of the programs were in schools, the location where children spend most of their time. According to the report, the advantages of programs in school buildings are that they are more likely to be accredited, and they spend a higher percentage of the budgets on staff salaries and benefits than programs not in school buildings. The disadvantage is that they are less likely to offer care during the summer, school holidays, school vacations, or teacher inservice days. In addition, they tend to be larger, have higher child/staff ratios, and charge higher hourly fees. While schools appear to provide convenient locations for before- and after-school care for children, there has not, to date, been a major movement toward increasing the number of before- and after-school programs in the schools (although specific programmatic efforts have promoted such care). Programs in schools have the disadvantages of being tied to school schedules, making them less attractive to parents. Since the programs are often run by outside organizations, it would not appear necessary or desirable that the schedules be the same. Although violence mars the school environment all too often, safety of children may be monitored more closely in school buildings than elsewhere. Schools may present an advantage in this regard.

Universality of Benefits

Should benefits be targeted to needy children and families or universally available to all? Given the underutilization of programs that exist and their high cost to parents, it might be concluded either that parents do not want to pay for them or that parents think they are inappropriate or inconvenient. On the other hand, given the need for increased supervision and exposure to supplemental programs as children grow into their teenage years and the concern about school drop-out rates and adolescent pregnancies, establishing universal programs after school merits consideration.

One of the advantages of a program that is universally available is that, since large numbers of individuals benefit, support is widespread. The Child and Dependent Care Credit in the income tax system is such a benefit. Because it is available to all it is widely supported and users are not stigmatized. As discussed earlier, parents do not even think of it as a direct subsidy. To the extent that programs for school-age children can also be made universal, support would be increased. States such as Indiana have already committed additional funding for before- and after-school programs.

It should be noted that a program of this nature would not be prohibitively expensive. The cost of serving all school-age children with an after-school program of $30 per week, with parents paying 86 percent of the cost, as they do now, would be about $116 million dollars.[6] Current *potential* federal funding for school-age programs is about $193 million.

In-Kind Benefits vs. Money

Should funds be targeted specifically for child-care expenditures or should low-income families' incomes be subsidized with no strings attached? Child-care vouchers are an example of in-kind benefits; the Earned Income Tax Credit (see Blank and London, this volume) is an example of direct financial assistance. Increasing the EITC helps low-income families by increasing their disposable incomes. The important question is whether families will spend part of this additional income on programs for their children. Given that the working poor currently pay for care and spend a substantial proportion of their incomes on it, I argue that increases in the EITC are unlikely to increase parental expenditures on before-and after-school programs. Lack of slots does not appear to be the problem. Money spent out-of-pocket is what appears to be the major hurdle. Since consumption by most low-income families is based upon current income, receiving a lump sum at the end of the tax year (Blank and London, this volume) is not useful for current spending.[7] Few such families can obtain credit until such funds arrive. Additionally, if families do not understand how the EITC operates and what benefits they will receive (Blank and London, this volume), it is unlikely to provide them with any incentive to spend more on child care. They may simply see it as a one-time windfall gain. Programs will have to improve their outreach, provide sliding-scale fees and scholarships, and demonstrate the value of such programs before they are likely to attract such families.

Children need both care and supervision. Economic, demographic, and other social changes have decreased the ability of parents to supervise their children during non-school time. Changes in the nature of society have increased children's exposure to harmful role models and involvement in risky behavior, particularly for unsupervised adolescent-age children. Though long-term studies are not available, research is beginning to show the short-term benefits of supervised after-school programs. While slots are available in most programs for children in the early grades, enrollments decline dramatically for young adolescent children. Parents tend to use a combination of extracurricular activities and lessons for these children. However, the group that could benefit from such activities—children in working-poor families—remains largely unserved. The major reasons are both financial and organizational, but this lack of use may also reflect the lack of safety of neighborhoods and, thus, the restricted mobility of children in these neighborhoods. If the opportunity to help these children develop the kinds of skills to increase their abilities and self-esteem is not taken, we will lose yet another generation to the streets.

Notes

1. Almost half of this increase is due to increased expenditures for Head Start.

2. Child care, which was obtained in the NCCS as of the previous week, would not be relevant to mothers not employed at the time; consequently employment is defined at the time of the survey rather than over the previous year. A person who has a job but is not at work during the survey week because they are on leave is still counted as employed.

3. I also explored using 100 to 200 percent of the poverty line as the lower and upper bounds for the second category. This group is much smaller in size than the group between 100 percent of the poverty line and $25,000 income annually, but the characteristics of its members are similar to those of families with incomes under $25,000.

4. In a small proportion of families children live with relatives, not parents; the few such families were excluded from the analyses.

5. There was only one significant difference. Families with incomes of $50,000 or more annually were less likely than any other group to report relatives available.

6. The cost per school-age child after school is estimated at $30 per week (Hofferth et al. 1991). Parents currently pay 86 percent of this, or $26, leaving the public sector to pick up $4 per child per week. $4 x 29 million = $116 million.

7. Although families can sign up to receive the EITC along with their regular wage or salary, apparently few do so (Committee on Ways and Means 1991).

References

Cahan, Emily. 1989. *Past Caring: A History of U.S. Preschool Care and Education for the Poor, 1820–1965*. New York: Columbia University, National Center for Children in Poverty.

Cain, Virginia, and Sandra Hofferth. 1989. "Parental Choice of Self-Care for School-Age Children." *Journal of Marriage and the Family* 51: 65–77.

Child Care Action Campaign. 1993. *Child Care and Education: The Critical Connection, Policy Statement.* New York: Child Care Action Campaign.

Committee on Ways and Means. 1991. *Overview of Entitlement Programs.* Washington, D.C.: U.S. Government Printing Office.

Hernandez, Donald. 1993. *America's Children: Resources from Family, Government, and the Economy.* New York: Russell Sage.

Hofferth, Sandra. 1993. "The 101st Congress: An Emerging Agenda for Children in Poverty." In *Child Poverty and Public Policy*, edited by J. Chafel. Washington, D.C.: The Urban Institute Press.

Hofferth, Sandra L., April Brayfield, Sharon Deich, and Pamela Holcomb. 1991. *National Child Care Survey, 1990*. Washington, D.C.: The Urban Institute.

Howes, Carollee, Michael Olenick, and Tagoush Der-Kiureghian. 1987. "After School Child Care in an Elementary School: Social Development and Continuity and Complementarity of Programs." *Elementary School Journal* 88 (no. 1): 93-103.

Kagan, Sharon Lynn, and Edward Zigler. 1987. *Early Schooling: The National Debate.* New Haven: Yale University Press.

Kuchak, JoAnn. 1983. *School-Age Day Care Study.* Silver Spring, Md.: Applied Management Sciences, Inc.

Levy, Frank, and Richard Michel. 1991. *The Economic Future of American Families.* Washington, D.C.: The Urban Institute Press.

Long, Thomas, and Lynette Long. 1982. "Latchkey Children: The Child's View of Self-care." Washington, D.C.: Catholic University of America (ERIC Document Reproduction Service No. ED 211 229).

Mayesky, Mary. 1979. "Extended Day Program in a Public Elementary School." *Children Today* (May-June).

Posner, Jill K., and Deborah Lowe Vandell. 1994. "Low-Income Children's After-School Care: Are There Beneficial Effects of After-School Programs?" *Child Development* 65.

Ribar, David C. 1991. Federal Child Care Assistance Takes its First Steps: 1933–1946. Working Paper 91–2. University Park, Penn.: Pennsylvania State University, Department of Economics.

Rodman, Hyman, David J. Pratto, and Rosemary Smith Nelson. 1985. "Child Care Arrangements and Children's Functioning: A Comparison of Self-Care and Adult-Care Children." *Developmental Psychology* 21: 413–418.

Ruggles, Patricia. 1990. *Drawing the Line: Alternative Poverty Measures and Their Implications for Public Policy.* Washington, D.C.: The Urban Institute Press.

Seppanen, Patricia, John Love, Dianne deVries, Lawrence Bernstein, Michelle Seligson, Fern Marx, and Ellen Kisker. 1993. *National Study of Before- and After School Programs.* Final Report. Washington, D.C.: U.S. Department of Education.

Seligson, Michelle, and Dale Fink. 1989. *No Time to Waste: An Action Agenda for School-Age Child Care.* Wellesley, Mass.: Center for Research on Women.

Seligson, Michelle, Andrea Genser, Ellen Gannett, and Wendy Gray. 1983. *School-Age Child Care: A Policy Report.* Wellesley, Mass.: Center for Research on Women.

Steinberg, Laurence. 1986. "Latchkey Children and Susceptibility to Peer Pressure: An Ecological Analysis." *Developmental Psychology* 22: 1–7.

Task Force on Youth Development and Community Programs. 1992. *A Matter of Time: Risk and Opportunity in the Nonschool Hours.* New York: Carnegie Corporation.

U.S. Bureau of the Census. 1987. "After-School Care of School-Age Children. December 1984." *Current Population Reports,* Series P–25, No. 149.

U.S. Bureau of the Census. 1994. *Statistical Abstract of the U.S. 1994.* Washington, D.C.: U.S. Government Printing Office.

Vandell, Deborah Lowe, and Mary Anne Corasaniti. 1988. "The Relation between Third Graders' After School Care and Social, Academic, and Emotional Functioning," *Child Development* 59: 868–875.

Willer, B., S. Hofferth, E. Kisker, P. Divine-Hawkins, E. Farquhar, and F. Glantz. 1991. *The Demand and Supply of Child Care in 1990: Joint Findings from the National Child Care Survey 1990 and A Profile of Child Care Settings.* Washington, D.C.: National Association for the Education of Young Children.

Zigler, Edward F., and Thomas J. Long. 1983. Testimony before the U.S. Senate Children's Caucus. Policy forum to examine problems confronting latchkey children (9 June).

7

The Right to Welfare of the Working Poor

JAMES P. STERBA

In 1990, 6.6 million workers who were in the U.S. labor force for more than half the year lived in families whose incomes were below the poverty level (Gardner and Herz 1992).This number represented about 6 percent of all persons in the labor force and about 20 percent of all those living in poverty in the U.S. (Gardner and Herz 1992; see also Durning 1990). President Clinton's welfare reform proposal and those offered by the Republican-controlled 103rd Congress require all able-bodied recipients to be employed after two years. But what if employment fails to lift people out of poverty as in the case of the 6.6 million U.S. workers who are working poor? Surely if there is a right to welfare then the working poor, who are presumably doing all that they can to meet their own basic needs, would be entitled to such a right. But do the poor, working or otherwise, have a right to welfare or should welfare be something that people are free to provide if they choose, not something that is required of them by their government? If welfare is not something the poor, even the working poor, have a right to, then any attempt to reform the U.S. welfare system would be misguided. If the poor do not have a right to welfare, then the U.S. welfare system should be abolished, not reformed.

To determine whether there is a right to welfare, I propose to critically evaluate the alternative conceptions of justice that are available to us to see whether they support such a right, particularly for the working poor. Now in philosophical debate at the end of the twentieth century, five major conceptions of justice are defended.

First, there is a libertarian conception of justice. In recent elections, libertarian party candidates have done very well. Ronald Reagan, George Bush, and Margaret Thatcher, whose views on economic issues are close to a libertarian conception of justice, were politically successful and did succeed in refashioning the economies of their respective nations. According to this conception of justice, liberty is the ultimate political ideal. Thus all assignments of rights and duties are ultimately to be justified in terms of an ideal of liberty.

Second, there is a socialist conception of justice. In the United States there has never been a viable socialist presidential candidate, but elsewhere there have been many successful socialist candidates. For example, the late Olof Palme led the Social Democrats back to power in Sweden and François Mitterrand, a socialist, served as President of France for nearly a decade and a half before cancer defeated him in 1995. According to a socialist conception of justice, equality is the ultimate political ideal. Thus all assignments of rights and duties are ultimately to be justified in terms of an ideal of equality.

Third, there is a welfare liberal conception of justice. This is the conception of justice endorsed, for example, by the left wing of the Democratic party in the United States, whose leaders have been Jesse Jackson and Ted Kennedy. According to this conception of justice, the ultimate political ideal is a blend of liberty and equality, and this blend can be characterized as fairness. Thus all assignments of rights and duties are ultimately to be justified in terms of an ideal of fairness.

Fourth, there is a communitarian conception of justice. This conception is somewhat difficult to associate with any particular political group, but it does seem to be reflected in a wide range of Supreme Court decisions in the United States today and has its roots in the republicanism of Madison and Jefferson. According to this communitarian conception of justice, the common good is proclaimed to be the ultimate political ideal, and this ideal is said to support a virtue-based conception of human flourishing.

Last, there is a feminist conception of justice. This is the conception endorsed by the National Organization for Women (NOW) and by numerous other women's organizations in the United States and elsewhere. According to a feminist conception of justice, the ultimate political ideal is a gender-free society. Thus all assignments of rights and duties are ultimately to be justified in terms of a gender-free society.

All of these conceptions of justice have certain features in common. Each regards its requirements as belonging to the domain of obligation rather than to the domain of charity; they simply disagree about where to draw the line between these two domains. Each is also concerned to give people what they deserve or should rightfully possess; they simply disagree about what it is that people deserve or rightfully possess. These common features constitute a generally accepted core definition of justice. What we need to do, however, is examine that part of each of these conceptions of justice over which there is serious disagreement in order to determine to what degree the disagreement is resolvable. In particular, we need to determine whether the disagreement is sufficiently resolvable to support a right to welfare.

Libertarian Justice

Libertarians frequently cite the novelist/philosopher Ayn Rand as an intellectual source of their view (Hospers 1971; Uyl and Rasmussen 1984). Ayn Rand defends a particular conception of human rights which regards individuals as ends in themselves and society as a means to the peaceful and orderly *voluntary* co-existence of individuals (Rand 1963). This conception is contrasted with an altruistic-collectivist ethics which regards each individual as a sacrificial means to the ends of others and society as an end in itself. According to Rand, the conception of human rights she defends is required for a free society and until recently characterized the political system of the United States.

In basic sympathy with Rand, contemporary libertarians such as John Hospers take liberty to be the ultimate moral and political ideal and typically define "liberty" as "the state of being unconstrained by other persons from doing what one wants." This definition limits the scope of liberty in two ways. First, not all constraints, whatever the source, count as a restriction on liberty; the constraints must come from other persons. For example, people who are constrained by natural forces from getting to the top of Mount Everest do not lack liberty in this regard. Second, the constraints must run counter to people's wants. Thus, people who do not want to hear Beethoven's Fifth Symphony do not have their liberty restricted when other people forbid its performance, even though the prescription does in fact constrain what they are able to do.

Given this definition of liberty, libertarians go on to characterize their moral and political ideal as requiring that each person should have the greatest amount of liberty commensurate with the same liberty for all. From this ideal, libertarians claim that a number of more specific requirements, in particular a right to life, a right to freedom of speech, press, and assembly, and a right to property, can be derived.

The libertarian's right to life is not a right to receive from others the goods and resources necessary for preserving one's life; it is simply a right not to be killed. So understood, the right to life is not a right to receive welfare. In fact, there are no welfare rights in the libertarian view. Accordingly, on the libertarian's understanding, the right to property is not a right to receive from others the goods and resources necessary for one's welfare, but rather a right to acquire goods and resources either by initial acquisition or by voluntary agreement.

By defending rights such as these, libertarians can support only a limited role for government. That role is simply to prevent and punish initial acts of coercion—the only wrongful actions for libertarians.

Libertarians do not deny that it is a good thing for people to have sufficient goods and resources to meet their basic nutritional needs and basic health care needs, but libertarians do deny that government has a duty to provide for such needs. Some good things, such as the provision of welfare to the needy, are requirements of charity rather than justice, libertarians claim. Accordingly, failure to make such provisions is neither blameworthy nor punishable.

Yet when the libertarian's own ideal of liberty is correctly interpreted, I have argued that it actually supports the rights of a welfare state rather than those of a minimal or nightwatchman state (Sterba 1985). For as long as libertarians think of themselves as putting forth a moral resolution for cases of severe conflict of interest, they cannot allow that it would be unreasonable *both* to require the rich to sacrifice the liberty to meet some of their luxury needs in order to benefit the poor and to require the poor to sacrifice the liberty to meet their basic needs in order to benefit the rich. But if one of these requirements is to be judged reasonable, then, by any neutral assessment, it must be the requirement that the rich sacrifice the liberty to meet some of their luxury needs so that the poor can have the liberty to meet their basic needs; there is no other plausible resolution if libertarians intend to be putting forth a moral resolution. What this shows, I contend, is that the libertarian's own ideal of liberty supports a right to welfare.

In his book, *Individuals and Their Rights,* Tibor Machan (1989, 100–111) criticizes my argument that a libertarian ideal of liberty leads to a right to welfare, accepting its theoretical thrust but denying its practical significance. He grants that if the type of conflict cases I describe between the rich and the poor actually obtained, the poor would have a right to welfare. But he then denies that the type of conflict cases I describe—in which the poor have done all that they legitimately can to satisfy their basic needs in a libertarian society—actually does obtain. "Normally," he writes, "persons do not lack the opportunities and resources to satisfy their basic needs" (Machan 1989, 107).

But Machan's response virtually concedes everything that my argument intended to establish. For the poor's right to welfare is not claimed to be unconditional. Rather it is said to be conditional principally upon the poor doing all that they legitimately can to meet their own basic needs. So it follows that only when the poor lack sufficient opportunity to satisfy their own basic needs would their right to welfare have any practical moral force. Accordingly, on libertarian grounds, Machan has conceded the legitimacy of just the kind of right to welfare that my argument hoped to establish.

The only difference that remains is a practical one. Machan thinks that virtually all of the poor have sufficient opportunities and resources to satisfy their basic needs and that, therefore, a right to welfare has no practical moral force. In contrast, I would think that many of the poor do not have sufficient opportunities and resources to satisfy their basic needs and that, therefore, a right to welfare has considerable practical moral force.

But isn't this practical disagreement resolvable? For who could deny that most of the 1.2 billion people who are currently living in conditions of absolute poverty "lack the opportunities and resources to satisfy their basic needs"? (Durning 1990, 24). And even within our own country, it is estimated that some 32 million Americans live below the official poverty index, and that one fifth of American children are growing up in poverty (Durning 1990, 29). Surely, it is impossible to deny that many of these Americans, especially the 6.6 million who comprise the working poor, also "lack the opportunities and resources to satisfy their basic needs." Given the impossibility of reasonably denying these factual claims, Machan would have to concede that the right to welfare, which he grants can be theoretically established on libertarian premises, also has practical moral force.

Socialist Justice

In contrast with libertarians, socialists take equality to be the ultimate political ideal. In *The Communist Manifesto* (1888), Karl Marx and Friedrich Engels maintain that the abolition of bourgeois property and bourgeois family structure is a necessary first requirement for building a society that accords with the political ideal of equality. In the *Critique of the Gotha Program* (1966), Marx provides a much more positive account of what is required to build a society based upon the political ideal of equality. In such a society, Marx claims that the distribution of social goods must conform, at least initially, to the principle from each according to his ability, to each according to his contribution. But when the highest stage of communist society has been reached, Marx adds, distribution will conform to the principle from each according to his ability, to each according to his need.

At first hearing, this conception might sound ridiculous to someone brought up in a capitalist society. The obvious objection is, how can you get persons to contribute according to their ability if income is distributed on the basis of their needs and not on the basis of their contributions?

The answer, according to a socialist conception of justice, is to make the work that must be done in a society as much as possible enjoyable in itself. As a result, people will want to do the work they are capable of doing because they find it intrinsically rewarding. For a start, socialists might try to get people to accept presently existing, intrinsically rewarding jobs at lower salaries—top executives, for example, to work for $300,000, rather than $900,000, a year. Yet ultimately, socialists hope to make all jobs as intrinsically rewarding as possible, so that after people are no longer working primarily for external rewards when making their best contributions to society, distribution can proceed on the basis of need.

Socialists propose to implement their ideal of equality by giving workers democratic control over the workplace. They believe that if workers have more to say about how they do their work, they will find their work intrinsically more rewarding. As a consequence, they will be more motivated to work, because their work itself will be meeting their needs. Socialists believe that extending democracy to the workplace will necessarily lead to socialization of the means of production and the end of private property. Socialists, of course, do not deny that civil disobedience or even revolutionary action may be needed to overcome opposition to extending democracy to the workplace.

However, even with democratic control of the workplace, some jobs, such as collecting garbage or changing bedpans, probably cannot be made intrinsically rewarding. Socialists propose to divide such jobs up in some equitable manner. Some people might, for example, collect garbage one day a week, and then work at intrinsically rewarding jobs for the rest of the week. Others would change bedpans or do some other slop job one day a week, and then work at an intrinsically rewarding job the other days of the week. By making jobs intrinsically as rewarding as possible, in part through democratic control of the workplace and an equitable assignment of unrewarding tasks, socialists believe people will contribute according to their ability even when distribution proceeds according to need.

Another difficulty raised concerning the socialist conception of justice involves the proclaimed necessity of abolishing private property and socializing the means of production. It seems perfectly possible to give workers more control over their workplace while the means of production remain privately owned. Of course, private ownership would have a somewhat different character in a society with democratic control of the workplace, but it need not cease to be private ownership. After all, private ownership would also have a somewhat different character in a society where private holdings, and hence bargaining power, were distributed more equally than they are in most capitalist societies, yet it would not cease to be private ownership. Accordingly, we could imagine a society where the means of production are privately owned but where—because ownership is so widely dispersed throughout the society and because of the degree of democratic control of the workplace—many of the criticisms socialists make of existing capitalist societies would no longer apply. Yet whatever the exact practical requirements of a socialist ideal of equality, it is obvious that a right to welfare, especially for the working poor, would be among them.

Welfare Liberal Justice

Finding merit in both the libertarian's ideal of liberty and the socialist's ideal of equality, welfare liberals attempt to combine both liberty and equality into one political ideal that can also be characterized as an ideal of fairness.

A classical example of welfare liberal justice is found in the political works of Immanuel Kant (1970). Kant claims that a civil state ought to be founded on an original contract satisfying the requirements of freedom (the freedom to seek happiness in whatever way one sees fit as long as one does not infringe upon the freedom of others to pursue a similar end), equality (the equal right of each person to restrict others from using his or her freedom in ways that deny equal freedom to all), and independence (that independence of each person that is necessarily presupposed by the free agreement of the original contract).

According to Kant, the original contract, which ought to be the foundation of every civil state, does not have to "actually exist as a fact." It suffices that the laws of a civil state are such that people would agree to them under conditions in which the requirements of freedom, equality, and independence obtain. Laws that accord with this original contract would then, Kant claims, give all members of society the right to reach any degree of rank that they could earn through their labor, industry, and good fortune. Thus, the equality demanded by the original contract would not, in Kant's view, exclude a considerable amount of economic liberty.

The Kantian ideal of a hypothetical contract as the moral foundation for a welfare liberal conception of justice has been further developed by John Rawls in *A Theory of Justice* (1971). Rawls, like Kant, argues that principles of justice are those principles that free and rational persons who are concerned to advance their own interests would accept in an initial position of equality.

Yet Rawls goes beyond Kant by interpreting the conditions of his "original position" to explicitly require a "veil of ignorance." This veil of ignorance, Rawls claims, has the effect of depriving persons in the original position of the knowledge they would need to advance their own interests in ways that are morally arbitrary.

According to Rawls, the principles of justice that would be derived in the original position are the following:

I. Special conception of justice
   1. A principle of equal political liberty
   2. A principle of equal opportunity
   3. A principle requiring that the distribution of economic goods work to the greatest advantage of the least advantaged

II. General conception of justice
   A principle requiring that the distribution of all social goods work to the greatest advantage of the least advantaged

The general conception of justice differs from the special conception of justice by allowing trade-offs between political liberty and other social goods. According to Rawls, persons in the original position would want the special conception of justice to be applied in place of the general conception of justice whenever social conditions allow all representative persons to benefit from the exercise of their political liberties.

Rawls holds that these principles of justice would be chosen in the original position because persons so situated would find it reasonable to try to secure for themselves the highest minimum payoff. In effect, they would want to follow the conservative dictates of the "maximin strategy" and *max*imize the *min*imum payoff. Rawls (1971, 150) describes their reasoning as follows:

> Now looking at the situation from the standpoint of one person selected arbitrarily, there is no way for him to win special advantages for himself. Nor, on the other hand, are there grounds for his acquiescing in special disadvantages. Since it is not reasonable for him to expect more than an equal share in the division of social goods, and since it is not rational for him to agree to less, the sensible thing for him to do is to acknowledge as the first principle of justice one requiring an equal distribution.

Rawls (1971, 157) goes on to argue:

> Thus, the parties start with a principle establishing equal liberty for all, including equality of opportunity, as well as an equal distribution of income and wealth. But there is no reason why this acknowledgment should be final. If there are inequalities . . . that work to make everyone better off in compari-

> son with the benchmark of initial equality, why not permit them. The immediate gain which a greater inequality might allow can be regarded as intelligently invested in view of its future return. If, for example, these inequalities set up various incentives which succeed in eliciting more productive efforts, a person in the original position may look upon them as necessary to cover the costs of training and to encourage effective performance.

Rawls's defense of a welfare liberal conception of justice has been challenged in a variety of ways. Some critics have endorsed Rawls's contractual approach while disagreeing with Rawls over what principles of justice would be derived from it. These critics usually attempt to undermine the use of a maximum strategy in the original position. None of these critics, however, deny that a right to welfare would be derived from Rawls's original position. Other critics, however, have found fault with the contractual approach itself, and if these critiques can be sustained, they would surely undermine the derivation of a right to welfare from Rawls's original position. One such critic is Ronald Dworkin.

Dworkin argues that hypothetical agreements, such as the agreement persons would make in the original position, do not (unlike actual agreements) provide independent arguments for the fairness of those agreements. Dworkin (1973, 200) writes:

> [Rawls's] contract is hypothetical, and hypothetical contracts do not supply an independent argument for the fairness of enforcing their terms. A hypothetical contract is not simply a pale form of an actual contract; it is no contract at all.

Dworkin (1973, 200) asks us to consider the following example:

> Suppose I did not know the value of my painting on Monday; if you had offered me $100 for it then I would have accepted. On Tuesday I discover it was valuable. You cannot argue that it would be fair for the courts to make me sell it to you for $100 on Wednesday. It may be my good fortune that you did not ask me on Monday, but that does not justify coercion against me later.

Dworkin contends that the fact that on Monday he would have accepted an offer of $100 for a painting he owned, because he did not know its value, in no way shows that it would be fair to force him to sell the painting for $100 after he subsequently learns that the painting is valuable. Accordingly, Dworkin holds that the fact that persons would hypothetically agree to do something in the original position does not provide an independent argument for abiding by that agreement in everyday life.

But while it seems correct to argue, as Dworkin does, that the hypothetical agreement in the painting case does not support a demand to presently sell the painting for $100, it is not clear how this undermines the relevance of the hypothetical agreement that emerges from Rawls's original position. For surely Rawls need not endorse the view that *all* hypothetical agreements are morally binding. Nor could Dworkin reasonably argue that this example and the few others that he gives support the conclusion that *no* hypothetical agreements are morally binding. Because if that were the case, we could argue by analogy from the fact that *some* actual agreements are not binding (such as an agreement to commit murder) to the conclusions that *no* actual agreement is morally binding, which, of course, is absurd. Consequently, Dworkin would have to provide some further argument to show that the specific agreement that would result from the original position is not morally binding. He cannot derive that conclusion simply from the premise that *some* hypothetical agreements (e.g., the one concerning the picture) are not morally binding.

Richard Miller (1974) raises another challenge to Rawls's contractual approach from the point of view of Marxist social theory. Miller maintains that if certain elements of Marxist social theory are correct then neither Rawls's principles of justice nor any other candidates for "morally acceptable principles" would emerge from the original position.

Miller (1974, 175) cites the following elements of Marxist social theory:

> (1) no social arrangement that is acceptable to the best-off class is acceptable to the worst-off class; (2) the best-off class is a ruling class, that is, a class whose interests are served by the major political and ideological institutions; and (3) the need for wealth and power typical of the best-off class is much more acute than what is typical of the rest of society.

What Miller is claiming is that if persons in the original position accepted these elements of Marxist social theory (and persons in the original position are presumed to have access to all available general information), then they would not choose Rawls's principles of justice nor any other "morally acceptable principles."

Let us suppose, however, that the needs and interests of a society are in extreme conflict, and that the conflict has the form of what Marx calls "class conflict." Let us consider the case in which the opposing classes are the rich, propertied capitalist class and the poor, relatively propertyless proletariat class. No doubt persons in the original position would know that in such a society compliance with almost any principles of conflict resolution could be achieved only by means of a stringent enforcement system. But why should that fact keep them from choosing any principles of social cooperation whatsoever? Surely, persons in the original position would still have reason to provide for the basic needs of the members of the poor, relatively propertyless proletariat class because they may turn out to be in that class, and thus would be inclined to favor a basic needs social minimum.

Of course, the members of the capitalist class who have developed special needs for wealth and power could claim that they would suffer acutely in any transition to a society with a basic needs social minimum. Yet persons in the original position, imagining themselves to be ignorant of whether they belong to the capitalist or the proletariat class, would have grounds to discount such considerations in deciding upon principles of social cooperation. They would realize that members of the capitalist class are not "compelled" to pursue their interest by depriving the members of the proletariat class of an acceptable minimum of social goods. They act as they do, depriving others of an acceptable social minimum, simply to acquire more social goods for themselves. Unlike members of the proletariat class, the members of the capitalist class could be reasonably expected to act otherwise. Accordingly, persons in the original position would recognize this and require whatever sacrifice from the members of the capitalist class would be necessary to restore to the members of the proletariat class the benefits of a basic needs social minimum. In this way, it would be possible to derive from Rawls's original position at least a right to welfare, especially for the working poor, even assuming conditions of class conflict.

Communitarian Justice

Another prominent political ideal defended by contemporary philosophers is the communitarian ideal of the common good. As one might expect, many contemporary defenders of a communitarian conception of justice regard their conception as rooted in Aristotelian moral theory. In the *Nicomachean Ethics*, Aristotle distinguishes between different varieties of justice. He first distinguishes between justice as the whole of virtue and justice as a particular part of virtue. In the former sense, justice is understood as what is lawful, and the just person is equivalent to the moral person. In the latter sense, justice is understood as what is fair or equal, and the just person is the person who takes only a proper share. Aristotle focuses his discussion on justice in the latter sense, which further divides into distributive justice, corrective justice, and justice in exchange. Each of these varieties of justice can be understood to be concerned with achieving equality. For distributive justice it is equality between equals; for corrective justice it is equality between punishment and the crime; and for justice in exchange it is equality between whatever goods are exchanged. Aristotle also claims that justice has both its natural and conventional aspects: this twofold character of justice seems to be behind Aristotle's discussion of equity, in which equity, which is a natural standard, is described as a corrective to legal justice, which is a conventional standard.

Note that few of the distinctions Aristotle makes here seem tied to the acceptance of any particular conception of justice. One could, for example, accept the view that justice requires formal equality, but then specify the equality that is required in different ways. Even the ideal of justice as giving people what they deserve, which has its roots in Aristotle's account of distributive justice, is also subject to various interpretations. For an analysis of the concept of desert would show that there is no conceptual difficulty with claiming, for example, that everyone deserves to have his or her needs satisfied or that everyone deserves an equal share of the goods distributed by his or her society. Consequently, Aristotle's account is primarily helpful for getting clear about the distinctions belonging to the concept of justice—distinctions that are common to all conceptions of justice.

If we turn to contemporary communitarians we find that rather than determining the particular requirements of their conception of justice, they have frequently chosen to defend their conception by attacking other conceptions of justice, and, by and large, they have focused their attacks on the welfare liberal conception of justice.

One of the best-known attacks of this sort has been put forth by Michael J. Sandel. Sandel claims that a welfare liberal conception of justice is founded on an inadequate conception of the nature of persons, according to which none of the particular wants, interests, or ends that we happen to have at any given time constitute who we are essentially. According to this conception, we are independent of and prior to all such wants, interests, or ends.

Sandel (1982, 179) claims that this conception of the nature of persons is inadequate because

> we cannot regard ourselves as independent in this way without great cost to those loyalties and convictions whose moral force consists partly in the fact that living by them is inseparable from understanding ourselves as the particular persons we are—as members of this family or community or nation or people, as bearers of this history, as sons and daughters of that revolution, as citizens of this republic. Allegiances such as these are more than values I happen to have or aims I "espouse at any given time." They go beyond the obligations I voluntarily incur and the "natural duties" I owe to human beings as such. They allow that to some I owe more than justice requires or

> even permits, not by reason of agreements I have made but instead in virtue of those more or less enduring attachments and commitments which taken together partly define the person I am.

Thus, according to Sandel, the conception of the nature of persons required by a welfare liberal conception of justice is inadequate because it fails to take into account the fact that some of our wants, interests, and ends are at least in part constitutive of who we are essentially. Without these desires, interests, and ends, we would not be the same persons we presently happen to be.

Sandel contends that welfare liberals are led to rely on this inadequate conception of persons for reasons that are fundamental to the conception of justice they want to defend. Specifically, welfare liberals want to maintain the priority of justice, and more generally the priority of the right over the good. For example, according to Rawls (1971, 31):

> The principles of right and so of justice put limits on which satisfactions have value; they impose restrictions on what are reasonable conceptions of one's good. We can express this by saying that in justice as fairness the concept of right is prior to that of the good.

To support these priorities, Sandel argues that welfare liberals endorse this inadequate conception of the nature of persons. For example, Rawls (1971, 560) argues:

> It is not our aims that primarily reveal our nature but rather the principles that we would acknowledge to govern the background conditions under which these aims are to be found and the manner in which they are to be pursued. *For the self is prior to the ends which are affirmed by it*; even a dominant end must be chosen from among numerous possibilities. . . . We should therefore reverse the relation between the right and the good . . .and view the right as prior.

What this passage shows, according to Sandel, is that welfare liberals, like Rawls, believe that the priority of justice and the priority of the right are grounded in the priority of the self to its ends.

At first glance, Sandel's case against welfare liberalism looks particularly strong. After all, Rawls actually does say that "the self is prior to the ends which are affirmed by it" and this claim seems to express just the inadequate conception of the nature of persons that Sandel contends underlies a welfare liberal conception of justice. Nevertheless, Sandel's case against welfare liberalism presupposes that there is no other plausible interpretation that can be given to Rawls's claim than the one that Sandel favors. But there is another interpretation according to which to say that persons are prior to their ends simply means that they are morally prior to those ends, that is, that they are morally responsible for those ends to the degree that they can or could have changed them. Of course, the degree to which people can or could have changed their ends varies, but it is that which determines the degree to which we are morally responsible for those ends and, hence, morally prior to them.

Nor does this interpretation deny that certain ends may in fact be constitutive of the persons we are, so that if those ends were to change we would become different persons. We can see, therefore, that nothing in this interpretation of Rawls's claim presupposes a self that exists prior to all its ends. Rather, the picture we are given is that of a self that is responsible for its ends insofar as its ends can or could have been revised. Such a self may well be constituted by at least some of its ends, but it is only responsible for those ends to the degree to which they can or could have been revised. So the sense in which a self is prior to its ends is simply moral: insofar as its ends can or could have been revised, a self may be called upon to change them or compensate others for their effects when they turn out to be morally objectionable. Clearly, this interpretation of Rawls's claim avoids any commitment to the inadequate conception of the nature of persons which Sandel contends underlies a welfare liberal conception of justice.

Another communitarian attack on welfare liberalism has been put forward by Alasdair MacIntyre. In a recent article, MacIntyre (1990) argues that virtually all forms of liberalism attempt to separate rules defining right action from conceptions of the human good. He (1990, 90) writes:

> This socially embodied divorce between rules defining right action on the one hand and conceptions of the human good on the other is one of those aspects of such societies in virtue of which they are entitled to be called liberal.

MacIntyre contends that these forms of liberalism not only fail but have to fail because the rules defining right action cannot be adequately grounded apart from a conception of the good. According to MacIntyre (1990, 92):

> Adequate knowledge of moral rules is inseparable from and cannot be had without genuine knowledge of the human good.

For this reason, MacIntyre claims, only some refurbished Aristotelian theory that grounds rules supporting right action in a complete conception of the good can ever hope to be adequate.

MacIntyre's critique relates to the way that the contrast between liberals and their communitarian critics is usually formulated. Usually, liberals are said to defend the view that society should be neutral with respect to conceptions of the good, while communitarians are usually said to defend the view that society should enforce a particular conception of the good. For example, according to Ronald Dworkin (1973, 127),

> [L]iberalism takes, as its constitutive political, that theory of equality [which holds that] political decisions must be, so far as possible, independent of any particular conception of the good life, or of what gives value to life.

By contrast, MacIntyre (1990, 92) contends that

> Any political society . . . which possesses a shared stock of adequately determinate and rationally defensible moral rules, publicly recognized to be the rules to which characteristically and generally unproblematic appeals may be made, will therefore, implicitly or explicitly, be committed to an adequately determinate and rationally justifiable conception of the human good.

But this way of putting the contrast—liberals favoring neutrality with respect to conceptions of the good, and communitarians favoring commitment to a particular conception of the good—has bred only confusion. What it suggests is that liberals are attempting to be value neutral when they clearly are not. Liberals, like their communitarian critics, are committed to a substantive conception of the good. The relevant difference between liberals and communitarians is that liberals are only committed to a partial conception of the good whereas communitarians aspire to a relatively complete conception of the good. So it would be best to view most forms of liberalism as attempting to ground moral rules on part of a conception of the good—specifically, that the part of a conception of the good that is more easily recognized, and needs to be publicly recognized, as good. For Rawls, for example, this partial conception of the good is a conception of fairness, according to which no one deserves his or her native abilities nor his or her initial starting place in society. Given this interpretation of liberalism, then, in order to properly evaluate the debate between liberals and communitarians, we would need to do a comparative analysis of their conceptions of the good with their practical requirements. Yet since the conception of the good so far specified and defended by communitarians, like Sandel and MacIntyre, is relatively formal, there is little reason to think that communitarians would reject the right to welfare endorsed by welfare liberals, especially as it applies to the working poor.

Feminist Justice

Defenders of a feminist conception of justice present a distinctive challenging critique to defenders of other conceptions of justice. In his *The Subjec-*

tion of Women John Stuart Mill (1869), one of the earliest male defenders of women's liberation, argues that the subjection of women was never justified but was imposed upon women because they were physically weaker than men; later this subjection was confirmed by law. Mill argues that society must remove the legal restrictions that deny women the same opportunities enjoyed by men. However, Mill does not consider whether because of past discrimination against women it may be necessary to do more than simply remove legal restrictions: he does not consider whether positive assistance may also be required.

Usually it is not enough simply to remove unequal restrictions to make a competition fair among those who have been participating. Positive assistance to those who have been disadvantaged in the past may also be required, as would be the case in a race where some were unfairly impeded by having to carry ten-pound weights for part of the race. To render the outcome of such a race fair, we might want to transfer the ten-pound weights to the other runners in the race, and thereby advantage the previously disadvantaged runners for an equal period of time. Similarly, positive assistance, such as affirmative action programs, may be necessary if women who have been disadvantaged in the past are now going to be able to compete fairly with men.

In *Justice, Gender, and the Family*, Susan Okin (1989) argues for the feminist ideal of a gender-free society. A gender-free society is a society where basic rights and duties are not assigned on the basis of a person's biological sex. Being male or female is not the grounds for determining what basic rights and duties a person has in a gender-free society. Since a conception of justice is usually thought to provide the ultimate grounds for the assignment of rights and duties, we can refer to this ideal of a gender-free society as "feminist justice."

Okin goes on to consider whether John Rawls's welfare liberal conception of justice can support the ideal of a gender-free society. Noting Rawls's failure to apply his original position–type thinking to family structures, Okin is skeptical about the possibility of using a welfare liberal ideal to support feminist justice. She contends that in a gender-structured society like our own, male philosophers cannot achieve the sympathetic imagination required to see things from the standpoint of women. In a gender-structured society, Okin claims, male philosophers cannot do the original position–type thinking required by the welfare liberal ideal because they lack the ability to put themselves in the position of women. According to Okin, original position–type thinking can only really be achieved in a gender-free society.

Yet at the same time that Okin despairs of doing original position–type thinking in a gender-structured society like our own, she herself purportedly does a considerable amount of just that type of thinking. For example, she claims that Rawls's principles of justice "would seem to require a radical rethinking not only of the division of labor within families but also of all the nonfamily institutions that assume it." She also claims that "the abolition of gender seems essential for the fulfillment of Rawls's criterion of political justice" (Okin 1989, 104). So Okin's own work would seem to indicate that we can do such thinking and that her reasons for thinking that we cannot are not persuasive. For to do original position–type thinking, it is not necessary that everyone be able to put themselves imaginatively in the position of everyone else. All that is necessary is that some people be able to do so. For some people may not be able to do original position–type thinking because they have been deprived of a proper moral education. Others may be able to do original position–type thinking only after they have been forced to mend their ways and live morally for a period of time.

Of course, even among men and women in our gendered society who are in a broad sense capable of a sense of justice, some may not presently be able to do such original position–type thinking with respect to the proper relationships between men and women; these men and women may only be able to do so after the laws and social practices in our society have significantly shifted toward a more gender-free society. But this inability of some to do original position–type thinking does not render it impossible for others, who have effectively used the opportunities for moral development available to them to achieve the sympathetic imagination necessary for original position–type thinking with respect to the proper relationships between men and women.

Like Susan Okin, I too endorse a gender-free society, but I claim that to identify feminist justice with a gender-free society is to characterize the ideal only negatively (see Sterba 1994). It tells us what we need to get rid of, not what we need to put in its place. A more positive characterization, I claim, is provided by the ideal of androgyny. Putting the ideal of feminist justice more positively in terms of the ideal of androgyny also helps bring out why men should be attracted to feminist justice.

The ideal of androgyny requires that traits that are truly desirable in society be equally available to both women and men, or in the case of virtues, equally expected of both women and men (see Sterba 1990). Support for the ideal of androgyny can be derived both from a right to equal opportunity that is a central requirement of a welfare liberal conception of justice and from an equal right of self-development that is a central requirement of a socialist conception of justice. I further argue that the ideal requires: first, all children irrespective of their sex must be given the same type of upbringing consistent with their native capabilities. Second, mothers and fathers must also have the same opportunities for education and employment consistent with their native capabilities. Yet since these equal opportunity requirements of an ideal of androgyny could not be achieved without a right to welfare, such a right, especially for the working poor, must also be understood to be a requirement of feminist justice.

Christina Sommers (1989) has criticized feminist philosophers like Okin and myself for what she considers to be an attack on the traditional family structures. She distinguishes liberal feminists from radical feminists. She contends that liberal feminists, like herself, want equal opportunity in the workplace and politics, but would leave marriage and motherhood "untouched and unimpugned." By contrast, Sommers contends that radical feminists are committed to an assimilationist or androgynous ideal that would destroy the (traditional) family and deny most women what they want. Sommers, however, never explains how it is possible to secure for women equal opportunity in the workplace and politics while rejecting androgyny in favor of maintaining existing gender roles. For example, how could women be passive, submissive, dependent, indecisive, and weak and still enjoy the same opportunities in the workplace and politics that are enjoyed by men who are aggressive, dominant, independent, decisive, and strong?

Marilyn Friedman (1991) also questions whether what Sommers supports is really what most women want. She quotes a 1983 survey which indicated that 63 percent of women preferred nontraditional family relationships, and points out that in 1977 only 16 percent of American households were traditional families in the sense of families consisting of a legally married heterosexual couple and their children, in which the man is the sole breadwinner and "head" of the household, and the woman does the domestic work and child care.

In responding to Friedman, Sommers (1991) explains that what she means by a traditional family is one that consists of two heterosexual parents and one or more children in which the mother plays a distinctive gender role in caring for the children. This definition obviously broadens the class of families to which Sommers is referring. But in her response, Sommers goes on to renounce any attempt to be promoting the traditional family even as she defines it. What she claims to be promoting is simply "the right and liberty to live under the arrangement of one's choice." According to Sommers, if people want to live in nontraditional families, they should be free to do so.

Yet however one assesses this debate between Sommers and Friedman, it is clear that while feminist justice seeks to give a new interpretation to equal opportunity between women and men, it also endorses, like our other conceptions of justice, a right to welfare, which is a prerequisite for equal opportunity. This right to welfare extends especially to the working poor, who given the feminization of poverty in the U.S. will be disproportionately women and their children.[1]

Practical Implications

In seeking to determine whether there is a right to welfare, I have critically evaluated five contemporary conceptions of justice—libertarian justice with its ideal of liberty, welfare liberal justice with its ideal of fairness, socialist justice with its ideal of equality, communitarian justice with its ideal of the common good, and feminist justice with its ideal of a gender-free society. I have argued that when these five conceptions of justice are correctly interpreted, they all can be seen to support a right to welfare, especially for the working poor.

The implications of this moral argument for public policy should be clear. If the poor, especially the working poor, have a right to welfare, then providing welfare is not something that governments can choose to do or not do, or that governments can choose to provide more or less of. If the poor have a right to welfare, then regardless of the cost to its more advantaged citizens, governments must provide an adequate welfare system in order to avoid unjustly violating the rights of the poor. Now given that most people endorse one or more of the five conceptions of justice that I have considered, and since all of these conceptions support a right to welfare, especially for the working poor, there should be widespread support for a welfare system that guarantees such a right to the poor, especially the working poor. For those trying to be just and moral, the call to fashion an appropriate public policy is compelling.

How might we do that? Certainly, we would all benefit if there were many prominent advocates of such a right who could help raise the level of discourse on this topic in the political arena. They could articulate the need for better policy at the local, state, and national levels. Concrete issues such as the negative portrayal of poor citizens must be challenged by providing images of the poor which are rooted in the empirical reality of their lives and not in the stereotypes perpetrated by ideologues on the right or left; ordinary informed citizens can write opinion pieces for their local newspapers, speak at public meetings, and work with others to alter the landscape. The common moral ground needs to be attended to and affirmed, helping the citizenry better understand that a right to welfare stems from our broadly agreed upon common values; moral leaders in every community have a special opportunity in this area. Efforts such as these may help to create the environment in which our public officials can work to design policy that enfleshes a right to welfare.

If we look to the U.S. Constitution, however, we find that it fails to guarantee a right to welfare. In *Wyman* v. *James* (1971), the issue before the Supreme Court of the United States was whether the Fourth Amendment prohibition of unreasonable searches applies to visits by welfare caseworkers to recipients of the program for Aid to Families with Dependent Children. The majority of the Court held that the Fourth Amendment does not apply in this case because the visitation is not forced or compelled since one can avoid the visitation by choosing not to accept the aid. What one cannot choose to do is to receive the aid but forego the visitation, and that is because there is no constitutional right to welfare. The only right to welfare is a right that is conditional upon the state or federal government's interest in providing welfare, and presently that interest requires the acceptance of a home visitation. If I am right, therefore, that a right to welfare can be seen to be required by each of the five conceptions of justice that I have considered, then surely this right would have to be guaranteed by any constitution that claims to be morally defensible.

Now it might be objected that this criticism of the U.S. Constitution is inappropriate because it attempts to evaluate the Constitution which for the most part was written two hundred years ago by appealing to contemporary conceptions of justice. But this is to miss my point. My criticism is not so much directed at the Constitution as originally written as it is directed at the Constitution as presently amended and interpreted. For whenever a society's constitution can be seen to be morally defective in light of its acknowledged conceptions of justice, it is incumbent upon the members of that society to amend, or at least reinterpret, their constitution to make up for its deficiencies. If I am right, therefore, that when these five conceptions of justice are correctly interpreted they require a right to welfare, especially for the working poor, then the U.S. Constitution will remain a fundamentally defective document until it too requires this right.

It might also be objected that greater injustice would be done if we assigned the responsibility for guaranteeing a right to welfare to the courts rather than to the legislature.[2] But this way of characterizing the alternatives fails to capture the alternative I would favor. For it is certainly possible for the

U.S. Constitution to contain a right to welfare such that the legislature would have the primary task of implementing this right and the courts only a secondary task of reviewing that implementation, generally improving upon it only in minor respects. This model for constitutional guarantees can be found, for example, in my own state of Indiana and I assume elsewhere. In Indiana, the state constitution guarantees a right to free education and the Indiana legislature has the primary task of implementing that right; the state courts only have a secondary task of reviewing that implementation.

Of course, I have been primarily concerned to argue that a right to welfare, especially for the working poor, is a fundamental requirement of the conceptions of justice we endorse. This is because the realization that such a right does follow from the conceptions of justice we endorse must be widespread in our society before we can realistically face the possibility of implementing such a right at the constitutional level. The task is challenging. But I believe it is one worth engaging: it builds on our best traditions and, to the extent that we all join in the efforts, it will result in a more just society.

Notes

1. On the feminization of poverty, see Diana Pearce, "The Feminization of Poverty," in *Feminist Philosophies*, edited by Janet Kourany, James Sterba, and Rosemarie Tong (Englewood Cliffs, N.J.: Prentice-Hall, 1991), 207–219.

2. I owe this objection to Robert L. Simon.

References

Durning, Alan. 1990. "Life on the Brink." *World Watch* 3: 22–30.

Dworkin, Ronald. 1973. "The Original Position." *University of Chicago Law Review* 40: 195–230.

Friedman, Marilyn. 1991. "They Lived Happily Ever After: Sommers on Women and Marriage." *Journal of Social Philosophy* 3: 57–65.

Gardner, Jennifer M., and Diane E. Herz. 1992. "Working and Poor in 1990." *Monthly Labor Review* 74: 20–28.

Hospers, John. 1971. *Libertarianism*. Los Angeles: Nash.

Kant, Immanuel. 1970. *Theory and Practice*. In *Kant's Political Writings*, edited by Hans Reiss. New York: Cambridge University Press.

Machan, Tibor. 1989. *Individuals and Their Rights*. La Salle, Ill.: Open Court.

MacIntyre, Alasdair. 1990. "Privatization of the Good." *Review of Politics* 52: 85–110.

Marx, Karl. 1966. *Critique of the Gotha Program*. Edited by C. P. Dutt. New York, International Publishers. (Orig. 1891.)

Marx, Karl, and Frederich Engels. 1888. *The Communist Manifesto*. London. (Orig. 1848.)

Mill, John Stuart. 1869. *The Subjection of Women*. London. (Orig. 1864.)

Miller, Richard. 1974. "Rawls and Marxism." *Philosophy and Public Affairs* 4: 167–180.

Okin, Susan. 1989. *Justice, Gender, and the Family*. New York: Basic Books.

Rand, Ayn. 1963. *The Virtue of Selfishness.* New York: New American Library.

Rawls, John. 1971. *A Theory of Justice.* Cambridge, Mass.: Harvard University Press.

Sandel, Michael J. 1982. *Liberalism and the Limits of Justice.* New York: Cambridge University Press.

Sommers, Christina. 1989. "Philosophers Against the Family." In *Person to Person,* edited by George Graham and Hugh Lafollette. Philadelphia: Temple University Press.

Sommers, Christina. 1991. "Do These Feminists Like Women?" *Journal of Social Philosophy* 3: 66–74.

Sterba, James P. 1985. "A Libertarian Justification for a Welfare State." *Social Theory and Practice* 11: 285–306.

Sterba, James P. 1990. "Feminist Justice and the Family." In *Perspectives on the Family,* edited by Robert Moffat, Joseph Grcic, and Michael Bayles. Lewistown, N.Y.: Edwin Mellon Press.

Sterba, James P. 1994. "Feminist Justice and the Pursuit of Peace." *Hypatia* 105: 64–98.

Uyl, Douglas Den, and Douglas Rasmussen. 1984. *The Philosophic Thought of Ayn Rand.* Chicago: University of Illinois Press.

8

An Editorial Comment: The Working Poor and the Prospect of Welfare Reform 1995 Style

THOMAS R. SWARTZ

Few deny the reality of Jim Sterba's conclusions: No matter how justice is viewed, America's working poor are deserving. They accept the challenge of self-determination. They embrace the work ethic. They, perhaps more than any other identifiable group in America, are willing to work for a better tomorrow. Yet in spite of their efforts they remain out of the mainstream. They remain poor. They work, but they are denied the rewards associated with being part of the middle class. They work, yet society is quick to judge them as losers in the economic game. They work, and they are often economically no better off than those who fail to work.

As many of the essays in this book note (Kasarda, Danziger–Gottschalk, and Blank–London) no matter how you measure the presence of the working poor, their numbers continue to grow in spite of a robust economy. Unlike the 1950s, 1960s, and mid-1970s, when younger generations eagerly anticipated that they would enjoy a level of income that far surpassed their parents and grandparents, workers at the bottom of the economic ladder increasingly have become aware that they are stuck at the bottom. They have played by the rules established by earlier generations, but these rules have worked against them.

Their plight is clearly seen in income distribution data. As Table 8.1 suggests, in the post-war years prior to 1979, growth in the overall economy was shared by all income groups. Real incomes for the bottom 20 percent of the families in the U.S. increased from an average income of $9,661 to $11,421, just as the real income of the relatively affluent—the top 20 percent of families—increased from $74,416 to $90,805. This pattern was abruptly altered after 1979. Families in the middle of the income distribution and those at the bottom found their real incomes to be lower in 1993 than they were in 1979.

Table 8.1
The Share of Aggregate Family Income Received by Each Quintile in Constant 1993 dollars.

	1993		1979		1967	
	Share	**Mean Income**	**Share**	**Mean Income**	**Share**	**Mean Income**
Bottom fifth	4.1%	$9,739	5.2%	$11,421	5.4%	$9,661
Second fifth	9.9%	$23,390	11.6%	$25,198	12.2%	$21,862
Third fifth	15.7%	$37,066	17.5%	$38,056	17.5%	$31,424
Fourth fifth	23.3%	$54,946	24.1%	$52,405	23.5%	$42,144
Highest fifth	47.0%	$111,017	41.7%	$90,803	41.4%	$74,416
Top 5 percent	20.3%	$191,612	15.8%	$137,482	16.4%	$117,738

Source: U.S. Bureau of the Census, unpublished data from the Current Population Survey Tables F2 and F2a.

Those at the top of the income distribution, however, continued to experience an increase in their standards of living.

Danziger and Gottschalk remind us that in the 1960s we likened this to the tides. In the earlier period a "rising tide" was expected to raise everyone's boat; unfortunately in the latter period there are "uneven tides." Some boats are lifted while others are left behind. Table 8.1 starkly reveals the consequence of these uneven tides. Prior to 1979, economic growth was shared by all income groups. True, the incomes of those families in the top 60 percent, even including those in the top 5 percent who were subject to very high marginal tax rates, grew more than the income of those in the bottom 40 percent, but the fact remains that all income groups were better off. In the post-1979 period we experience a perverse distribution of income, the rich became richer at the expense of the poor. The share of aggregate income falls for those families in the bottom 60 percent of the income distribution, it grows modestly for those in the fourth quintile, rises sharply for those families in the top 20 percent, and skyrockets for those in the top 5 percent (see Table 8.1). The loss in purchasing power is dramatic. In Table 8.2, we see that families in the bottom quintile are 14.7 percent worse off, those in the second quintile are 7.2 percent worse off, and those in the third quintile are 2.6 percent worse off. Many of the families in the second quintile and some of those in the bottom quintile are our working poor.

Weigert, in her introductory essay, suggests that the reasons for the deteriorating economic situation of those in the bottom of the income distribution are many and varied. She notes that some argue that it can be traced to the

Table 8.2
Shares of Aggregate Real Family Income 1967 to 1993
Winners and Losers (1993 dollars)

	Real Income Growth 1979–1993	Real Income Growth 1967–1979
Bottom Fifth	−14.7%	+18.2%
Second Fifth	−7.2%	+15.3%
Third Fifth	−2.6%	+21.1%
Fourth Fifth	+4.8%	+24.3%
Highest Fifth	+22.3%	+22.0%
Top 5 percent	+39.4%	+16.8%

Source: Calculations based on U.S. Bureau of the Census, unpublished data from the Current Population Survey, Table F-2a.

loss of union jobs, others contend that it is traced to deregulation, immigration, technological change, and/or the globalization of the American economy. Education and training is the common thread that is woven through these various explanations. If you have the right education, college or the appropriate advanced job training, you can succeed in this new world. But even if you have these credentials there are no guarantees. This is a necessary, but not a sufficient condition for success. Danziger and Gottschalk tell us that regardless of race/ethnicity, those with only a high school degree experienced a 12 percent decline in their mean earning from 1979 to 1989, while those with a college degree earned at least 8 percent more in 1989 than they did in 1979. (See Table 4.3, Danziger and Gottschalk this volume). Danziger and Gottschalk also tell us that 16.6 percent of males and 25.1 percent of women with college degrees earned less than $15,000 in 1992, when the poverty line for a family of four was $14,335. (See Table 4.1, Danziger and Gottschalk this volume).

The Republican Welfare Agenda

It is clear that the past decade and a half has been hard on those families that fall into the category of the "working poor." What is less obvious is that their future prospects are even more bleak. If the Republian majority of the 103rd Congress is successful in implementing their *Contract with America*, America's working poor today are in line to be negatively and significantly impacted. In light of the very insightful analysis provided in the first seven chapters of this book, a review of the welfare proposals that are currently on the table is particularly appropriate.

The proposals, as they have been articulated by Speaker Gingrich, have two broad initiatives: a substantial reduction in federal spending on welfare and devolution of this responsibility to state governments. These initiatives are expected to generate a $40 billion savings in welfare expenditures over a five-year period. This is particularly important for the GOP leadership, since these moneys are earmarked to fund a significant federal tax cut. Given the high priority the 103rd Congress has placed on balancing the budget, if taxes are to be cut, spending must also be cut.

Privatizing Public Welfare

The harsh reality is that $40 billion can only be generated if welfare entitlements are abridged. These entitlements include Aid to Families with Dependent Children (AFDC) and nutrition programs such as the Food Stamp program. The proposed cuts in the former impact our current working poor most directly. It should be noted, of course, that cuts in the latter program will also impact these families, but in this case the loss in economic well-being will be the same for those who work as it is for those who are solely dependent on AFDC.

In the winter and early spring of 1995, several distinct proposals emerged. Each is intended to reduce welfare dependency. Some proposals do this directly by cutting the welfare rolls. In this category, the most extreme legislation would deny any welfare assistance to unwed teens and their offspring. Presumably, this would entail a lifetime denial of welfare benefits. The least draconian cuts are what popularly have become known as "two years and off." In the Republican version of this proposal a hard line is drawn. After a two-year support period, welfare recipients will be forced off the welfare rolls and expected to make their own way in the private labor market. No provision is made for an extended training period nor is the government obligated to become the employer of last resort. A number of other proposals, most focused on systematically limiting cash payments, are located between these two extremes.

Since there is little empirical, historic evidence to evaluate the consequences of these radical changes in our social protection system, one can only speculate as to how welfare recipients will respond. Some will turn to private charity: the Salvation Army, homeless shelters, church-sponsored programs, etc. Others will turn to friends and family for help. And as intended, significant numbers will attempt to find jobs in the private labor market. It is this latter response that is of special interest.

Those summarily cut from our welfare rolls will compete for the same low-skill, low-pay jobs that are currently held by our existing working-poor labor force. Without federal or state intervention, it is not difficult to anticipate how markets will respond. In brief, the new entrants add a depressing effect on the wage rate of this segment of this labor market.

History tells us that the prospects for those currently in this market and for those who are trying to enter this market are not good. The best that can be hoped for is that we can *grow* our way out of this problem. But this is not a likely scenario. We have already learned that a "rising tide" will not raise all boats. A rising tide can stabilize the lower end of the labor market and at the margins create some jobs, add to overtime opportunities, and put some upward pressure on the wage rate; but these positive influences will be overwhelmed by depressing effects of the new entrants.

In the 1950s, 1960s, and early 1970s growth in the overall economy acted as a ratchet, pulling the wages of low-income workers upward as the economy grew. We no longer benefit from this "ratchet effect." Indeed, the new economic world may be better characterized as a ratchet set in reverse. As the general economy grows this ratchet sustains a wage platform for low-skill workers somewhat above the minimum wage level. When the economy recesses, this ratchet lowers that wage platform back down to the minimum wage floor. One wonders whether or not the Republican leadership have considered the consequences of their programs when the national economy is in a state of recession.

Let us for the moment assume that good fortune smiles on us and our economy is in a period a robust economic growth when our welfare rolls are systematically reduced. Will our former welfare recipients be able to *work* their way into the middle class? We know some of the obstacles they will encounter. At the prevailing minimum wage level, it will take two workers, working full-time in year-round work, to earn enough to escape poverty. That is, at a $4.25/hr. wage rate, two workers working 40 hours per week for 50 weeks will generate $17,000 in annual income. By the year 1997, the first year that a policy of "two years and off" would be in place, the poverty threshold for a family of four is likely to be close to but a bit less than $17,000. However, this assumes a two-earner family. A one-earner family, earning $8500 per year, is in a much more precarious position.

The prevailing wage rate is not the only obstacle these individuals will face in their effort to enter the middle class under the Republican proposals. There is, for example, no indication that other social services such as medical care and day care will be liberalized to accommodate their needs. In fact, some of the newly elected members of Congress speak of further cuts in these programs. The analysis provided by Hofferth suggests that the child-care needs of the working poor need to be expanded, rather than reduced. This is of particular concern for female-headed households that have been the focal point of a number of Republican proposals. The consequence seems clear. If large numbers of women who serve as the heads of households are suddenly forced into the labor market, they will in turn place an increased demand upon existing child-care facilities. If more services are not made available, the children of some of these heads of households and some of the children of the existing working poor who currently have access to adequate child care may find it impossible to place their children in facilities they can afford. More children will be exposed to inadequate care or left to fend for themselves, unsupervised. Faced with this prospect, a significant number of working poor mothers may simply opt out and become jobless and homeless.

Devolution of Welfare

The second broad welfare reform initiative of the Republican leadership of the 103rd Congress is to shift the responsibility for establishing welfare programs to state governments. Here the intent is to give states greater flexibility to create programs that serve the needs of their constituents rather than implementing programs that are formulated with national minimum standards. Proponents of devolution go on to argue that operating these programs at the state level would eliminate one level of bureaucracy, and this in turn would lower costs.

The federal government would continue to bear a large portion of the fiscal responsibility for these programs, although at a lower level of participation than they have in the past. States for their part would not receive funds unencumbered. These funds would be passed back to the state governments in the form of block grants. Although the block grant categories have not as yet been articulated, it can be assumed that seven or eight block grants will be established. One block grant would likely fund cash payments—AFDC being by far the most significant program that will be collapsed into this block grant, another might underwrite the costs of child care, including perhaps foster care, "group houses," and adoption, and still another would provide funds for nutrition programs such as food stamps and school lunches.

It is important to note that these block grants, and others that undoubtedly will be established, will only be made available to states that have agreed to a series of mandates proposed by the Republican leadership. Some of the preconditions that have been discussed are: i) the two years and off proposition, ii) an overall lifetime maximum participation of five years; iii) exclusion of benefits of both legal and illegal aliens; iv) an outright denial of benefits to all unwed mothers less than eighteen and mothers who do not help identify their baby's father, and v) a denial of additional benefits to support additional children born to unwed mothers on welfare.

The use of a block grant mechanism, particularly a block grant mechanism which incorporates some or all of the preconditions just outlined, will lead to the uneven treatment of welfare recipients across the country. This, of course, is the intent of those who have framed these proposals. Ironically, it was this very unevenness that prompted earlier congressional action which imposed the mandatory minimum standards that the new reformers rail about.

Those states that select to scale back their existing welfare programs severely will impact their working poor most directly. If the private sector in these states cannot absorb the new entrants, labor surpluses will appear and aggregate income will fall. This negative impact and its associated multiplier effects will not be evenly distributed across states, rather it will be concentrated in those urban and rural communities that currently experience economic stress. Those individuals who can move, generally those who are relatively more affluent, will flee to those areas which are economically more viable. They will leave behind some rural communities, some urban neighborhoods, and some cities that will increasingly become what one community activist—Monsigneur Geno Baroni—in the 1960s characterized as "black, brown, and broke." Welfare program dollars will no longer act as a built-in stabilizer. Economic stagnation will take root and employment opportunities for the "working poor" will disappear.

The Democrat Response

Paradoxically, when President Clinton first articulated his program to end "welfare as we know it," his proposals were considered too extreme, too radical, too insensitive to the needs of those currently on welfare. Pundits, both inside and outside of the Washington, D.C. "beltway," held out little hope that these initiatives would ever be enacted by Congress. Less than a year later, the Clinton agenda was characterized by the new Congress as too restrained, too conservative, too paternalistic to those on welfare. The same pundits who argued that his reforms would not be enacted because they went too far, now argue that they do not go far enough.

Setting political rhetoric aside, what we do know is that the Clinton proposals do have dramatically different consequences for the working poor compared to the Republican alternatives. They also have dramatically different consequences for the average American taxpayer. Forty billion dollars will not be saved here. In fact, if enacted, the Clinton program would probably require an increase in federal funding over the next five years.

The Clinton initiative attempts to both "push" and "pull" welfare recipients off of the welfare rolls. To achieve the former, he too suggests a "two years and off" policy. To achieve the latter, he would employ wage incentives.

The Clinton Push *Policy*

Welfare dependency, becoming trapped in a cycle of poverty, is a frightening prospect for middle America. No one wants to see the children of those in poverty condemned to live the rest of their lives in this limited state. Whether or not dependency exists is an empirical question which will not be addressed here. What is important for our purposes is the general perception that there *is* dependency. Both the Clinton and the Republican response is motivated by that perception.

Redressing existing dependency and assuring that future welfare recipients are not seduced into a life of welfare is a high priority of both Clinton and the Republican leadership. Both also agree that this priority can be accomplished by forcing individuals off the welfare rolls in two years. Where their policies differ is in what happens at the end of two years. In crass terms, the GOP policy is a policy of "sink or swim." A welfare recipient has two years to prepare for employment and to find employment. If at the end of that two-year period welfare recipients cannot find jobs, they are no longer the concern of the public sector. The Clinton proposals are far more accommodating. At the end of two years welfare recipients must be in training or in private sector jobs. If they are not in a job-training program or employed, the public sector becomes the employer of last resort.

Fortunately, Blank and London have provided us with a comprehensive review of public policies designed to impact the work behavior of poor households. What is important to note is that public assumption of the training and employment responsibility has dramatically different consequences for the working poor compared to the Republican proposals. This is particularly true for those who are currently employed in the private sector. If their labor market becomes glutted, the excess supply of workers are siphoned-off to the public sector. A job will exist and an income stream will be assured for the new entrant. The community at large will not be subjected to the multiplier effects of a sudden loss of income.

The Clinton Pull *Policy*

The most important initiatives of the Clinton agenda for welfare reform are focused on stimulating work incentives. Two of these initiatives, the Earned Income Tax Credit (EITC) and the minimum wage, have again been comprehensively discussed in the Blank–London essay. It is important to underscore, however, the intent of these policies compared to the policies proposed by the Republican leadership.

Clearly the single most important welfare initiative of the Clinton Administration is the EITC. Early in his administration, Congress enacted a significant increase in the EITC. This increase, which will be phased in over several years, is designed to make work more attractive by supplementing the market wage for low-wage earners. It is an explicit market-based policy. Benefits from this program can only be enjoyed if the recipient works. The policy should be endorsed by the new Congress since it is in concert with their stated goal of increasing labor force participation.

But this is an expensive program and as Blank and London suggest, it is a program about whose consequences we know little. Do low-skill, low-wage workers understand the relationship between their market wage and their after credit income, particularly an after credit income that will not be received until they file for a tax refund? Even sophisticated taxpayers have failed to see this linkage in other tax credit schemes enacted in the past. Will the complicated nature of the EITC provide a convenient justification to eliminate it and in the process save billions of dollars which can be devoted to other priorities of the new Congress?

The second "pull" policy of the Clinton Administration is the minimum wage. The inflation-eroded minimum wage, which was last increased in 1992, is near its historic low in real terms. Although, as Blank and London note, there is ample empirical evidence to suggest that a moderate increase to the $5.00 an hour level would have relatively small disemployment effects, the Republican leadership has judged this proposal to be "dead-on-arrival." Indeed, some on the Republican side of the aisle, Congressman Dick Armey in particular, have pledged to eliminate it completely.

Unlike the EITC, low-income workers understand the consequences of a minimum wage. If the real purchasing power of the minimum wage is allowed to continue its erosion with the passage of time or if it is eliminated completely, it is hard to believe that there will not be disincentive effects.

A Final Thought

A growing mood of cynicism toward government has taken root in American society. Editorialists, talk show hosts, and television commentators repeatedly tell us that government can do nothing right, therefore it should do nothing at all. It is a modern day articulation of *laissez faire*: allow them to do it. But who is the "them" that speaks for this policy? Who wins and who loses if we continue along this path? Will those who cling to the bottom rung of the economic ladder, our working poor, continue to "play" this market game? How will today's poor children, Betty's grandchildren, whom Eli Anderson tells us about, judge us? How will we judge ourselves?

Contributors

ELIJAH ANDERSON is the Charles and William L. Day Professor of the Social Sciences at the University of Pennsylvania, where he has been a member of the faculty since 1975. He presently serves as the associate director of the Center for Urban Ethnography. He received his master's degree from the University of Chicago and his doctorate in sociology was awarded by Northwestern University in 1976. An expert on the sociology of Black America, he is the author of numerous articles on the African-American experience, including "Sex Codes and Family Life among Inner-City Youth" (The *Annals,* January 1989) and "Of Old Heads and Young Boys: Notes on the Urban Black Experience" commissioned in 1986 by the National Academy of Sciences' Committee on the Status of Black Americans. He is the author of *A Place on the Corner: A Study of Black Street Corner Men* (University of Chicago Press, 1978) as well as the ethnographic study, *Streetwise: Race, Class, and Change in an Urban Community* (University of Chicago Press, 1990), for which he won the 1991 Robert E. Park Award of the American Sociological Association.

Considered an outstanding teacher, Anderson was honored in 1983 with University of Pennsylvania's top teaching prize, the Lindback Award for Distinguished Teaching. His teaching and research interests involve "The Social Psychology of Organizations," "Field Methods of Social Research," "Social Interaction," and "Social Organization."

REBECCA M. BLANK and REBECCA A. LONDON. Rebecca M. Blank holds doctorate in economics from M.I.T. and is a Professor at Northwestern University in the Economics Department. She directs the Urban Poverty Program, an interdisciplinary research and graduate training in the Center for Urban Affairs and Policy Research. Prior to coming to Northwestern, she taught at Princeton University and served for a year as a Senior Staff Economist with the Council of Economic Advisors, the in-house economic advisory staff to the White House in Washington, D.C.

Her own research focuses on the interaction between macroeconomic effects, government anti-poverty programs, and the behavior and well-being of low-income families. Recent research includes a study of the comparative effectiveness of anti-poverty efforts in the U.S. and Canada; a study of the reason why economic growth was relatively ineffective in reducing poverty rates over the 1980s; a study of the use of part-time jobs among low-income women; and a study of the timing of recipiency among AFDC and food stamp users. Professor Blank has published extensively in economics and policy-related journals, and serves on a variety of professional and advisory boards.

Rebecca A. London has a master's degree in economics from Northwestern University. She is currently a doctoral student in Human Development and Social Policy at Northwestern. Co-author of a study of Chicago's poverty population, she is now working on a study of the determinants of single mothers' work-welfare choices.

Sheldon Danziger and Peter Gottschalk. Sheldon Danziger is Professor of Social Work and Public Policy, Faculty Associate in Population Studies, and Director of the Research and Training Program on Poverty, the Underclass and Public Policy at the University of Michigan. He received his doctorate in economics from the M.I.T. From 1974–1988 he was a member of the Faculty of the School of Social Work and the Institute for Research on Poverty at the University of Wisconsin. He was Director of the Institute for Research on Poverty from 1983–1988.

His research focuses on trends in poverty and inequality and the effects of economic and demographic changes and government social programs on disadvantaged groups. He is the co-editor of several volumes—*Fighting Poverty: What Works and What Doesn't* (Harvard University Press, 1986), *The Distributional Impacts of Public Policies* (Macmillan, 1988), *State Policy Choices: The Wisconsin Experience* (University of Wisconsin Press, 1988), *Uneven Tides: Rising Inequality in America* (Russell Sage Foundation, 1993), and *Confronting Poverty: Prescriptions for Change* (Harvard University Press, 1994). Danziger is co-author with Peter Gottschalk of *America Unequal: How Slow Growth and Rising Inequality Have Diminished the Prospects of the Poor and the Middle Class* (Harvard University Press and the Russell Sage Foundation, 1995).

Danziger often consults with government agencies and testifies before Congressional committees. During 1994 he was a visiting scholar in the Office of the Assistant Secretary for Planning and Evaluation in the U.S. Department of Health and Human Services. His professional activities include membership on the Panel on Poverty and Family Assistance of the National Research Council, the Council of Advisors of the National Center for Children in Poverty, the National Advisory Committee of the Institute for Research on Poverty, and the Russell Sage Foundation Advisory Committee on Poverty Research.

Peter Gottschalk is Professor of Economics at Boston College. He received his doctorate in economics from the University of Pennsylvania. He is currently a Research Affiliate for the Institute for Research on Poverty at the University of Wisconsin, Madison, and was previously a Russell Sage Foundation Visiting Scholar and a Brookings Economics Policy Fellow.

Gottschalk's main area of research is labor economics, with a special emphasis on income distribution and poverty. His current work includes studies of intergenerational patterns in welfare participation, turnover in AFDC caseload, and international comparisons of changes in inequality.

SANDRA L. HOFFERTH is Research Scientist at the Institute for Social Research, University of Michigan. She received her doctorate in sociology from the University of North Carolina in 1976. From 1983 to 1988 Hofferth served as Health Scientist Administrator in the National Institute of Child Health and Human Development. Until her move to Michigan, she had served as Senior Research Associate in the Population Studies Center at the Urban Institute in Washington, D.C. Hofferth has been engaged in work related to children, youth, and families for fifteen years. She recently completed the analysis of two national studies of child care. The first, *The National Child Care Survey 1990*, describes the early education and care arrangements used by parents for their children under age thirteen. The second, *A Profile of Child Care Settings, Early Education and Care in 1990*, described early childhood programs from a program perspective. A recent publication in the *Journal of Human Resources*, "Price, Quality and Income in Child Care Choice," examines the relative importance of different characteristics of care in parental choice of child care arrangements. Hofferth was awarded the 1991–92 Jensen Lectureship, jointly sponsored by the American Sociological Association and Duke University, for research contributing to the goal of providing social action with a more rational grounding in rested knowledge.

Besides her work on early education, Hofferth has reviewed and conducted research on a variety of family issues, such as kin networks, children's living arrangements, maternal employment, fertility decisions, and the consequences of adolescent pregnancy and childbearing. She has also been active in the policy arena. She testified three times on the Hill during the late 1980s Congressional debates on child care legislation. She has published eight books, monographs, and edited volumes, and over thirty articles and book chapters. Dr. Hofferth is Secretary-Treasurer of the Family Sociology Section of the American Sociological Association.

JOHN D. KASARDA is a Kenan Professor of Business Administration and Director of the Kenan Institute of Private Enterprise at the University of North Carolina at Chapel Hill. He received a master's degree in business administration with distinction from Cornell University and his doctorate from the University of North Carolina.

Dr. Kasarda has published more than fifty scholarly articles and eight books on urban development, demographics, and employment and serves on the editorial boards of a variety of major professional journals. He has also served as a consultant on national urban policy to the Carter, Reagan, Bush, and Clinton administrations and has testified numerous times before the U.S. Congressional committees on urban and employment issues.

JAMES P. STERBA is Professor of Philosophy in the Philosophy Department and Faculty Fellow in the Institute for International Peace Studies at the University of Notre Dame where he teaches moral problems and political philosophy. He received his doctorate in philosophy from the University of Pittsburgh. He has written more than 120 articles and published fourteen books, including *How to Make People Just* (1988), *Contemporary Ethics* (1989), *Feminist Philosophies* (1990), *Morality in Practice*, Fourth Edition (1992), *Earth Ethics* (1994), *Contemporary Social and Political Philosophy* (1994), *Morality and Social Justice* (1994), and *Social and Political Philosophy: Classical Western Texts in Feminist and Multicultural Perspectives* (1994). He is president of the North American Society for Social Philosophy, past president of the American Section of the International Society for Social and Legal Philosophy and past president of Concerned Philosophers for Peace, and has lectured widely in the United States and Europe. He is currently at work on a project that employs a peace-making rather than a war-making model of doing philosophy which attempts to reconcile divergent social and political perspectives such as libertarianism with socialism, liberal feminism with postmodern feminism, just war theory with pacifism, and anthropocentrism with nonanthropocentrism.

THOMAS R. SWARTZ is a Professor of Economics at the University of Notre Dame. He came to South Bend in 1965 after completing his doctorate from Indiana University. He has served as a fiscal consultant with federal agencies, the State of Indiana, and a number of local governments. He has authored, co-authored, or co-edited five books, three monographs, and more than twenty-five chapters of books or professional articles, and delivered more than thirty papers here and abroad. His recent books include *Urban Finance Under Siege*, (1993) and *Taking Sides*, Seventh Edition (1995), both edited with Frank J. Bonello.

KATHLEEN MAAS WEIGERT is Faculty Liaison/Academic Coordinator at the Center for Social Concerns, Concurrent Associate Professor of American Studies, and Faculty Fellow at the Joan. B. Kroc Institute for International Peace Studies at the University of Notre Dame. She received her doctorate in sociology from the University of Notre Dame. A member of the faculty of Notre Dame since the early 1970s, she has served in a variety of teaching and administrative positions. She is the co-designer with Professor John Howard Yoder of the University's Concentration in Peace Studies, the first concentration in the College of Arts and Letters (approved: 1983). She has given workshops, presented papers, and published in the areas of experiential education, nonviolence, and education for justice and peace. She is currently part of a research team undertaking a Lilly-sponsored three-year study of pluralism among Catholics.

Index